Faster, Smarter, Greener

Faster, Smarter, Greener

The Future of the Car and Urban Mobility

Venkat Sumantran, Charles Fine, and David Gonsalvez

The MIT Press

Cambridge, Massachusetts

London, England

© 2017 Massachusetts Institute of Technology

All rights reserved. No part of this book may be reproduced in any form by any electronic or mechanical means (including photocopying, recording, or information storage and retrieval) without permission in writing from the publisher.

This book was set in Myriad Pro by the MIT Press. Printed and bound in the United States of America.

Library of Congress Cataloging-in-Publication Data

Names: Sumantran, V., 1958- author. | Fine, Charles H., author. | Gonsalvez,
   David J. A. (David Joseph Anthony), 1956- author.
Title: Faster, smarter, greener : the future of the car and urban mobility /
   Venkat Sumantran, Charles Fine, and David Gonsalvez.
Description: Cambridge, MA : MIT Press, [2017] | Includes bibliographical
   references and index.
Identifiers: LCCN 2017001168 | ISBN 9780262036665 (hardcover : alk. paper)
Subjects: LCSH: Transportation, Automotive--Technological innovations. |
   Automobiles--Technological innovations. | Automobile industry and
   trade--Technological innovations. | Urban transportation--Technological
   innovations.
Classification: LCC HE5611 .S86 2017 | DDC 388.3/21--dc23 LC record available at https://lccn.loc.
gov/2017001168

10 9 8 7 6 5 4 3 2 1

To Girija and Ramani

Contents

Preface

For last year's words belong to last year's language
And next year's words await another voice.

—*T. S. Eliot*[1]

Mobility has served as the lifeblood of human civilization. Over the course of the twentieth century, often referred to as the century of the automobile, cars have moved drivers and riders with a combination of utility, efficiency, and variety, unrivaled in the industrial age. Yet as new cars are welcomed by the millions, the world appears poised on the edge of a new horizon for mobility, one that promises to be *faster, smarter,* and *greener.*

This book studies a world that is changing—a world in which people's values, priorities, demographics, and lifestyles are evolving faster than ever before. The chapters that follow traverse a spectrum of technology, entrepreneurship, social change, and governance that engages the human desire for transformed mobility architecture, and anticipate necessary and desirable changes that society will make to move toward such future-relevant, vibrant, and sustainable mobility.

This book peers into this evolving world of wondrous variety, ingenious innovations, engaging enterprises, and ecologically minded communities and proposes a mobility architecture for the challenges of the times. We propose an architecture that is robust, adaptable, and efficient along with a framework that may serve as a template for societies as they transform and adjust their mobility systems. People's journeys are seldom limited solely to economic goals—there is joy in traveling across new landscapes. Similarly, our book not only deals with mobility as a topic of vital importance to the global economy, it also offers the reader a window seat from which to observe a rapidly evolving mobility landscape.

The century of the automobile

The automobile has been central to human mobility systems for over a hundred years. From its origins, when horseless carriages required a flagman to walk ahead of each car, the automobile has been responsible for a remarkable evolution in mobility experiences. Automotive production evolved from a cottage industry relying on a small number of craftsmen to becoming arguably the biggest industrial sector of the global economy. Cars have sped past the sound barrier on the ground and have carried astronauts on the moon. And now cars can communicate with each other to avert accidents and even drive themselves in urban traffic.

Along the way, a love affair blossomed between people and cars. Through symbiotic evolution, the auto industry reshaped urban and suburban landscapes and changed how we live, work, and play. For many, the automobile made personal mobility available round-the-clock. And access to efficient mobility has propelled economic development and a better quality of life in many parts of the world. When early humans began to walk upright, a new vantage was gained and bipedal mobility multiplied survival options. Cars afforded humans yet another level of mobility. *Cogito ergo zoom* is a mantra we have lived by ever since.[2]

When Peter Drucker, referring to the auto industry, coined the phrase "industry of industries," could even he have foreseen how powerful the impact of the automobile would become?[3] The raw numbers are staggering. If the auto industry were a country, its annual revenue, exceeding $3.5 trillion, would earn it the number four rank among nations. The industry accounts for more than 50 million employed across the value chain. The global vehicle population registers at more than 1.1 billion, which means there are almost as many cars on Earth today as there were people when the automobile was invented.

Troubled waters

Yet the sheer success and omnipresence of cars have created a new set of problems. In urban areas, which contribute more than 85 percent of global GDP, population densities are crowding out space for automobiles. Congestion is a pain point that sits high on the list of most city administrators. Societies have awoken from a reverie to realize that we have been designing cities for cars when we should have been designing cities for people. Accelerated urbanization in emerging economies and a wave of urban renewal in mature economies are pressuring urban planners to rethink and redesign cityscapes and regulations, sometimes aimed at curbing the use of personal vehicles.

Cars have often been the most efficient and quickest mode for point-to-point travel in cities. This assumption is less frequently true today. For some, escalating cost, congestion, and inconvenience are turning this beloved asset into a liability. As Thoreau reflected, "When the farmer has got his house, he may not be the richer but the poorer for it, and it be the house that has got him."[4] One might say this about many urban car owners.

People's passion for cars has cooled for other reasons as well. The scale of the human impact on our planet is becoming more evident with each passing decade. The levels of increase in greenhouse gas emissions and depletion of resources are not sustainable. Cars have become cleaner and greener in dramatic fashion. Yet the sheer increase in the global vehicle population means that this progress is insufficient. Governments are restricting profligate development, constraining vehicle designs, and limiting the use of personal cars, which will become increasingly expensive to develop, own, and operate.

Even as the long love affair between people and the driving machine seems to be waning, a new romance is blooming. Smartphones are the new object of love and adoration. Phones have supplanted cars as a portal to social interactions, communication, and entertainment and even as a space for intimacy. The smartphone has changed customer expectations broadly with respect to personalization, connectivity, and information-integrated system technologies by offering a breathtaking new array of possibilities.

Cultural attitudes are changing too. A few decades ago, in many countries, obtaining a driver's license was a rite of passage for many teenagers. Not anymore. Vehicle ownership, vehicle use, and the number of licensed drivers are all declining in most developed economies. Many young adults are choosing to abandon the suburbs their parents populated and moving to rejuvenated cities with a wide array of bars, cafés, theaters, and restaurants and myriad opportunities for social interaction. Cars rank lower in priority for many of this tribe compared to earlier generations.

A perfect storm

These social changes have whipped up a perfect storm, requiring us to reenvision future mobility.

Even leaders from traditional industry behemoths are speaking with uncharacteristic candor. According to Mark Fields, former CEO of Ford Motor Company, "We are on the cusp of a mobility revolution."[5] Nissan's Europe chairman, Paul Willcox, adds that automakers are facing "a decade of disruption."[6] Ian Robertson, a board member of BMW and head of BMW's global sales and marketing functions, cautions that "the next ten years are probably going to involve more change and more dynamics than we have seen in the last century."[7] Analogies with the demise of Kodak and Polaroid, companies that underestimated the disruptiveness of digital imaging, are invoked to assure investors and customers that the auto industry has awoken to the magnitude of changes ahead. Traditional auto companies surely will not give up without a fight, but the challenges they face are formidable. Only the nimble few, who fundamentally redefine their roles and strategies will survive in a very different future mobility landscape.

The track record of human civilization provides hope that individuals and their institutions will adapt. From the onset of the Ice Age through centuries of calamities, famines, and floods, people have evolved and survived. The one sure source of strength and optimism is humankind's ability to cooperate and innovate to work itself out of tight spots. Technology, innovation, new forms of cooperation, and new business models give us multiple ways to respond.

Innovations to redefine mobility

Heeding society's alarm at the degradation of our planet's environment, regulators are pushing automakers to lower carbon emissions and vehicular pollution. In response, automakers have harnessed a range of technologies to address fuel efficiency and tailpipe emissions. Carbon emissions from some concept cars are reaching levels that are a tenth of those released by conventional cars just a decade ago. Other tailpipe emissions have been reduced even more dramatically—to less than 2 percent of the values of emissions spewed by cars from the 1970s. New breeds of electric vehicles promise far greater range, better efficiency, and much lower operating costs while technically meeting zero-emission mandates. Some nations have set forth a vision to achieve zero traffic fatalities on their roads. Sustainability, an imperative increasingly espoused by society, has gained a more central role in driving the development agenda in many industries and communities.

Now connectivity has joined sustainability at the top of the agenda. Whether at home, at work, in the park, or on the streets, innovations in communication have allowed us to be immersed in an ocean of connectivity, data, and analytics, even while we are on the move. Interfaces in smartphones, smart things, and smart wearables help us summon information, assistance, guidance, services, and even assets. This ubiquitous connectivity provides a path to dramatically improve our transportation experiences and efficiency. Smartphone applications can plan a journey, hail a car, keep people connected while traveling, and pay for the trip through an e-wallet. These modern opportunities are available not only in industrialized economies but also in many emerging economies. China, India, and Indonesia, to name a few, are leapfrogging into a digitized world with astonishing rapidity. Most traditional automakers are responding by turning their cars into mobile connected spaces that can also be personalized. Many technologies from consumer electronics are being integrated into cars and car-related services. Several automakers and their suppliers have unleashed a flurry of apps and mobility solutions suitable for modern customers operating in a digital economy. However, these incumbents face competition from new-age communication behemoths such as Apple, Google's parent Alphabet, and China's Tencent, which see a chance to play the role of disruptor by leveraging their platforms to dominate the consumer's interface with cars and mobility systems.

For the younger generation, dubbed digital natives, connectivity innovations are as natural as the seemingly new sharing economy. The Internet has fostered a newly accessible marketplace for assets, offering consumers a chance to share everything from apartments to garden implements, household appliances, and cars. Modern travelers increasingly prefer to adopt the role of users of services rather than owners of assets. For many of the connected netizens in emerging markets, stepping straight into the user role with Uber or Didi or Grab may be the most natural path to improved mobility, bypassing both the owner role and the driver role. And for those occasions when use of a car is critical, local short-term car rentals offer a solution in the form of a rental billed by the minute, where you want it, when you want it, all handled through the smartphone. In the "use, don't own" realm, traditional automakers are not standing still. Many have acquired significant stakes in customer-facing startups such as taxi alternatives and peer-to-peer car-sharing and vanpooling services. In a wide-open marketplace, other mobility stakeholders, including rail and transit operators, have also attempted to enter with a range of urban mobility solutions.

Such a variety of options, provided in a mode of mass customization, has come to be expected by today's consumers. To provide this mass customization, companies must leverage big data and analytics to extract granular information about customers and options, supply and demand. Advances in the industrial Internet allow products and services to be configured, one at a time, to individually serve customers who expect and will pay for customization and personalization in travel services. Intelligent personal advisers in the form of apps that harness web-crawling bots can likewise sift through a multitude of possibilities to craft an individualized travel itinerary, even if the destination is nothing more than a new eatery across town.

And just around the corner is the age of self-driving cars. Prototypes have gained maturity remarkably quickly over the past decade. As vehicles become better able to drive themselves, the technology promises to allow drivers to become passengers and free up their time for alternative productive uses. Here too, new entrants—interlopers, to some—such as Tesla's electric vehicles with their Autopilot functions and Google's self-driving podcar, are provoking shifts in R&D investment and priorities among traditional automakers the world over. Shedding their traditional wariness of wading into domains that pose high liability risk, numerous automakers also have set their sights on the holy grail of full autonomy with aggressive investments and acquisitions. Always connected, self-driving cars have gone from science fiction to roving prototypes in a mere decade. Summoning and using a car in the near future may come to resemble the way we summon and use an elevator. The transition to driverless cars may be as profound as the shift modern society made when it switched to the horseless carriage.

Yet all technological progress comes packaged with new challenges. As George Bernard Shaw observed, "Science never solves a problem without creating ten more."[8] Technology has sometimes widened the gulf between the haves and the have-nots. Mobility is a vital activity, and societies need to ensure that access to it is not beyond the reach of any demographic segment of society. Some of society's investments in mobility infrastructure can be quickly rendered obsolete, so careful planning and execution are necessary. And the all-digital world has brought new awareness of the risks of cyber intrusions, for data theft, and hacking via a connected auto can be more threatening than traditional Grand Theft Auto. Thus, future mobility architectures need to safeguard many societal imperatives.

Re-envisioning mobility

These innovations, nurtured in a rich but sometimes chaotic entrepreneurial ecosystem, will drive migration to a new and better era of mobility, as long as the appropriate government actors—national, regional, and local—complement privately funded initiatives with enlightened oversight and intelligent public investment. Along the way, the discourse must shift from *cars* to *mobility*. That is, a wider range of actors, public and private, complementing the automakers, will provide mobility components and solutions. No single entity will be able to provide an end-to-end mobility system, so collaboration and integration will be essential to offer a seamless service to consumers.

Urban society will look beyond cars to a broader range of options. This shift will require mobility users to be open to multiple modes. Walking, bicycling, ride sharing, and taking public transit such as buses, subways, and trains are all valuable complements to individual driving, each with its own merits and purpose. We can expect a blurring of the divide among public, personal, and shared modes of transit.

As exciting as these innovative products and services will be, perhaps the greatest opportunities for dramatically changing the ecology of transportation are expected to come in the realm of integration and coordination. Just as the toughest filament of carbon fiber is of little use without the resin matrix in which it is embedded, transportation modes need to be effectively linked.

Our approach to comprehending this future is determinedly holistic. Discrete but connected solutions offer better opportunities to deliver superior results for complex user needs. A multisolution mobility landscape will open up, with two simple goals—to delight the customer and to align with societal priorities. Toward this end, a society leveraging dynamic entrepreneurship will access a full spectrum of technologies, business models, and transport modes. These options will span a range of economic value propositions so that low-cost modes will coexist with premium and exclusive modes. Personal mobility devices such as cars, bicycles, and microcars will coexist with buses and metro transit systems. The quickest path between two points may involve a drive by car to a metro station, then travel by mass transit to a city center, followed by the use of a shared bicycle for the last mile. Uber, Zipcar, Sidecar, Turo, Car2Go, BlaBlaCar, Grabtaxi, Velib, Boris Bikes—personal urban transportation is acquiring a whole new vocabulary. Urban mobility experiences will become increasingly heterogeneous. A multiplicity of innovative modes suitable for various purses and contexts will compete to lure travelers with their speed, economics, and convenience. Each mode or combination of modes will be characterized by its signature for cost, availability, environmental impact, and time efficiency. Around the world, sustained investment in physical infrastructure and digital infrastructures, augmented by the world of smart devices and handheld apps, has given a huge boost to connecting these diverse modes of transportation.

For individual journeys, consumers will rely on "intelligent advisers" in the forms of apps residing in or accessible through their smartphones, wearable digital devices, or built into their cars, with up-to-date analytics that can recommend personalized, profile-specific travel choices and routes. Mobility as a service (MaaS) is a paradigm that captures the essence of use-as-needed systems, providing the potential for more efficient use of resources and capital. Various assets for mobility need not be owned, yet they will be made available for use as needed by consumers. In such well-managed systems, asset utilization can be high, and mass customization can tailor transport solutions to suit specific communities and individuals.

Adjusting societal focus from cars to mobility also leads to another important transformation in thinking. An earlier generation believed that roads and infrastructure should be paid for by general fund taxes, including taxes on fuels. However, to encourage behaviors that are consistent with the need to limit pollution and congestion, targeted user fees, taxes, and subsidies—for roads, bridges, cars, buses, trains, parking spaces, and even urban access—will be needed to help shape the use of mobility services and the use of assets and infrastructure. Such pricing mechanisms will further influence consumers' choices of modes, travel patterns, and investments in cars, bicycles, and housing, for example. If designed well, these new mechanisms should influence travelers to choose modes aligned with societal priorities.

Society, through its arms of governments, regulators, and city administrators will have to join automakers, entrepreneurs, and technologists to craft this far more comprehensive mobility map. Societies need convenient, user-friendly mobility for people and goods. We need clean air and safe roads. We also need productive organizations that can provide jobs and economic development. And we need a planet that can continue to sustain and nourish life as we know it.

The CHIP mobility architecture

Future society will demand connected, heterogeneous, intelligent, and personalized (CHIP) mobility. CHIP mobility for a digitally powered society will be logical and efficient. This future preserves the freedom of personal choice, even as it upholds fairness. Those who use more assets and resources, including urban road and parking space, will be expected to pay more. Customers can enjoy flexibility and variety even as society ensures sustainability and urban harmony. "Mobility where I want it, when I want it, uniquely fitting my budget and my context"—this is the expectation of customers and society. CHIP mobility serves this expectation.

This vision provides a sustainable future course for mobility to help humanity continue its journey toward a better quality of life. Mobility has not only been the grease that sped economic development, it has also been the spice that added flavor to our lives, making them fuller and richer. The next generation deserves an exciting future, but also a sustainable one.

Recognizing the great diversity of conditions and needs across the world, we envision CHIP mobility as an architecture that is adaptable for a range of environments. Global context varies not only from continent to continent but also from cities to suburbs. Local cultures and lifestyles will predispose societies to prefer certain solutions. Democracy and freedom have emphasized the importance of individual choice and expression. To ignore this would be imprudent. We examine the building blocks of mobility that are advancing, boosted by technology, regulations, and customer preferences. We review the novel ways in which these building blocks are juxtaposed and connected to deliver mobility solutions applicable to different priorities. From this analysis we offer guidelines as to how the CHIP architecture may be adapted and the prerequisites for strategic success.

Innovative mobility solutions are a social and economic necessity that must transcend traditional industry boundaries. These solutions must align with national and global goals for sustainability and still cater to individual needs. This mandate is a tall order. Getting to this future state, will require us to discard many of the assumptions that underpin current mobility. The traditional auto industry is unlikely to enjoy the dominant role it played for the last generation. Governments and city administrations must play a constructive, collaborative role to enable CHIP mobility. They will be joined by a range of new-generation entrepreneurs and investors such as Google, Apple, Uber, and Tencent, technology startups, and app developers, all of which have visions of being the disruptor and redefining future mobility.

We make no attempt to offer simple prescriptive recommendations. We cannot expect such a future to arrive gift-wrapped, all in one bundle. In our view there is no perfect solution under these conditions. Rather, CHIP mobility will evolve through the messy processes of capitalism and democracy, often tinged with disruption and, regrettably, sometimes corruption. After all, any road to the future is bound to have a few construction zones along the way. We expect much trial and error—and much political wrangling—as societies move toward a more sustainable future.

We anticipate a period of heightened experimentation, mimicking the process undergone by biological systems, during which industries, entrepreneurs, and governments explore a multiplicity of combinations, constructed from an ever-expanding set of building blocks. Fluid adaptations across time and geography are a characteristic of many life forms. As such, we do not expect a single "winner" mobility model. Rather, we expect continued differentiation and variation—genetic mutations—across travel modes, business models, and evolving regulations.

As Darwin noted, "It is not the strongest of the species that survive, nor the most intelligent, but the one most responsive to change."[9] The CHIP mobility architecture is a model for a flexible, responsive mobility ecosystem that can evolve and adapt to a wide variety of domains and challenges. As such, we believe it is an architecture that Darwin would have been delighted to observe and citizen travelers will find pleasing to their needs.

About this book

The scope of the book is deliberately limited to human mobility. We have refrained from extending the discussion to the world of freight and logistics, even though there are many topics of overlapping interest and relevance.

The bulk of our discussion is oriented toward the urban context. Noting that a lot of commuting also occurs across the city-suburb boundary, we address several solutions that are relevant to these commuters. We concede that huge changes are under way in rural manifestations of mobility as well. But the preponderance of economic activity and population concentrations in urban locales led us to pay greater attention to these domains. Further, we believe that many of the technological advances, such as vehicle connectivity and autonomy, as well as business solutions, such as car sharing, will be driven by innovators and demand in the urban context, though they will eventually have an impact in rural areas as well.

Although our research and coverage are heavily dependent on the mobility patterns and technologies being deployed in postindustrial developed economies, we also take note of many important innovations occurring outside these regions—affordable mobility in India, electric vehicles in China, and motorcycle taxis in Southeast Asia, for example. We observe the dichotomy of the industrialized and emerging economies from several angles. First, some of the interesting entrepreneurs (Google, Uber, BlaBlaCar) have developed their innovations in the industrialized world, but their ideas are rapidly being spun (by numerous players) across a very broad global landscape. Second, the industrialized economies have plunged deep into a pattern of mobility that is worryingly unsustainable. We hope the lessons learned here may help deflect emerging economies from such a trajectory while motorization is still low, to avoid future expensive remediation. Along the way, we hope the successful examples of transforming urban mobility, such as we see in London, Hong Kong, and Singapore, may be emulated in cities like Mumbai or São Paulo. In all cases, we seek to identify sustainable solutions that can be customized to the needs of the wide variety of land-scapes across the globe.

The book is organized into three parts:

In part I we review the contours of the world that are changing all around us and stimulating the need to transform existing mobility systems. Accelerated urbanization, growing concern for the environment, and continuously evolving cultural attitudes will require our future mobility architecture to be different.

In part II we examine humans' irrepressible instinct to innovate and find solutions to mobility challenges. Innovative responses can leverage the digitized economy, lead to a variety of greener and more personalized solutions, and improve our products and services. They form the building blocks of the CHIP mobility architecture.

In part III we synthesize the CHIP mobility architecture and outline a framework to identify stakeholder roles required to realize society's vision for faster, smarter, and greener mobility.

Throughout, we have endeavored to include numerous external viewpoints to complement our own. These inputs, some of which are presented in boxes, have widened the range of perspectives we bring to the discussion. They help refine and amplify the many takeaways presented in the chapters.

This book takes on a core challenge of our age. How can we shape the trajectory of mobility so that it becomes sustainable? What is the role of the traditional automotive companies? What is the role of the Internet generation entrepreneurs? What is the role of government? How should rules be written to support this new future? How can they be enforced? Who will pay for them? How can society's mobility expectations be addressed?

If you are drawn to these questions, we are confident that the chapters ahead will unfold a tapestry that analyzes the challenges and proposes solutions to the above.

Come, take us for a test ride!

Acknowledgments

This book is the outcome of three independent but intertwined journeys. Our respective careers have afforded us a certain breadth and depth of exposure to the automotive and associated industries accumulated over three-plus decades. Tracing the evolution of our society and its perspectives, our engagement has gradually morphed from being very auto-focused to embracing the full diversity of tools and solutions that aid human mobility today. Effort specifically dedicated to this book was spread over three years, during which time we have been very fortunate to broaden our perspectives through interactions with a large number of people with varied backgrounds who have contributed in a variety of ways to help us shape and present the ideas we offer. Our approach has required us not only to look at future mobility but also the key factors that will shape it. As a result, we had sought out counsel, perspectives, and experiences not only from people connected with mobility but also many who had little to do with the subject professionally—a list that includes sociologists, futurists, and urban planners. Their opinions too have enriched the contents of this book.

A number of people remained close to this project through its evolution, and our discussions with them proved invaluable. We are especially grateful to Venkatesh Prasad, Richard Spitzer, Nagi Palle, Jim Womack, Kasturi Venugopal, and Jay Parikh for their intelligent and thought-provoking debates as we shaped the ideas presented here.

The auto industry itself is a deep source of experience, and we benefited from the insights of several industry leaders, including Carlos Ghosn, Rick Wagoner, Bob Lutz, Carlos Tavares, Anand Mahindra, Andy Palmer, Bernd Bohr, Mark Reuss, Don Runkle, and Mark Schulz. Thanks are also due to Larry Burns, Carl-Peter Forster, Klaus Entenmann, Christoph Grote, Johann DeNysschen, and Phil Murtaugh. The Society of Automotive Engineers has been a leading platform for global mobility practitioners, and we similarly benefited from extensive discussions with three of their past presidents, Dan Hancock,

Andy Brown, and Cuneyt Oge. Many senior executives in the auto industry also devoted time to debating ideas with us, and we are thankful to Bill Jordan, Dave Vanderveen, Dirk Lembregts, Bob Inman, and Jon Owen for their support.

The industry has long depended on a number of experts in specific technical domains who anticipate trends and shape future technologies. We gained valuable insights from Bernard Charles, Helmut List, Stephan Pischinger, and George Gillespie.

Our book highlights some topics in boxes. We are grateful to Wolfgang Bernhart, Wilfried Aulbur, John Hagel, Sarwant Singh, Martyn Briggs, Gary Silberg, Andrew Savarie, Don Devereaux, Donna Miller, Divya Venugopal, Phil Gott, and Egil Juliussen for their valuable contributions to this material.

S. Ramadorai, Rodney Brooks, Robin Chase, Amory Lovins, Marina Gorbis, Geoff Wardle, Gopal Srinivasan, and Lakshmi Narayan, each in their own way, have been peering into the future of human society. We thank them for the insights they readily shared with us.

Much of the technology in the mobility industry has flowed from suppliers, and their perspectives have also been important. We are thankful to Dirk Hoheisel, Michael Ruf, Jeff Owens, and Jean Brunol for sharing their outlook from this vantage. At the same time, the book has identified an important role that will be played by a new genre of technologists and suppliers, many of whom originate from Silicon Valley. We acknowledge the assistance of Kent Helfrich, Marty McEnroe, Kerry Champion, Marty Thall, and Avneesh Agrawal.

Mobility is a domain that is home to a number of highly experienced analysts and consultants, and our discussions with many of them are deeply appreciated. They include David Andrea, Prakash Krishnaswamy, Chris Borroni-Bird, Tim Armstrong, Murli Iyer, Gary Lapidus, Rainer Scholz, Rakesh Batra, Thomas Schmelzer, Frank Haertl, Marco Hecker, Anantha Krishnan, Sean McAlinden, Jay Baron, Mahender Singh, Amy Mills, Anne Asensio, Monica Menghini, Stephen Dyer, Jian Sun, and Sven Beiker. Karl Ludvigsen is an old friend, prolific author, and industry insider whose delightful anecdotes and deep insights we treasure.

We have had access to corporate information through many official sources, including Wieland Bruch and Michael Fischer (BMW), James Ryan and Nada Filipovich (Daimler), Mark Gilles (Volkswagen), Simon Sproule (previously at Tesla), Stephen Lynn (Catapult), , Zhaoming Chua (EasyMile), Michael Austin (BYD), Christy Petty (Gartner), Nashwa Naushad and Shreya Gadepalli (ITDP), Jana Hartline (Toyota), Katelyn Chesley (Zipcar), and Larry Kinsel and Kathy Adelson (General Motors).

The perspectives of regulators, governments, and think tanks have contributed to some of the balance the book has sought to deliver. We are grateful to Margo Oge, Sue Zielinski, Komal Anand, Clayton Lane, Walter Hook, and Rachel Tang.

Throughout the course of the book, we have sought to present the thesis with rigor. We were helped in this effort by input from a number of talented academics, including Yossi Sheffi, Erik Brynjolfsson, Venkat Ramaswamy, Bhaskar Ramamurthy, Stefan Bratzel, Ferdinand Dudenhoeffer, Uwe Clausen, and Dieter Rombach. Among students, we acknowledge the assistance of Nachiket Joshi.

In academia, the size of one's intellectual debts can often be a measure of wealth. By that metric, Charlie Fine is grateful indeed for the tall stack of IOUs he has accumulated. His dissertation committee at Stanford, David Kreps, Evan Porteus, and Steven Wheelwright, supported his exploration of the Toyota manufacturing phenomenon, which shaped his earliest understandings of the modern automotive industry. At MIT, Dan Roos nurtured the International Motor Vehicle Program, which enabled Charlie to learn with and from a powerful collection of mentors and colleagues, including Dan Whitney, Takahiro Fujimoto, Kim Clark, John Paul MacDuffie, Susan Helper, Fritz Pil, Mari Sako, Andrew Graves, and Koichi Shimokawa. Former students in MIT's LFM/LGO program, Milo Werner and Doug Field generously shared their insights regarding the challenges and successes faced by Tesla Motors, and led to a case co-authored with Milo, Don Rosenfield, and Loredana Padurean.

Fine-tuning the content and narrative benefited from the generous time and effort expended by Sampath Kumar, Thomas Abraham, Sathya Prasad, and Sundaram Parthasarathy. Sathiyaseelan Gangasalam, an accomplished industrial designer, lent his keen understanding to an exquisite rendering of the book's cover image.

The considerable task of preparing the manuscript would not have been possible without the efficient assistance of Saurabh Jain and Priya Rao. At the MIT Press we are grateful to Emily Taber, Deborah Cantor-Adams, Marjorie Pannell, and Katie Hope for enthusiastically and efficiently steering the manuscript through the production and marketing processes.

Last but most important, at all times we have been buoyed by the support, strength, and encouragement of our spouses, Venil Sumantran, Wendy Fine, and Maria Aguerri Gomez. Not only had they indulged our three years of effort on this book, they have helped us sharpen many of our ideas and discussion through curious and challenging debates.

I   The World Is Changing

Part I opens with a review of two large and thriving metropolises that have evolved in two very different sets of conditions and shaped by very different policies. They represent two divergent trajectories that are supported by very different mobility architectures. Their destinies to date have been largely influenced by their mobility framework, illustrating the relationship between policies and investment and their eventual outcomes.

In chapters 2 through 4 we turn to the role played by urbanization and population densification in determining suitable transportation options. We evaluate how these options affect the resulting environmental footprint. For baby boomers, cars have been central to mobility; to a digital native, "mobility" has a wider range of connotations. We assess how changing cultural values and priorities will alter society's expectations of future mobility.

These chapters help identify key requirements for the CHIP—connected, heterogeneous, integrated, and personalized—mobility architecture, which are then explored in more depth in subsequent chapters of the book.

1 A Tale of Two Cities

We are our choices.

—*Jean-Paul Sartre*

Los Angeles, the city of Angels

On March 16, 2016, the headline in the *Los Angeles Times* blared: "Los Angeles area can claim the worst traffic in America. Again."[1] Commuters on Interstate 101 spent an additional fifty-eight minutes in traffic for their typical commute compared to free-flowing transit times. Against a posted 65 mph speed limit, average traffic speeds were observed to be 17 mph. Over a full year, the millions of Los Angeles commuters each sacrifices an average of almost 5.5 days stuck in traffic, which is more than the four days of vacation the average American takes each year.[2]

Detroit may have earned its moniker of Motor City, being home to U.S. automakers, but it was Los Angeles that usurped the number one spot for celebrating car culture. Ford in Dearborn built the 1932 Ford Deuce Coupe, but it took hot-rodders in Los Angeles and the Beach Boys' song to celebrate its reputation across the world for over three generations. More recently, the genre of movies represented by *Fast and Furious* have glorified a culture of tuning and "slamming" Japanese performance cars. Enthusiasts in Southern California have lifted the sport of "drifting" out of obscurity in Japan and made it a global motorsport event.

Los Angeles is also home to numerous advanced concept studios for global automakers, including GM, Ford, Daimler, Nissan, and Toyota, which seek the free-spirited talent they sometimes find lacking in their native Detroit, Stuttgart, or Tokyo. The Art Center College of Design, located in the L.A. suburb of Pasadena, is the preeminent finishing school for many of the renowned auto designers of the world. Los Angeles and Southern California talent, drenched in sunshine, are the globally acknowledged fashionistas of car culture.

However, Angelenos pay a heavy price for their obsession with cars.

The sprawling urban form

Ironically, railroads promoted early growth and development in Los Angeles.[3] But even as a railhead town, home to railroad companies and builders, the city struggled with getting urban transit systems to work effectively. Transport provided by early streetcars was unreliable and inconvenient. In the early twentieth century, the city embraced cars as *the* modern solution for transportation. In 1920, L.A. County had a car population of roughly 160,000. A decade later that figure had grown fivefold.

Not only was car culture celebrated and nurtured, L.A.'s urban form evolved in consonance. While New York City and Manhattan Island faced geographic constraints to sprawl, as did Hong Kong and Singapore, Los Angeles faced no such limitation. Sprawl may be loosely defined as the expansion of urban areas into surrounding rural hinterland, through low-density habitation, under market forces. In Los Angeles, liberal investment in highways and the popularity of the car allowed people to spread out. Cheap oil, much of it also extracted locally, lubricated such expansion. Los Angeles evolved into a cluster of more than seventy-two suburbs, including such well-known names as Santa Monica, Century City, Pasadena, Glendale, Beverly Hills, and Long Beach. Car-centric California served as the crucible for urban developments such as super-service stations and drive-in markets.[4]

The L.A. metropolitan area is home to more than 10 million people. That is not a problem in itself: since many cities around the world manage such large populations. However, L.A. is an exceptional megacity that evolved without a disproportionately concentrated core. The community planner Eric Eidlin describes L.A.'s urban form as "density without downtown, sprawl without suburbia."[5] The city's large, sprawling urban area has a very high population density, almost three times as much as Houston's and twice as much as Detroit's.[6] L.A. is uniformly crowded over a very large area but lacks an ultra-high-density core.

Such sprawl poses unique challenges for mobility, which must serve numerous contiguous high-density locales. L.A.'s problems were compounded by residents trying to satisfy their mobility needs with personal cars after ineffective public transit led to the closure of many streetcar services. According to Karen Anderton of Oxford University's Transport Studies Unit, "Although countless cities across the world are decades ahead in terms of transit provision and have much to teach Los Angeles, the U.S. model of suburban sprawl and expansion was based on the symbolism and iconic status that Los Angeles gave the automobile in the twentieth century."[7]

Angelenos' love of the car was supported by significant expenditure on highways, resulting in the densest network among large U.S. cities. L.A. offers almost twice as many highway lane-miles per square mile as Detroit.[8] Predictably, perhaps, adding highway capacity only led to more travelers choosing to commute by car, a problem described by Paul Sorensen, an authority on urban planning affiliated with the University of California, as a "triple convergence."[9] The new highways attracted commuters who changed routes of travel, time of travel, or modes of travel, quickly saturating the additional capacity.

Over the past four decades, the pace of highway construction in L.A. has decreased. Continued population growth and economic expansion have therefore contributed to travel demand further outstripping highway capacity.

Public sympathy favored personal cars. Thus, proposals to fund and subsidize new mass transit projects were repeatedly voted down by taxpayers. The city experimented with subways and elevated railways in the first half of the twentieth century, but none of these endeavors was sustained. L.A. did develop an extensive bus transit system, but these vehicles compete for road space with ever more cars. Even with modern interventions, such as priority at traffic signals, these "rapid" bus lines averaged less than 12 mph.

A bias to the personal car was encouraged by local builders and zoning approaches that mandated adequate inexpensive parking for residents. Compared with New York or San Francisco, L.A. provides a larger number of parking spots at significantly lower price points. Many global cities have used the lever of controlling price and availability of parking to manage traffic and congestion, but L.A. has chosen not to do so.

Overall, L.A. residents drive more, on a per capita basis, than residents of other megacities. According to Christopher Hawthorne, architecture critic at the *LA Times*, "We want the cultural amenities and economic clout of a major metropolis but the traffic patterns of a garden-variety suburb."[10]

Awakening to the smog
Western travelers to Beijing, Shanghai, or New Delhi often arrive armed with travel and weather apps that monitor air quality and pollution and are advised against stepping outdoors on days when alerts are sounded. These

Figure 1.1 A view of the Los Angeles skyline, typically smothered in smog.
Source: Flickr. Photograph by J. Barreiros (CC BY-SA 2.0)

are by no means rare occasions. Yet many travelers are unaware that in the 1970s, they would have experienced similar restrictions in Los Angeles.

Smog is the outcome of a variety of industrial and automotive emissions that release nitrogen oxides into the atmosphere, along with particulates and other volatile organic compounds, as a result of burning fossil fuels. In L.A., this issue had become a topic of headlines as early as the 1940s, as industrialization and auto sales started to ratchet up. Soupy smog defined ambient air quality. Hospitals were inundated with patients seeking assistance for respiratory ailments. Children suffered the worst, and smog exposure was linked to permanent lung damage and impaired physical development.

By 1950, air pollution had got the attention of citizen groups, who demanded action from local governments. The actions that followed were built on a combination of regulations and science. Controls were imposed on industries, on burning waste in landfills, and on automobile emissions. By 1959, air quality standards defining tolerable air pollution levels had been announced, and in 1967 Governor Ronald Reagan established the California

Air Resource Board (CARB) to tackle the problem statewide. Because of the acute nature of the problem, California was granted a waiver to depart from national regulatory norms to advance more stringent standards. Progressively, pollutants from a host of sources were targeted for reduction. Over time, California embraced the most stringent automotive emission standards of any region around the world. Uniquely among U.S. states, California also issued automakers a mandate to supply a small fraction of their sales fleet as zero-emission vehicles (ZEVs), usually electric vehicles, with no tailpipe emissions. This mandate was intended to foster R&D in the industry and to promote the development and sales of electric cars. Although the ZEV requirements had little effect, collectively, these efforts seemed to halt the air quality deterioration over the course of the next few decades, and even offer some relief. In 1979, levels of ozone, a contributor to smog, exceeded current norms on 234 days. By 2015, that threshold was exceeded on only 67 days.

Policy changes and new investments

Over time, regional policies heeded the factors that were driving L.A. in an unsustainable direction. In a city bordered by the Pacific to the west and eventually spreading as far east as the San Bernardino Mountains, urban planners were forced to manage zoning more carefully. The result was a focus on redeveloping central areas of the city and on placing further developments along newly planned transit corridors.

To coax people out of their cars, the Los Angeles County Metro Transit Authority launched new rail services linking some of the main population centers. Although these services were limited in comparison with the mass transit services in other megacities, they signaled a change in direction. With a limited budget and service scale, L.A. chose to deploy bus rapid transit along several dedicated corridors. By some measures, L.A. has the most extensive bus transit in the U.S. Fares were kept low to motivate users to take public transit. Bike infrastructure has since been expanded to pair with the bus transit network. A new Mobility Plan 2035, approved by the Los Angeles City Council, anticipates greater use of dedicated bus lanes, with linkage to a network of bike lanes.

Too little, too late?

Yet for Angelenos, mobility remains a painful topic, and these initiatives are judged by many to be too little, too late. L.A.'s fundamental urban form has given rise to a host of challenges that are not easily solved by taking incremental steps. Policy measures have not gone far enough, and unlike many cities that have employed pricing and fee structures to alter commuter habits, L.A. has been reluctant to deal with this topic, fearing citizen backlash. Tentative changes to policies regarding zoning or parking have had limited impact. Compared with many peer cities, investment in transportation infrastructure and new mobility solutions in L.A. has been half-hearted. Migration to more sustainable mass transit or nonmotorized modes has been slow.

The Greater Los Angeles metro area sprawls over 4,850 square miles, making it the largest metropolitan region in the U.S.; it supports the highest density of vehicles among U.S. urban areas. Compared to New York, where 30 percent of trips are made using public transit, in L.A. that figure is less than 6 percent.[11] Even after the recent initiatives, L.A.'s 10 million residents are served by no more than ninety-three metro rail stations (compared with 370 above- and below-ground rail stations in London). Fewer than 10 percent of the 4.4 million employed in the greater L.A. area work in the downtown L.A. zone, leaving the city to grapple with a highly dispersed working population. The 2016 INRIX traffic study once again placed Los Angeles at the top of the list of global cities with the worst congestion.[12] Notwithstanding very strict auto emission standards, pollution is on the rise again. While many cities in Europe, including London, experience even more traffic congestion, in those cities cars are seldom the primary travel mode. In many cities traffic congestion has in fact been manipulated to steer people to higher-capacity modes. In L.A., commuters have few options to forsake their cars for an alternative travel mode.

The lessons are clear and painful. Urban form is a key determinant of mobility choices. Zoning policies and investments in infrastructure and technologies can shape the resulting mobility network. These mobility networks influence economic productivity and environmental sustainability, which in turn contribute to the quality of life residents may enjoy. City and regional planners must think decades ahead of their urban growth curves to design and adopt systems that will accommodate expansion or suffer the price of extreme congestion and pollution when the growth inevitably arrives.

In contrast to car-centric L.A., we next turn to a far older city, one that has embarked on an ambitious journey to integrate contemporary mobility solutions within its age-old architecture. London, a city with permanent settlements predating the Roman Empire, has taken a very different course, one that promises its residents faster, smarter, and greener mobility.

London: More than double-deckers

The iconic London double-decker buses are a staple on picture postcards so popular with tourists to the city. Behind this quaint vehicle is a much larger story suggesting how cities might address their urban mobility and congestion challenges.

For the average Briton, history and traditions matter a lot. Hence, through much of history, and even after devastating destruction in two world wars, London's charm has barely changed. Beefeaters continue to play the role of sentinel at the Tower of London, something they have done since 1485.[13] A large part of the city's physical infrastructure has roots that go back several centuries. The roads date back to medieval times, the Tube lines to the 1800s, and the river bus service to the reign of King Richard I in 1197. No wonder foreign tourists lap it up!

Limiting sprawl

In 1801, London's population was estimated at about 1 million people. The Industrial Revolution then triggered massive migration to cities and by the end of the century, London's population had grown to 6.5 million.[14] Like many cities, London briefly witnessed a loss of population to its suburbs in the mid-twentieth century before the urbanization trend reemerged to take the city's population to over 8 million in the early twenty-first century. Forecasters expect London's population to swell beyond 10 million by 2050.

Greater London today spans an area of almost 600 square miles (one-eighth the area occupied by Greater Los Angeles), bisected by the river Thames. Like many cities, London too felt the pressure of burgeoning population, particularly in the postwar years when population growth was extremely rapid. By the Town and Country Planning Act of 1947, London imposed a green belt around the city. This restriction was intended to limit urban sprawl and preserve a countryside surrounding the city where development would be restricted. In a sense, the law supplied pressure to encourage rejuvenation and the productive use of neglected areas within the city. The green belt remained a controversial subject, with many advantages and disadvantages. But it was successful in limiting uncontrolled expansion of the city boundary even if it did significantly increase the cost of housing within the city.

The Metropolitan Green Belt was often the target of developers, who sought access to valuable land in close proximity to the city. In some instances, such as the Thames Gateway project, at one time among the largest development projects in Europe, allowances were made, and in this case they brought many brownfield sites into productive use. Extending 40 miles from Canary Wharf eastward it encompassed areas that would form a part of London's Olympic Village.

Nevertheless, London has largely prevailed in its effort to limit urban sprawl. This urban form has had a major effect on the way the city functions and on its mobility infrastructure and systems.

Molding personal travel modes

London's approach to serving the mobility needs of its vibrant and expanding community was characterized by encouraging public travel modes and gradually disincentivizing personal modes.

London's road network originated in the early Roman roads, which were rebuilt and expanded in the Anglo-Saxon period. Congestion on London roads was observed as early as 1740, and periodically over the centuries many notable investments were made to expand the network of roads. Yet each project was soon overwhelmed by ever increasing traffic. By the 1960s, any further attempts to construct large highways to crisscross the city were abandoned in favor of public transport. Only the M25 ring road was completed, allowing travelers to bypass London if necessary. Yet even today, roads remain an important aspect of urban mobility, and 80 percent of all travel in London happens on its roads.[15]

The horse-drawn omnibus service made its debut in 1830s, complementing the hackney carriage. Competition soon erupted between rival operators, who served a rapidly expanding population of users. The city also recognized very early that the demand for transportation would need to be augmented by using space beneath the humming city. In 1863 the first London Underground line was operational, and this would evolve into the Tube, in modern use covering more than 270 stations along eleven separate lines.

London also began to manage vehicular traffic, mainly because of congestion and pollution. Policy and pricing played important roles in making this system work. In 2003, London garnered global attention with its imposition of a Congestion Charge for vehicles entering the central area of the city. While relatively unpopular at the time, the £5 daily charge for any car or van entering Central London had a dramatic effect. While many complained the fee was a stealth tax in addition to existing road use charges, all funds received from the scheme were to be reinvested in public transport services. As a result of these measures, vehicular traffic dropped by one-sixth, traffic delays were reduced, and air quality improved.[16] Concurrently, London altered commuter behavior and catalyzed modal shifts through control of capacity and pricing of parking. In London's Canary Wharf business district, parking capacity was limited to fewer than 5,000 spaces to serve an estimated working population of more than 100,000.

A common failing of many large cities is the lack of adequate coordination among their various functions. This is especially true for mobility, which involves many modes and often diverse agencies that are insufficiently coordinated. London's Traffic Management Act created a framework for regulating and controlling activities related to highways. By 2001, this framework had become the One Road Network, which functions as a forum for connecting diverse governmental departments and provides information on such topics as road inspection, parking enforcement, permits, and safety.

On an even larger scale, Transport for London, a local government body responsible for the transport system in Greater London, was formed in 2000 with the initial goal of delivering to London's commuters a user-friendly transit system that was high on efficiency and low on net carbon emissions. The system was designed to promote greater use of public transit, which in turn was expected to lead to a reduction in private car use and ease congestion.

As a system operator, Transport for London, while by no means perfect, has traversed this journey with considerable success. In the process it has contributed to the transformation of mobility into a service-led rather than an asset-led business.

Transport for London is the executive body of the Greater London Authority. It was formed by aggregating several predecessor organizations covering most transportation modes in the city. Over time, it has emerged as one of the largest integrated transport systems in the world. A strategic plan was drawn up for a twenty-year period, through 2020. Over time, Transport for London has integrated a wide range of services, including bus, the London Underground or Tube, local rail and light rail, river services, taxi and private hire cars, bus coaches, cycle hire, and road and traffic management. Integration among these modes was a key factor in enabling more effective multimodal connectivity.

Even by global standards, Transport for London is working with a large-scale template. The system manages the operations of more than 8,700 buses in London covering 700 routes.[17] The Tube contributes 270 stations that are linked by 402 kilometers of tracks. This network is augmented by 124 kilometers of surface rail network serving more than 100 stations. Furthermore, Transport for London is responsible for 580 kilometers of main roads and all of London's 4,600 traffic lights. Plans are also under way to include car-share services within the integrated framework. More than 26 million trips are now made daily across the network managed by Transport for London, and the average trip is 9 kilometers. Importantly, Transport for London has taken many steps in fostering easy connectivity across these diverse modes.

Since Transport for London's initiation, user data reveal growth in the use of all public transport services in excess of population growth and a decline in car use, helped by congestion charges. Between 1993 and 2013, London saw a reduction in the mode share of private transport from 46 percent to 33 percent.[18] Private car trips declined from 10.4 million to 9.6 million trips per day over the same period, the almost 22 percent growth in population notwithstanding. The main beneficiary was public transport, whose share of daily trips grew from 30 percent to 45 percent.

Seeking to ensure that shifting people to public modes would also lead to cleaner mobility, Transport for London has set in place a move to ensure that by 2020, all buses will be electric and all double-deckers will be hybrid-electric. Cycling trips have also doubled, though this figure grew from a low base of 1 percent to 2 percent of mode share. By 2014, Transport for London was operating more than 10,000 bicycles in its network. These are often referred to as "Boris bikes" in honor of Boris Johnson, the erstwhile mayor of London who supported the launch of the bicycle-sharing scheme.

Figure 1.2 London will soon be served by a fleet of pure-electric double-decker buses to lower vehicular pollution in the city.
Source: BYD Co.

To maintain momentum, control costs, and remain attractive to users, Transport for London has frequently updated its technology platforms. The first such step was to enable smart ticketing across the capital with the launch of the Oyster card in 2003. The card provided increased convenience, as well as reduced complexity in the fare structures. Indeed, Oyster fares were launched at half the price of cash fares as both an incentive to use the card and to encourage mass adoption. As a large fraction of users switched to the Oyster card, the costs for operating the system dropped significantly. By 2014, more than 85 percent of the journeys taken on London's public transport were made using the Oyster card and over 70 million cards had been issued—nearly eight times the population, reflecting the high proportion of non-Londoners using the system. Travel on London's buses was also made cashless. By 2015, more than 40 percent of London's pay-as-you-go fares were using the next generation of contactless cards, demonstrating the rapid ramp-up of a new payment technology.

Of course, it takes money to invest in, manage, and maintain such a network. Transport for London's budget for 2014–2015 was almost £11 billion, with just 40 percent of that coming from fare revenues. The remainder came from grant funding or subsidies, which amounted to about 25 percent, and cross-rail funding, adding another 13 percent, from a combination of private and public sector contributors. In short, each of the 8.6 million residents of London sees the expenditure of the equivalent of £1,300 on transport services—a significant investment indeed. London has a disproportionately high percentage of tourists who contribute to the local economy and also use local transport. The net benefit to London's economy is seen to be very positive.

Financial viability remains an important aspect of transportation design for all cities. Efficient, low-carbon mobility often requires some level of subsidy. Such subsidies are often justified on the basis of improvements in air quality and congestion. Cities like London increasingly face payment of penalties to national and regional governments for failure to comply with clean air norms. A subsidy for cleaner, more efficient transport may be seen as a better use of that money.

Transport for London has also understood the kinds of changes in consumer behavior that car sharing can bring, in terms of reducing car ownership, private vehicle usage, and emissions in particular, and has encouraged many parallel service providers. London is the world's second largest market for car sharing, where the largest operator, Zipcar, had more than 1,800 vehicles available for its station-based car-sharing service by 2016. Autolib, the Paris-based point-to-point service, has drawn up plans for significant expansion in London. BMW's DriveNow free-float service was launched at the end of 2014 as the only flexible car-sharing operator in the market to also facilitate one-way rentals within four boroughs in North East London, with close to 300 vehicles. Other automakers such as Ford have also announced plans to enter this space. Transport for London has anticipated that users will demand connected, heterogeneous modes to enhance their mobility experience.

Transport for London's performance is monitored and evaluated by an independent watchdog appointed by the UK Parliament, London Travel-Watch. That entity's report from 2015–2016 concludes that "TfL are delivering well against their own targets and customer satisfaction is high."[19] Urban transport administrators from almost any country would be envious of such a summary.

In comparing London's very different evolutionary pattern of mobility with that of Los Angeles, we can make several observations. We identify four key factors: urban form, culture, coordination, and technology investment:

- Many major cities in Europe, London included, were built up well before automobiles existed, and their urban form dictates many narrow city streets that are not hospitable to cars. In contrast, many American cities, especially in the sun belt—Miami, Houston, Phoenix, Los Angeles—grew up with cars as the primary transportation mode. Sprawl was an outcome of this mobility architecture.

- In part, some differences are cultural. Los Angeles and Southern California have reigned supreme in the kingdom of car cultures and voters there have regularly voiced their preference for auto mobility.

- In a strategic move, London vested all administrative powers related to urban mobility under one umbrella, Transport for London, and this organizational approach has helped coordination across trains, the Underground, buses, bikes, and even the roadway system. Many global cities including Los Angeles have failed to achieve such coordinated orchestration of various departments and services.

- Compared with Los Angeles, London has continuously and aggressively invested in technologies that have made public transport easy and convenient for users.

Yet, all these favorable initiatives in London may be no more than an initial down-payment of a fuller set of CHIP mobility initiatives to achieve the objectives of sustainable, healthful, and user-friendly urban transportation.

Early in 2017, it was already evident that London was still significantly lagging behind in its goals to tackle air pollution. Levels of nitrogen oxides in the air, attributable to a large population of diesel-powered cars and heavy vehicles, flared up far too often. Mayor Sadiq Khan and TfL faced calls to move even faster on many of their emissions mitigation initiatives resulting in Mayor Khan's pledge to double funding and accelerate the transformation.

Box 1.1 An analyst's view

Martyn Briggs heads mobility research and consulting at Frost and Sullivan and has studied Transport for London and similar systems in detail. According to him, "TfL represents the implementation of a visionary strategy and unique integration of multiple transportation modes into one entity. They also seem to have converged on an acceptable combination of carrot and stick—they are encouraging shifts away from private car use in a congested city like London, through a combination of improved services and disincentives for personal modes."[20]

A modern and key element of Transport for London's approach has been to embrace external service providers and link them to Transport for London's own data systems, even when such services may compete with buses or the Tube. Briggs believes that "this mentality of enabling third party and private sector growth of tech-enabled mobility business models is also visible by recent developments in the private hire trade, where Uber accounts for around 40 percent of the market for such services in London and continues to grow."

According to Frost and Sullivan's analysis of the evolution of Transport for London, the main building blocks have been the following:

- Creating a central company responsible for managing all forms of transportation: Private contracts are tendered for routes to encourage competitiveness and are pegged to various service levels and patronage.
- Creating disincentives for private car use, initially through congestion charging and increasing prices continually.
- Prioritizing low-emission vehicles: Air quality is a real challenge in London, causing up to 10,000 premature deaths per year, and a ULEV zone will be launched in 2020 to mitigate this issue.
- Promoting and investing in public transport: All congestion charge revenues are ring-fenced for public transport.
- Investing in technology, principally ticketing and information.
- Enabling new mobility businesses that add value: Car-hailing and car clubs have been among the first to really take off, but there is high potential in London for other services as well, in years to come, owing to the vast population and land area.

In closing

The lessons of Los Angeles and London are useful for many developed cit-ies as well as for those in emerging economies that are stepping onto the escalator of growth and development. Urban growth triggers higher popu-lation densities and increases in per capita output. The resulting demands for greater mobility options need to be addressed systemically. Shortages of public investment in mass transit can leave residents to fend for themselves and default to greater reliance on personal cars, sometime accompanied by a search for suburban housing.[21] The L.A. story can repeat itself in many emerging economies.

To avoid such an adverse spiral requires a combination of thoughtful urban form, intelligent zoning policies, discriminating prices for road use and parking, and aggressive investment in transportation infrastructure. Enlightened policy must also be open to newer options that leverage tech-nology and business model innovations, such as autonomous vehicles and ride-sharing apps. The entire toolbox of infrastructure, technology, policy, pricing, and incentives will be required to address the challenges. Any city that attempts to tackle the issue with a limited set of instruments, as we have seen with Los Angeles, will face an uphill battle.

London's journey aligns well with our advocacy for CHIP mobility and pro-vides an encouraging yet cautionary benchmark for megacity mobility ser-vices. In London we see connected, heterogeneous, intelligent, personalized mobility. Many Londoners seem willing to view and use their transportation services very differently from the traditional reliance on personal cars. When infrastructure is brought into alignment with these views and technology is leveraged to enable ease of use, radically more efficient mobility becomes possible. However, London's journey may still be viewed as a beginning and in relation to the magnitude of the climate problem that needs to be addressed. Success of these initiatives can only be realized when they are sustained and as technological solutions, entrepreneurship, pricing and funding mechanisms are brought into alignment.

The challenge that every city mayor, transport planner, or investor faces is that no two cities are alike, and different solutions will be more viable and sustainable in different locations. However, as we show through this book, the building blocks and the configurations of CHIP mobility are intrinsically variable and can be adapted to suit various contexts. London represents one successful start toward systematic arrangement of the building blocks—one successful illustration of the principles.

As Keats said, "Heard melodies are sweet, but those unheard / Are sweeter." We believe other cities in developed economies and many more in emerging economies have an opportunity to create new expressions and manifestations of the CHIP mobility framework and to deploy an even fuller spectrum of technologies, policies, and business solutions in their own quest to serve their customers faster, smarter, and greener mobility.

2   An Urban Century

A city is more than a place in space, it is a drama in time.

—*Patrick Geddes*[1]

In *The New Urban Sociology,* Mark Gottdiener refers to our times as the "first urban century in human history."[2] At the dawn of the twentieth century, the world was mostly rural. By the close of that century it was mostly urban. The evolution of human civilization is the result of the collective use of human cognition, intelligence, and effort. The more we cooperate, the more we accomplish. Cities and urban environments have proven vital for this.

Thomas Friedman's book *The World Is Flat* has gained critical acclaim for elaborating the thesis that in commerce and technology, the modern world offers a far more level playing field.[3] Even as Friedman's thesis was gaining currency, some prominent urbanists and social scientists were beginning to assert that the world was actually becoming more "spiky."[4] They had noticed localized pockets of heightened activity and influence among vast expanses of relative barrenness. Massive population migrations have converged in such cities as Paris, Tokyo, New York, and Shanghai, drawn by a gravitational field of attractive work and social and cultural opportunities. Academics and urbanists such as Richard Florida and Edward Glaeser argue that measured by population concentration, economic power, and creative output, cities represent localized peaks of human activity.[5] Cities seem to get stronger as they grow bigger. This concentration of human activity presents a monumental challenge to implementing effective urban livability and mobility strategies.

The stakes are high. In 2010, according to the World Bank, the world's top fifty cities together would have formed the world's second largest economy, with a GDP in excess of $9.5 trillion based on purchasing power parity. This grouping would also have housed 500 million people and would have been the third largest greenhouse gas emitter, after the U.S. and China. As we grapple with the task of getting our planet onto a sustainable trajectory, adaptable, well-planned, people-friendly cities can become effective localized change agents.

The magnet of cities

The Industrial Revolution of the nineteenth century spurred a mass migration of labor to cities in search of better-paying jobs. Cities bulged with growing populations. England witnessed the fraction of urban dwellers grow from 17 percent in 1801 to 72 percent by 1891.[6] The magnitude and the speed of change to a fundamental form factor of society—characterized by the degree of urbanization, nature of jobs, living patterns—speak to the power of disruptive transformations. Within a century, the Industrial Revolution had transformed an agrarian society into an urban society.

Similar migrations were evident in other parts of the world. In the United States, the twentieth century saw urban population double, from 40 percent to 80 percent.[7] New York City, a beacon to so many migrants from overseas, as well as those from the hinterland, did not cross the population threshold of 1 million until 1871. By 1925 it had ballooned to 6 million. Across the Atlantic, in Europe, two out of every three persons lived in urban areas.[8] The magnet of cities would sustain population agglomeration across the world through the century.

The same phenomenon transpired in the developing economies in the latter half of the twentieth century. The big cities on China's eastern seaboard swelled with migrants from the interior provinces. In India, a largely agrarian economy also began facing the challenge of rapid urbanization.[9] Globally, fewer than one person in six lived in urban locations in 1900. By the end of the twentieth century, half the world's population was urban. The share of urban population is expected to climb further, to 66 percent, by 2050, when there will be as many urban dwellers as there are people living on Earth today.[10]

This larger urban population is also increasingly concentrating in larger cities. Satellite townships merged with other satellite townships as the boundaries of cities expanded to absorb them. Around the world, cities are getting bigger, and there are more of them. At the start of the twentieth century, only sixteen cities had a million inhabitants. By 2010, 449 cities could meet this criterion, most in the emerging economies.

Motivations for urbanization

Urbanization has enabled economies of scale for the production and delivery of goods and services. Such scale boosts the viability of investment in infrastructure and technology. Furthermore, greater concentrations of population make it easier for producers of goods and services to access both large labor pools and large consumer populations, allowing higher efficiency and lower costs of production. For urban residents, population agglomeration leads to larger social networks, a wider choice of goods and services, and a better selection of jobs. These factors nourish one another and help compound the advantage. Evidence from the U.S. reveals that doubling the size of a city increases productivity across sectors by 3 to 8 percent.[11] In fact, economic development and per capita incomes seem to accelerate when nations reach the point that more than half their population is urban, at which stage greater efficiencies are unleashed.[12]

Arguing that the benefits are more than just economic, Ed Glaeser has posited that "cities magnify humanity's strengths."[13] Larger and denser populations create opportunities for competition, cooperation, innovation, and entrepreneurship. According to the UN's 2014 *World Urbanization Prospects,* increasing urbanization of the population has been accompanied by a longer life expectancy, lower fertility rates, and a reduction in poverty.[14] Furthermore, urban populations have higher levels of literacy, have better access to health care, and enjoy higher levels of cultural and political participation.

However, population concentration can also give rise to serious adverse outcomes. Overcrowding, crime, economic polarization, housing shortages, and inadequate sanitation can all contribute to urban squalor. In the U.S., Detroit, Newark, Philadelphia, and other cities have at times suffered the consequences of decay in once prosperous population centers. As population influxes have exceeded the ability of some global cities to provide basic housing and infrastructure, vast shantytowns have developed. Even in the twenty-first century, we find evidence of this struggle in emerging economies, as in the favelas of Rio de Janeiro or the slums of Mumbai, which remain mired in poverty, even though there is no lack of aspiration or entrepreneurship. A world galloping toward greater urbanization needs to safeguard against such trajectories.

Escape to the suburbs

Evolution is never predictable. Life forms evolve through nature's myriad mutations. Cityscapes too have seen mutations and experimentation. As the large metropolises of the Western world struggled to receive the population flows resulting from the opportunities provided by the Industrial Revolution, many who could afford to leave migrated to the greener suburbs. So, for a brief period in modern history, in some pockets within developed economies, urbanization slowed or even reversed.

Ironically, the word *suburb* traces its origins to the Roman period, when the affluent populations occupied the hills around Rome and the less affluent occupied the base areas of these hills—hence the terminology of "below" the urban areas. In the twentieth century it was the affluent, not the poor, who migrated to the suburbs, emancipated by improved mobility and connectivity.

Migration to suburbs by the wealthy had been observed in London even before the turn of the twentieth century.[15] Since living patterns are often shaped by mobility options, these new suburbs often sprouted along railway lines and highway corridors. In the twentieth century, a similar trend was evident in cities such as New York, where the well-heeled bolted from cramped inner-city life to the elegance of Westchester County, Long Island, or Greenwich, Connecticut. Newly constructed highways and rail connections to the Grand Central Terminus meant that affluent bankers and lawyers could commute to their jobs in Manhattan and be away from the madding crowds by nightfall. After reaching a population of 7.9 million by 1970, New York City then experienced a reversal of growth, losing almost a million inhabitants in the following decade.

Flight to the suburbs represented an American middle-class family dream, with the promise of independent lots, single-family residences, and a green backyard. And after World War II there was an additional attraction: suburban lots offered space for a garage for that new symbol of affluence, the personal car.

With the aid of modern technology, including automobiles, telephones, and television sets, distances shrank, and a person's effective range expanded. Thus the suburban family sacrificed little to gain the advantages of more space and quieter surroundings. The great suburban explosion in the U.S. in the postwar years was mainly helped by the spread of interstate highways and road networks. Equally responsible was the rapidly expanding reach of the automobile, whose popularity was aided by mass production and easier affordability. Suburban life gained a further boost with the advent of better telecommunications and the age of the Internet. These suburban families lived the thesis portrayed by Frances Cairncross in her book *The Death of Distance*.[16]

The evolution of the suburbs and the flight of the middle class had several social and economic consequences. The suburban migrants often left behind city centers that then rapidly withered, beset by a declining tax base and a rising crime rate. New jobs were being created in belts away from city centers. According to a study conducted by the Brookings Institution, in the U.S., "as people and jobs continued to suburbanize and spread out the number of jobs near the typical city resident fell."[17] Economists and urban planners spoke of the "donut hole of decay" in abandoned city centers.[18] The less affluent city dwellers who could not afford to migrate to the suburbs had to make do with poorer infrastructure.

Pendulum swings and the rediscovery of cities

For many of these migrants, the allure of the suburbs had a finite life, and communities soon began to pay a price for serving dispersed populations. Travel and commute times started to climb as suburbs spread out further and travel speeds slowed because of increasing congestion. Vehicular traffic typically grew faster than the infrastructure to support it.

Even cultural attitudes demonstrated a reversal of trends. Baby boomers fled the cities in which they had been raised for the attraction of the suburbs. Subsequently, many of the millennial generation are rebelling against the manicured lawns and suburban lifestyle of their boomer parents and seeking the more vibrant city life. Sociologists have pointed to such trends as later marriages and longer periods of single living as contributing to the attractiveness of cities, which offer more options for entertainment and social interactions. According to one study, 62 percent of millennials indicated a preference for mixed-use urban communities close to shopping, work, and restaurants.[19]

The nuclear family has also shrunk. Even after millennials found partners and formed families, they could make do with less space than their parents, rendering city living more affordable. Many cities have found that after suitable renovation, previously run-down urban habitats emerged as economically attractive residential areas.[20] In some, modern loft-style apartments have become popular in what used to be industrial neighborhoods. They ooze upscale charm even though some offer limited floor space. Decent urban living is also possible even on a relatively limited budget. Many U.S. cities, including Detroit, Baltimore, Philadelphia, Cleveland, and Pittsburgh, are witnessing a gentrification of parts of the city center.[21]

It's not just the millennials who are attracted to cities. As their children became young adults, many baby boomers found themselves empty nesters and needing less space. This population found the vibrancy of renewed cities to be a far cry from the unattractive inner-city neighborhoods they had fled in their younger years, and they have followed their offspring back to the cities.

Another economic factor was also at play in influencing migration to cities. As a result of a steep rise in the cost of gasoline to more than $4 per gallon ahead of the 2008 recession in the United States,[22] transportation became the second largest expense for suburban households. Migration back to the city meant less time and money spent commuting. The redevelopment of city blocks accessible by modern transit systems was a factor drawing residents from the suburbs.

Taken together, these factors weakened the pull of the suburbs just as the attraction of city living was once again ascendant. Starting in the 1990s, most city centers that had lost population since 1950 started to record population growth again.[23] By 2014, growth in U.S. cities had outpaced growth outside cities for the first time since the 1920s.[24] In her book, *The End of the Suburbs*, Leigh Gallagher postulates that the decline of the suburbs will only accelerate.[25]

The mushrooming of suburbs remains a notable diversion in the evolution of social organization. It blossomed in reaction to the rapid and poorly planned densification of cities and was supported by expensive suburban infrastructure investment. It offered an interesting, though expensive, alternative to high-density aggregation, made possible by highways, personal cars, and cheap oil. The phenomenon of the suburb resurfaces periodically wherever the hassles of unplanned densification in cities outweigh the adverse cost impact of moving out of cities. In other words, poor urban planning can encourage suburban migration that ultimately works against the long-term economic and environmental goals of communities.

Notwithstanding the seductive appeal of the suburbs to some, if we look globally at secular trends, the overwhelming evidence points to the relentless advance of urbanization. According to International Association of Public Transport data from twenty metropolitan cities around the world, average urban density increased from 64.5 inhabitants per urban hectare in 2001 to 68.2 by 2012.[26]

Refocusing on cities

For much of the world, cities have an abiding appeal, and urbanization has progressed unabated. Even in a world where networking and social interactions are enabled virtually, physical proximity is still highly prized for many tangible and intangible benefits. The impact of distance may have been minimized in some spheres by technology, but nearness still seems to count for a lot. One could be located in Bangalore, India, and contribute to the output of a Silicon Valley technology company. In this sense, the impact of distance has collapsed. Yet the fact that financial professionals preferentially congregate in New York, London, or Hong Kong and technologists congregate in Bangalore or San Francisco or Boston implies that specific locales and their position in economic and social networks are by no means irrelevant. Such ecosystems flourish because of the colocation of many assets that contribute to better work and social opportunities. The *Economist* summed up the dynamics that motivated suburban exodus and the subsequent rediscovery of cities by stating, "In the 20th century, tumbling transport costs weakened the gravitational pull of the city; in the 21st, the digital revolution has restored it. Knowledge-intensive industries such as technology and finance thrive on the clustering of workers who share ideas and expertise."[27]

In similar ways, Los Angeles, Paris, and Tokyo, as well as the megacities of the developing world, such as São Paulo, Shanghai, or Mumbai, offer distinct advantages for their inhabitants. As Ed Glaeser observes, "The city is humanity's laboratory, where people flock to dream, create, build and re-build."[28] Higher population densities enable the combinatorics of such experimentation, as we discuss in the next section.

Urbanization and its economic impact

In many emerging economies, population used to be treated as a major liability and a key factor that contributed to impoverishment. In an era of knowledge and service economies, populations are increasingly treated as assets for creativity and output and, equally important, as consumers of products and services. From this perspective, high population concentrations can lead to high economic potential. Dharavi, in Mumbai, for example, is one of the largest slums in Asia and also one of India's largest leather craftsmanship centers. In India more than 63 percent of slum dwellers own a mobile telephone, and such consumption, even in lower economic segments, is powering India to have become, by 2015, the third largest global market for mobile phones, with more than 314 million mobile Internet users.[29] In Dharavi, mobile phones are used to amplify social and economic benefits, which are seen as outweighing the relatively large fraction of income that is spent on the phones.[30] Their users are preparing for a world that leverages connectivity to create economic value. Large aggregations of people, as in cities, can have strong effects on the economics of both production and consumption.

The McKinsey Global Institute goes so far as to claim that urbanization will be the twenty-first century's biggest driver of global economic growth.[31] The authors of the McKinsey report, *Urban World: Mapping the Economic Power of Cities,* note first the increasing global propensity for population aggregation and second that per capita GDP is far larger in urban areas than in rural areas. In 2015, the 55 percent of the global population that was urban was estimated to contribute about 85 percent of global GDP.[32] In fact, few countries have crossed the $10,000 per capita income level without recording at least 60 percent urban population.[33] In South Africa, Johannesburg alone contributes one-fourth of the national GDP, while São Paulo and London contribute almost one-third of their respective countries' GDP.[34] Cities can be powerful change agents to aid national agendas. Michael Berkowitz, managing director of the Rockefeller Foundation and president of their initiative titled "100 Resilient Cities," summarizes this sentiment by saying, "Cities both present our biggest risk and our greatest opportunity. Get cities right and you can really change the world."[35]

Many city administrations have worked proactively to forge economic development and attract investment rather than waiting for states or central governments to push the right buttons. Chennai, in southern India, had historically nurtured a limited ecosystem of automakers and suppliers. Since 1990, with a focused plan, the city set its sights on becoming the Detroit of the East. By 2012, it had attracted Ford, Hyundai, Renault-Nissan, BMW, Daimler, Isuzu, and Yamaha. The clustering of so many automakers and their suppliers has made Chennai a vibrant auto hub, which in turn has led to the creation of many well-paying jobs and the expansion of the local economy. Chennai factories now produce more cars each year than the factories in Detroit.

The mayors of cities of the size and economic importance of London, Paris, New York, and Shanghai wield enormous power and have increased their roles in the domains of policy making, urban and environmental planning, and job creation. Boris Johnson and Michael Bloomberg may have been merely mayors of their respective cities of London and New York, but they enjoyed greater prominence in global politics than many heads of state do. The economic value managed from within their cities is greater than the GDP of many nations. Mayor Bloomberg summed up the situation by saying, "Mayors don't have to wait for national governments, or a new global climate agreement to act. They can take action today, and increasingly they are."[36] Both London and New York are examples of cities that have significantly pushed the agenda of environment-friendly mobility, leading to alteration of their cityscapes, well in advance of the imposition of national regulations.

To support continued urbanization around the world, especially in emerging economies, a lot more urban infrastructure is on the way. Arthur Nelson, a professor of urban planning at the University of Arizona, reminds us that "in the U.S., nearly half of what will be 'built infrastructure' in 2030, doesn't exist today."[37] Globally, the built-up area of cities will triple between 2000 and 2030.[38] That is equivalent to adding 400 cities the size of Greater London. The Asian Development Bank estimates that between 2010 and 2020, Asian cities will consume an additional $8 trillion in infrastructure spending, almost equivalent to China's entire GDP, while adding 44 million residents to cities every year.[39] We are essentially at a very opportune juncture. With so much new infrastructure being put in place, there is excellent opportunity to embed a future-ready mobility infrastructure within this expenditure.

Beijing, already a megacity with a population in excess of 21 million, is poised to grow to supersize dimensions.[40] By 2030, analysts estimate, Beijing's boundaries will merge with those of the port city of Tianjin and the province of Hebei to the north. This greater metro region will cover more than 80,000 square miles, or roughly twice the land area of South Korea. It is expected to be home to a population of more than 130 million, slightly more than the population of Japan. The new megacity will combine the financial strength of Beijing, the transportation logistics of Tianjin, and the technology orientation of Hebei. It will face competition from another mega-metropolis, the Pearl River Delta, which subsumes nine prefectures in the province of Guangdong, including Guangzhou and Shenzen, and is on pace to become the third largest urban area in the world.

Urban areas of such scale and economic power are unprecedented in human history. The risks inherent in high concentrations of population remain, and unless these are carefully managed, there could be very adverse consequences for humanity. To grow sustainably, cities must have stable, just, and inclusive governance in addition to appropriate infrastructure investments. The economic model of a city may seem straightforward to steer and manipulate, but managing its sociology model requires a great deal of skill. Political outcomes do not always follow economic logic.

Apart from presenting a challenging problem for governance, a city's ability to function well rests heavily on the design and operation of its mobility systems. Environment, economic development, and mobility remain at the top of the list of factors that attract investment to cities.

The New Urbanism: Designing cities for people

Through the 1970s, motorization was in full bloom. Car ownership soared and, at least in the developed world, almost every suburban household had access to a car. With the rapid increase in suburb-to-city commuting, ambitious urban highway projects in Europe and the U.S. were seen as key to fostering better mobility. Most cities witnessed new urban freeways, flyovers, tunnels, and grade separators.

New Urbanism was a contrary approach promoted by a newer breed of thinkers who were dismayed at the transformation of cities into concrete jungles that dehumanized city life. Their prescription for modern urban environments had four main elements: (1) high-density, vertical cities, (2) mixed land use, mingling residential and commercial blocks with green spaces, (3) pedestrian-friendliness, and (4) mass transit. The New Urbanists were vehemently opposed to traditional urban planning, which seemed to give priority to cars rather than people in designing cities and their infrastructure.

The two opposing philosophies clashed over their vision for cities. Basic elements of city design, such as the size of city blocks, and use of land look very different when oriented toward cars rather than people. The New Urbanists opposed plans to isolate people, who would travel cocooned in their cars, from their habitat. They sought to integrate people into their local communities through activity on streets and in local stores. To the New Urbanists, conventional urban planning was leading to a world in which cities would increasingly become problems rather than solutions for future society. Their approach called for a greater emphasis on the softer aspects of urban livability. So, in addition to the macroeconomists' justification of cities for the sake of economic efficiency, the New Urbanism drew attention to sociability and principles of equity in the evolution of cities.

New York is perhaps the American city in which it is easiest to manage without a personal car. This did not happen by accident. It took a major confrontation on these battle lines to change the course of development in that city.

The 1956 Federal-Aid Highway Act, signed by President Eisenhower, funded a large number of construction projects across the country. Robert Moses was an influential urban planner who had made notable contributions to the infrastructure planning of several major cities. To him, urban planning was all about improving communication and making mobility efficient. The new interstates and urban highways were to play a key role in propelling the nation forward. In his view, "Cities were created for and by traffic. A city without traffic is a ghost town."[41] After the construction of the Long Island Expressway and several radial highways leading out of New York City, he turned his sights to cross-town traffic within the city. For this he envisioned a set of north-south and a couple of east-west connectors that would run through many of the historic districts in New York, such as Greenwich Village and SoHo. Many buildings and dwellings there would have to be razed and the residents relocated to distant boroughs to conform to the new master plan. The plan would divide people and would segregate housing from commercial districts and low-income from high-income boroughs.

Jane Jacobs, a journalist and New York City resident, emerged to lead the fight against the kind of urban renewal planned by Robert Moses. For Jacobs and her supporters, the livability aspect of the city was of primary importance. The author of *The Death and Life of Great American Cities,* Jacobs argued not only for the value of cities in promoting development and entrepreneurship but also for the organic evolution of communities of high population density, which to her equated with high degrees of pedestrian permeability.[42] Scenes from the traditional boroughs of New York and from large European cities such as London, Paris, and Amsterdam show people frequenting city streets for shopping, walking to work, and social interactions. To Jacobs, these were important aspects of quality of life and contributed to the city's social capital. The challenge that had to be addressed, she held, was not a transportation problem but rather one of dealing with a vibrant city of many hues, races, economic groups, and traditions. Jacobs and her followers viewed New York City as a living organism that evolved and was molded by the millions of its citizens, who were actors in a real-life play.

Jane Jacobs and her group ultimately prevailed, and the city administration voted down the interstate construction plan proposed by Robert Moses. It set New York on its course of development and would serve as a reminder several decades later—cities needed to be planned for people, not cars.

Four decades after the Jane Jacobs victory, New York City mayor Michael Bloomberg picked up the issue to further the next wave of change. His administration was credited with rolling out several broad-ranging initiatives

Figure 2.1 New York's transformation of the Times Square area was an attempt to give more of the city back to people and their activities. Cars made way for pedestrians, changing patterns of land use.
Source: Institute for Transportation and Development Policy, New York.

for urban rejuvenation. When their plans to have Times Square turned over to pedestrians were unveiled, there were serious apprehensions that commercial activity would suffer from the drop in motorist traffic. In reality, the pedestrian zone transformed the area into one where people interactions were fostered. Sidewalk cafés and more pedestrians actually increased footfalls in retail stores and led to an overall increase in economic activity. The addition of almost 600 kilometers of bike lanes and bike-sharing facilities were related measures. As Janette Sadik-Khan, a transport commissioner in the Bloomberg administration who served as a lightning rod for her impassioned championing of such transformation, noted, "City streets used to serve as places for social interactions before the auto culture hijacked its use for cars."[43] According to Bloomberg, "The results of that experiment have been tremendously positive for public safety, for our economy and for traffic flow."[44] New York City is expecting to add another million residents in the next twenty-five years. Apart from New York, many other U.S. cities, including Memphis, San Antonio, Miami, and Portland, are also adopting New Urbanist principles as they rejuvenate their urban centers.

By and large, most of Europe and Japan had been spared the rampant expansion into suburbs following the trails of highways and inexpensive automobiles. Europe has also experienced the current wave of densification of urban areas. Between 2001 and 2011, the population of city centers grew by 37 percent.[45] There too the recent trend of millennials migrating to urban centers has accelerated. The number of twenty-two- to twenty-nine-year-olds living in large urban centers in England and Wales tripled between 2001 and 2011.

Such cities as Copenhagen, Amsterdam, and London have also explored practices advocated by New Urbanism, with impressive results. Significant investments in urban renewal projects in Amersfoort in the Netherlands, Hammarby Sjöstad in Stockholm, and Adamstown in Dublin were guided by these pedestrian-friendly, public-transit-oriented, compact urban design templates.

Cities: Economic hot spots and environmental cool spots

In 2015, cities accounted for approximately 75 percent of global energy–related greenhouse gas emissions.[46] The Global Footprint Network together with the San Francisco Planning and Urban Research Association released an interesting report documenting the carbon footprint of various cities and countries.[47] Their unit of measure was the ecological footprint, which is

Figure 2.2 Carbon footprint map showing the New York City region in a cool green shade compared to neighboring suburbs. Lower energy demands for transportation work in New York City's favor.
Source: © 2015, Regents of the University of California, University of California, Berkeley. All rights reserved.

derived from publicly available data on resource production, trade, and consumption. One might think of this simply as the amount of land area needed to sustain a person. At the macrolevel, against a global average of 4.5 acres (1.8 global hectares [gha]) per person, the U.S. average was estimated at 16.5 acres (6.7 gha) in 2007. Many factors influence this number.

First, cities in colder climates have a higher carbon footprint resulting from home and workplace heating. The ecological footprint is also related to affluence and expenditure per capita. Since urban regions typically house people with higher average per capita income than rural regions, this difference would normally suggest an increase in carbon footprint per capita in cities. So it is surprising to learn that the average New York City resident has a 15 percent lower carbon footprint (6.1 gha) than her counterpart in San Francisco (7.1 gha). Indeed, New York City's figure is lower than the U.S. average, the much higher average income in that city notwithstanding. New York City's superior performance is aided by the factor of population density, which is inversely correlated with carbon footprint. After food and sustenance, the second highest category contributor to carbon footprint is transportation. According to the U.S. Energy Information Administration, urban households in the U.S. drive about 7,000 miles less each year than their rural counterparts. In New York City, in 2011, it was estimated that more than 55 percent of households did not own a car, compared to fewer than 10 percent for the national average. Not surprisingly, the major factor that tilts the balance in favor of New York City is transportation.

If cities can simultaneously be economic hot spots and carbon emission cool spots, then it is no surprise that both economists and environmentalists quickly find common ground in pitching cities as the model for future social design.

The symbiotic relationship between urban design and mobility architecture

In our tale of two cities, Los Angeles and London demonstrated how urban form and sprawl are interconnected with culture, patterns of living, environment, and mobility. Population density, economic activity, and their effects on urban form are not easy to measure with precision. One approach is to consider the density in a core city center, such as Manhattan in the case of New York, or, alternatively, the density across a greater metropolitan region, including, in the case of New York, the city's adjacent counties in New York State, New Jersey, and Connecticut. Another approach considers where people live and where jobs exist, and their relative juxtaposition. All these factors are relevant in assessing the interplay between urban form and mobility architecture. The following observations underpin our thesis for urban mobility:

a. Compact cities with higher levels of productivity (GDP) per unit area make it economically viable to provide better connectivity of public transport services. European and wealthy Asian cities have demonstrated the cost-effective and sustainable transport systems aided by typically more compact forms and excellent public transit infrastructure. Cities such as Hong Kong, Singapore, and Tokyo sustain a much higher GDP output per square mile and operate with a much lower dependence on cars than do Rome or Los Angeles.[48]

b. Higher population densities penalize the transit time achievable with personal cars when measured on a door-to-door basis, and hence promote public transit. A detailed analysis of thirty-two cities distributed across the U.S., Europe, and Asia underscored how higher urban densities correlate with higher use of transit systems and lead to lower cost of urban transport.[49] Conversely, urban sprawl correlates with higher use of cars and higher budgets for transport.

The cost to the U.S. economy attributable to the inefficiency of urban sprawl was estimated at almost $1 trillion, or 2.6 percent of GDP, in 2014.[50] China, still expanding at prodigious pace, could save an estimated $1.4

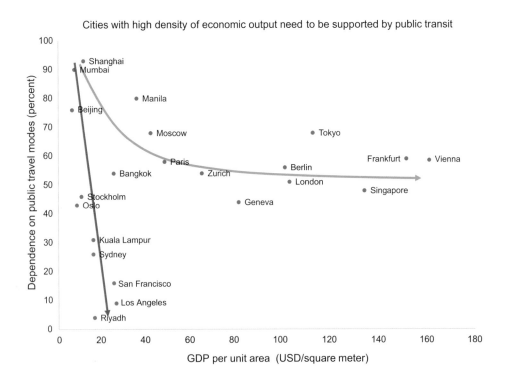

Figure 2.3 Modal share of public transport. Cities in emerging economies may take one of two trajectories as their economic development accelerates. Cities with high levels of economic intensity will face limits to the level of personal car use.
Source: Data from UITP, Brussels.

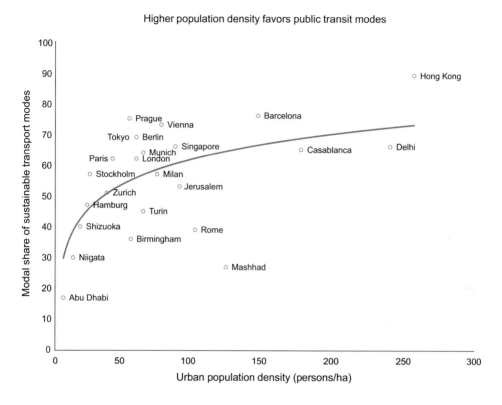

Figure 2.4 As cities are called upon to support higher population densities, there is a limiting effect on the use of personal cars and public transit modes are favored.
Source: Data from UITP, Brussels.

trillion in infrastructure spending until 2030, or almost 15 percent of GDP in 2013, if that nation pursued a more compact urban form than what is currently in the works.[51]

The mobility choices people make are strongly influenced by cultural attitudes and affluence. In the postwar years, there was a clear correlation between income levels and the use of personal cars. The automobile was an expensive asset for much of the global population, and as personal incomes grew, families aspired to a "higher" level of mobility. In the postwar U.S., fueled by fast-rising incomes compared to the rest of the world and with little pressure on land use, most cities evolved with significant urban sprawl and dependence on the car.

Yet the wealth of cities alone does not reliably explain the degree of dependence on cars. Particularly in Europe and Asia, many cities and countries soon adopted policies that would limit sprawl and reshape mobility patterns.

Munich, like London, is another example of a large city that has used policy to reshape way of living and mobility. Munich has a higher average income but a lower degree of dependence on cars than Hamburg, a difference influenced mainly by Munich's higher population density.[52] Its development in the postwar period was carefully planned, and the Munich Regional Planning Association involved local citizen groups to develop policy and avoid sprawl. Seeking to nurture a city in equilibrium, the planning association incentivized redevelopment of sites within the city perimeter to encourage denser form with higher economic activity within compact boundaries. It also preserved green city spaces and planned a comprehensive public transportation system.

To Ed Glaeser, "Transportation technologies have always determined urban form."[53] However, we believe that transportation policy and infrastructure investment also play strong roles in the evolution of cities. Roughly two-thirds of all travel is undertaken in urban environments, and the quantum of urban travel is expected to triple by 2050.[54] It's little wonder that in many surveys, mobility heads the list of priorities for city administrations. Fluid mobility systems boost economic productivity and enhance residents' quality of life.

The cost incurred for mobility in pursuit of economic output is a bit like friction. In the EU-28 nations, private households spend almost 13 percent of their total consumption on transportation.[55] Compact urban forms supported by efficient mobility can impose a low cost, as in the case of Copenhagen, where households spend 9 percent of household expenditure on transport. On the other hand, an inefficient mobility architecture can extract a high price. In Lagos, this figure grows to 28 percent.[56] Unfortunately, for most cities the cost of mobility is expected to climb in the coming decade as economic growth outpaces investment in transport infrastructure. Based on existing investments, in New York City, already a benchmark for the U.S. on many scores, it is expected that this fraction will climb from 15 percent to 18 percent of GDP by 2030. Paris, which has recently committed significant city metro investments, is expected to see a minor improvement, declining from 14 percent to 13 percent. It will take a lot of focus on efficient transportation infrastructure by cities to ensure that economic growth is not squandered through runaway transportation costs.

Congestion is a large and growing component of this friction. In 2013, the cost of traffic congestion in the U.S., Germany, France, and the UK alone was estimated to total $200 billion, or almost 1 percent of GDP.[57] This cost excludes the impact of carbon dioxide emissions, estimated at an additional $350 million. When specific cities are examined, the data are even starker. A study conducted by the Indian Institute of Technology, Madras, reported in 2017 that the cost of traffic congestion in New Delhi was estimated at $10 billion annually or almost 3 percent of the GDP of that region.[58] As a proportion of regional GDP, congestion is estimated to account for the loss of 1.1 percent for New York City, 1.5 percent for London, almost 8 percent for São Paulo, and a staggering 15 percent for Beijing.[59] Even more alarming is that the figures for OECD nations could climb by 50 percent by 2030 unless aggressive remedial actions are undertaken.

But there is more to cities and societies than just economic value. As we have seen, livability and social capital are important aspects. In the summer of 2016, a tragic, congestion-induced chain of events unfolded on the Indonesian island of Java.[60] As crowds made their annual journey to their hometowns to mark the end of the holy month of Ramadan, very heavy traffic converged at one traffic intersection, where a road construction project was under way. The subsequent traffic jam, which lasted from Sunday until the following Tuesday, snaked through 21 kilometers of a three-lane highway. More than twelve people, including a toddler, lost their lives from a combination of dehydration, exhaustion, and carbon monoxide inhalation.

No nation can afford a trajectory of development that favors freedom for personal mobility at the expense of the health and safety of the polity. Yet the tragedy in Java could be visited on any number of fast-growing cities in the emerging economies if we fail to heed such warnings. In Mexico City, two new vehicles enter circulation for every child that is born. In India, the number of private vehicles is growing three times as fast as the human population.[61]

Enrique Peñalosa, former mayor of Bogotá, Colombia, later became president of the Board of Directors of the Institute for Transportation and Development Policy in New York. An ardent supporter of urban mobility solutions, he feels that "urban mobility is peculiar and is different from other urban challenges like education or housing—it tends to get worse as societies become richer."[62] Going forward, it will be imperative to manage the evolution of urban mobility trajectories for large and fast-growing economies like those of China and India. They will see a phase of rapid per capita income growth leading to improved affordability, hence favoring personal motorized mobility. The results of poor urban planning, delayed infrastructure, or flawed investment can be extremely wasteful and significantly slow down economic growth.

Road safety is another concern for urban planners, apart from congestion. In 2011, 70 percent of all road accidents in Europe occurred in urban areas, and 38 percent of all road traffic fatalities were reported in urban conditions.[63] Motorized modes (such as cars, buses, and trucks) and nonmotorized modes (such as walking or cycling) in close proximity to one another, as often happens in cities, make for a more difficult environment in which to ensure safety. We examine the sustainability aspects of mobility in greater detail in chapter 3.

Across a distribution of towns and small cities in the U.S., these socioeconomic concerns are being taken up as popular public cause. A movement called Complete Streets aims to highlight changes needed for infrastructure spending and road design to ensure "safe, comfortable, integrated transportation network for all users, regardless of age, ability, income, ethnicity, or mode of transportation."[64] The U.S. Department of Transportation has taken a role in fostering the movement by vetting and assessing new city investment plans using a rating system that is based on Complete Streets principles.

Mobility impact on land use

In the coming decades, as cities engage in transforming their mobility architecture, they will face many challenges. A core issue in dense urban areas will be the allocation of valuable space. Social, economic and environmental goals will compete more acutely as cities determine how urban spaces may be used. As we develop our framework for CHIP mobility, these factors will need to be embedded within it.

New Urbanism's call for liberal allocation of green spaces in urban environments is endorsed by the World Health Organization, which recommends 9 square meters per capita.[65] Stockholm in Sweden has evolved such that its citizens are able to enjoy as much as 88 square meters. Even a dense bustling metropolis like London affords its residents 27 square meters, while New York City allocates 23 square meters. On the other hand, cities such as Buenos Aires and Shenzen, with fewer than 2 square meters per capita, face serious health risks to their populations.

All cities, even those in Europe and Japan with good public transit, are obliged to set aside a significant fraction of expensive real estate for roads. Tokyo allocates almost 15 percent of its urban area to roadways, while London allocates almost 24 percent.[66] In most U.S. cities the figure is higher: typically between 30 and 40 percent is allocated to roads and sidewalks. The experience of Los Angeles has shown that more roads only invite more drivers. As a result, in a study of thirty-two global cities, data revealed that the average driver in the U.S. cities in the study drove almost 150 percent more than her European counterpart.[67]

The Catalan capital of Barcelona, in Spain, found itself falling significantly behind an imperative to comply with EU air quality standards. Pollution from autos has been a major source of this problem. The city has embarked on a mission that attempts to tackle the core issue of allocation of urban space for vehicles based on the finding that 85 percent of public areas in a typical city neighborhood was being used by vehicles. A pilot project was initiated in the neighborhood of Eixample.[68] This neighborhood of the city had been developed in the late nineteenth century in the form of regular grids, with the objective of allowing the city to "breathe" for both health and emotional benefits. The growth of vehicular population in the twentieth century gradually undermined that objective, as roads that formed the grids were choked with cars. The project, launched in 2016, involved aggregating nine city blocks (in a three block by three block grid) into a superblock (*superilles* as they are locally known) within which vehicles are allowed limited access. This was seen to reduce vehicular traffic within the superblock by 40 percent, improving local air quality and allocating use of the freed space for cafes and pedestrian activities. This experimental project underscored the relationship between urban form, utilization of space and choice of mobility modes, and was slated for evaluation in several other localities of that city.[69]

Personal transport also forces a city to allocate land area for other purposes. Anyone who attempts to find a parking spot in New York City might conclude that the city devotes very little space to private car parking, even though more than 900 acres are allocated to a combination of street parking and parking garages.[70] To set that figure in perspective, all of Central Park occupies less than 850 acres.

Bill Ford, chairman of Ford Motor Company, notes that the U.S. can count more than 800 million parking spots, yet in a city like San Francisco, only 14 percent of drivers looking for parking are likely to find a spot on their first try. Cruising around looking for a parking space is estimated to account for almost 30 percent of congestion in many U.S. cities. Yet astonishingly, 99 percent of all car trips in the U.S. end in free parking at the destination.[71] Maybe Milton Friedman was wrong when he claimed there was no such thing as a free lunch.[72]

Even in Paris, where street parking is expensive, it is estimated that 60 percent of cars are parked at any given time.[73] There are approximately 900,000 cars registered in Paris, requiring the city to allocate close to 5 percent of its land area for parking. As the urban population continues to climb and development focuses on creating compact cities, personal mobility will make unacceptably large demands on expensive urban land unless vehicle density can be shrunk with intelligent, effective policies and attractive alternative modes are offered to travelers.

The urban perspective on future mobility

The thesis we are building for future mobility is critically dependent on how we wish to live, work, and play. Urbanization crucially shapes this thesis. We therefore offer a few key observations about urban living that will likely mold future mobility architecture.

Since the start of the Industrial Revolution, people have been on a course of increasing urbanization. Anthropologists now join economists and environmentalists in calling for higher densities to improve societal productivity and reduce the per capita environmental footprint. There is a natural element in the evolution of civilizations and cities. Yet too often, the haphazard and unplanned evolution of cities leaves monumental problems in its wake. The world needs urban planning to achieve a better quality of life and better productivity. We need compact urban forms with local neighborhoods designed around people, not cars. Urban forms and mobility systems enjoy a symbiotic relationship. Urban designs determine which forms of mobility are effective, and conversely, mobility investments and technologies influence urban form. Planners need to work these birelational influences in tandem.

Urban regions are critical actors in the global economy. They disproportionately influence economic activity and environmental impact. Mobility system design is a unique and powerful agent: it can address both the economic and the social objectives of city living. Because cities differ, these blueprints need to be uniquely tailored to local conditions and needs. Mobility is a necessity, and the range of modal offerings and their affordability must be designed not to exclude any sector of population.

Future cities must increasingly favor shared and public mobility as they confront scarce resources such as space and energy and a growing density of population. At the same time, residents of democracies will demand a choice of modes to suit unique individual needs. Good policies and the appropriate pricing of assets and resources will play critical roles in providing residents with appropriate choices. These choices must be fairly priced or incentivized in alignment with societal priorities.

Future mobility architecture for cities must be flexible, affordable, and sustainable. This does not happen by itself. Planning, orchestration, and oversight are obligatory. The challenge for city administrators, therefore, is to dynamically align their policies, deploy investments, and provide fiscal motivators in ways that are aligned with needs and designed to encourage sustainable practices. In chapter 12 we delve more deeply into specific actions that cities may take to customize the CHIP framework to their needs so that they may achieve these goals.

3   A Softer, Greener Footprint

I am surrounded by city. I lack air.

—*Octavio Paz, "Return"*[1]

It was supposed to be the start of spring, yet a pall of acrid smog hung over Paris. On that day in March 2015, air pollution in Paris spiked, earning the city the distinction of being the world's most polluted large city, worse than even Beijing or Shanghai.[2] In an unprecedented action, the city of Paris imposed restrictions on the use of personal cars in the city center. Increasing levels of smog, attributed to increased vehicular pollution, combined with local weather conditions frequently pushed the air quality below acceptable thresholds. The ban on personal automobiles would be repeated several days that spring and summer, whenever levels of pollution breached defined limits. That year, Parisians had to learn to get used to such interruptions, and to the idea that one could not always count on using one's car.

Troubled by seeing the cherished skyline of Paris and the Eiffel Tower increasingly obscured by atmospheric pollution, in September that same year, Paris followed the lead of Brussels in observing a car-free day, to be implemented one Sunday each month. Egged on by the group Paris sans Voiture (Paris without Cars), it was imposed by Mayor Anne Hidalgo, who was enthusiastically preparing Paris to host the UN World Climate Conference in 2015.[3] Her stated objective was "to show that Paris could operate without cars." She was building on the steps taken earlier by her predecessor, Bertrand Delanoë, who had supported bike sharing and popularized the zero-emission Autolib car-sharing service across Paris. For both, their beloved Paris needed to be resuscitated.

To be fair, France, along with most of Europe, had steadily advanced auto emission standards for new vehicles, tightening levels of permissible particulate and nitrogen oxide (NO_x) emissions. At stage Euro 6, emission standards in Europe were among the toughest in the world. Yet the sheer number of cars, including a large and growing number of diesels, meant that the progress made was inadequate, and more desperate measures, such as restricting use of vehicles, became unavoidable.

Paris is not alone. Over the past decade, policies have been put in place by cities such as Vienna, Barcelona, and Stockholm, motivated by similar goals—to achieve a reduction in personal vehicle usage in cities, mainly to improve air quality and reduce congestion.

The problem is also being felt in emerging nations, even though overall vehicle ownership is still at very low levels. Vehicular population and pollution are growing at alarming rates. In Beijing, the number of cars grew more than fourfold between 2000 and 2010.[4] The effects of smog there and in other large cities, such as Shanghai, Mexico City, and New Delhi, has led to local restrictions being imposed on vehicle use to reduce exhaust emissions. In Beijing, the local administration resorted to a lottery for people to gain the right to buy and register an automobile. Shanghai has turned to auctioning license plates to stem the rate of vehicle population increase. In India, by the winter of 2015, the administration in New Delhi had imposed a rule restricting the use of cars to odd- or even-numbered license plate numbers on alternate days. The city government had been compelled by the country's highest court to intervene to lower dangerous levels of atmospheric pollution.

Across the world, transportation is leaving deep scars on the environment. The current architecture for mobility is simply not sustainable. In this chapter, we examine how societies have gradually become sensitized to the topic of environmental protection and how regulations have evolved to deflect our dangerous trajectory. In part II of the book we review how technological and business model innovations may accelerate the switch to a more sustainable mobility architecture.

Awakening to a disquieting reality

If ever there was a pivotal book to awaken a recalcitrant society to a looming environmental reality, it may well have been Rachel Carson's *Silent Spring*.[5] By the end of the 1950s, with postwar prosperity spreading, society had grown accustomed to the idea that development was unarguably positive. Bigger homes, more powerful cars, and more consumption had been perceived as natural consequences of progress and improved standards of living. Carson's book provided a strident wakeup call and caused many people to pause and consider the impact of humans on the ecology of Earth. In 1974, the Club of Rome published its seminal report, *The Limits to Growth*, which predicted that society would soon run out of certain critical resources needed to feed its insatiable appetite.[6] It painted a grim picture of the Earth's ability to sustain the ascending aspirations of its booming population.

Concurrently, concerns arose over how humankind was harnessing technology in ways that might ultimately be detrimental to its own survival. World War II had accelerated applications of the technologies of destruction and left society suddenly apprehensive of the vastly increased powers at its disposal. The consequences of nuclear radiation from atomic tests and the atom bombs used at Hiroshima and Nagasaki were terrifying. In the words of the U.S. nuclear scientist Robert Oppenheimer, "We knew the world would not be the same. A few people laughed, a few people cried, most were silent." The next generation learned of the effects of exposure to Agent Orange defoliants in Vietnam on both local populations and combatants. This discovery buttressed unsettling evidence of the increasing powers available to humans to wield. Even away from the theaters of war, the "green revolution" that was advancing farm productivity was often achieved with the aggressive use of agricultural pesticides, which were silently working their deleterious effects on the habitat.

Sometimes all it takes is a different perspective on the challenges to trigger change. Neil Armstrong and Buzz Aldrin landed on the Moon in 1969. Their pictures of Earth, shot from space, had a dramatic effect. To a world still awed by the unleashing of nuclear power, these photographs conveyed the image of a delicate blue planet—a view hitherto unseen. Viewed from the vastness of space, Earth did not seem imposing; rather, it looked vulnerable. Slowly, starting in certain sectors of the population, society began to understand the scope of humans' impact on a fragile planet.

Global action on climate change

As we had seen in chapter 1, the Los Angeles smog had served as the canary in the coal mine and motivated early efforts to tackle airborne pollution in the U.S. The initial targets were local, and remediation efforts were aimed at the more visible aspects of climate degradation. By 1967, both the U.S. and the UK had enacted their own versions of legislation, their respective Clean Air Acts, to address the combination of smog, sources of pollution, and air quality.

The first Earth Day was celebrated on April 22, 1970, and successfully galvanized wider public interest in the environment in many parts of the world. Later that year, President Nixon created the Environmental Protection Agency (EPA), which was tasked with monitoring and focusing its efforts on human health and the environment. Across the globe, momentum was building, and each step seemed to advance collective engagement to halt the dangerous slide. The UN Conference on the Human Environment of 1972, held in Stockholm, was another milestone. For the first time, nations gathered to discuss the need for collective action on the environment, leading many nations, especially those in Scandinavia, to create a Ministry for Environment to coordinate action.

Since then, global leaders, administrators, and scientists have met periodically to develop the science, assess the trajectory, and attempt to forge consensus on actions. As science advanced comprehension of the manifestations of environmental impact, efforts were directed toward mitigation. For example, after studies revealed that the Earth's ozone layer was being eroded by the use and release of certain chemicals, leaving humans vulnerable to solar radiation, the 1987 Montreal Protocol established a regime to control and eventually eliminate this class of chemicals, which are typically used in refrigeration and air-conditioning units.

Carbon dioxide emissions and global warming

Carbon emissions have come to dominate much of the world's recent debates on environment. As carbon dioxide (CO_2) from human activity concentrates in the atmosphere, it accentuates a global greenhouse effect. The accumulation of CO_2 acts as a thermal blanket, causing the Earth to retain more heat from the sun. In 1800, levels of CO_2 in the atmosphere were estimated at about 280 parts per million (ppm). By 2015, levels had breached 400 ppm, causing the World Meteorological Organization to caution that these effects could not be reversed easily and would be felt for generations.[7] According to most scientific reports, humans' current developmental trajectory is on course to cause average global temperatures to rise by anywhere from 3 to 5 degrees Celsius by 2100, compared to temperatures in a pre-industrial world. Such a change is expected to seriously disrupt agriculture and food supplies and lead to sea level increases that would inundate many coastal cities. Such changes would result in the massive disruption of habitat for millions of people.

The global agenda on climate change has advanced very slowly, requiring very substantial effort for meager progress, every step of the way. In 1992, the Earth Summit in Rio de Janeiro specifically sought agreement on

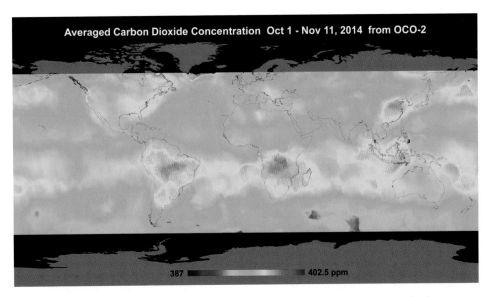

Figure 3.1 Contours of atmospheric CO_2 in the Earth's atmosphere. Breaching levels of 400 ppm will have a lasting impact on the food supply and coastal habitation.
Source: NASA/JPL-Caltech.

stabilizing greenhouse gas concentrations in the atmosphere to slow global warming. The Kyoto Protocol, adopted on December 2, 1997, sought to take the next step, requiring signatory nations to reverse their own increases in carbon emissions and commit to a 5 percent reduction within a decade. Unfortunately, the agreement was never ratified by many governments. In the end, signatories accounted for less than 15 percent of global emissions.

A major roadblock was the issue of balancing the competing interests of industrialized nations, which had begun to confront the environmental consequences of modern technologies, and emerging economies, which were still struggling to adopt these technologies to meet the basic needs of their citizens. These emerging nations aspired to a similar quality of life enjoyed by their affluent brethren, and the global challenge was to map out a course that would allow them to reach this state without traversing the same unsustainable path taken by their predecessors. The general solution was to meet somewhere in the middle, where the industrialized nations would commit to meaningful cuts and the emerging nations would be assisted in steering a more sustainable course of development.

As the agenda shifted from a discussion of the nature of the problem to a discussion on what needed to be done, the participants in the negotiations found the going even more arduous. Gaining agreement on the priority of specific topics was hard enough. Gaining consensus on actions to be taken, especially as the actions implied nonuniform costs and benefits, was even harder. It takes a compelling issue and coordinated global leadership to secure convergence on action. Frustration at a series of global conferences sowed the seeds for a more serious and harmonious approach by the time of the 2015 Paris Climate Change Conference. Balancing the need for concrete action along with respect for sovereignty issues, the accord, which went into effect before the end of 2016, had many significant outcomes.[8] It established a creative way of setting goals: there would be nationally determined contributions that were effectively voluntary targets. There were clear obligations to report on progress toward these goals and to incrementally improve the goals to meet longer-term milestones. Trading of credits was also allowed and subject to better auditing. Even so, the accord relied greatly on voluntary action, and there were limited ways to deal with individual countries' failure to meet their goals. In other words, society's best hope for a course correction rests on a shaky agreement that is weak on obligating compliance.

On the positive side, the Paris accords have led to a new set of internal targets to be cascaded by respective signatory governments. Thus, compared to 1990 levels, the EU would cut its emissions by 40 percent by 2030. The U.S. would trim its emissions by 26–28 percent by 2025 compared to 2005 levels. China, still developing its industrial base, pledged to allow its emissions to peak by 2030 and then decline from there. If these commitments are met, and there are many reasons to doubt if they will be, there is a good chance of holding back global temperature rise to within limits thought to be tolerable. Global efforts to reach these goals are expected to have a significant impact on the transport sector and the auto industry in the coming decades.

The quantum of improvement committed to by the U.S., Europe, Japan, and China by 2030 oblige the auto industry to transform itself in a manner not witnessed since the energy crisis of the 1970s. Reducing emission levels will require revamping product technologies, introducing different mobility patterns, and finding new ways to price the impact of fuel costs and environmental costs. For a world heavily dependent on personal cars, these changes will be revolutionary. Yet, serious doubts have arisen as to whether this motivation will survive in the face of a transformed geopolitical landscape. The crucial issues are discussed below.

Impact of mobility on energy demand and environment

In many cities and countries around the world, the current mobility architecture imposes an unacceptably high cost on the environment, health, and the global economy. According to a UN report, a combination of negative externalities arising from people and freight movement, including untoward environmental impacts, traffic fatalities, and congestion, could account for 6–10 percent of global GDP.[9]

As more nations accelerate their internal state of development, our appetite for energy to fuel mobility demands is expected to grow considerably. Globally, transport accounts for 25 percent of delivered energy consumption,[10] more than the total energy consumed in all buildings, offices, and homes. According to the International Energy Agency (IEA), if global growth continues at current rates, demand for primary energy will see an increase of 40 percent by 2030 compared to 2007.[11]

Crude oil constitutes 40 percent of the world's energy source. For more than half a century, society's dependence on crude oil supplies has not only meant dealing with the vagaries of wild swings in oil prices; it has brought with it a combination of geopolitical costs and turmoil that have extracted an even higher price from humankind. Yet this oil dependence shows no sign of waning. The growth of the global economy has been lubricated by affordable energy, and the auto industry has been a major beneficiary. Between 1948 and 1972, as the U.S. and Europe took to motorization, oil consumption more than quadrupled in the U.S., from about 6 million barrels per day to about 26 million barrels per day. Even more rapid was the growth in Western Europe, where, in the same period, consumption increased from about 1 million barrels per day to 14 million barrels per day. Transport's share of global crude oil consumption grew from 45 percent in 1973 to 64 percent in 2013.[12] Global dependence on crude oil is set to grow further with motorization in such fast-growing countries as China, India, and Indonesia. Access to oil supplies will remain a geopolitical flashpoint.

Switching to alternative energy sources is easier said than done; it requires a lot of time and investment. Despite the urgency and the motivation, the pace of switching global energy sources remains glacial. Fossil sources, including coal and oil, continue to supply three-fourths of the world's primary energy needs. The situation will look about the same by 2040, according to forecasts by the U.S. Energy Information Administration,[13] though by that time a combination of renewables, accounting for 17 percent, and nuclear energy, accounting for 6 percent, should make a small dent in the fossil fuel demands. Even as administrators redouble efforts to bring online additional capacity of renewable power, the sustained dependence on carbon-based fossil fuels means that mitigating actions must focus intensely on conservation and efficiency.

Near-term projections are not encouraging. The fight to stave off global warming and achieve the goals of the global climate accords that have been signed is an uphill struggle. The global emission of CO_2, mainly from burning fossil fuels, is expected to increase by 35 percent between 2012 and 2040. This is a sobering prospect for a planet that is already witnessing accelerated melting of polar glaciers.

The combination of the utility and versatility of road transport, cars in particular, is tough to beat. Road travel is globally popular for its flexibility and utility. In Europe, for example, notwithstanding the availability of multiple well-connected modes and an excellent train network, it was estimated that in 2008, 83 percent of all passenger-kilometers and 73 percent of all freight-kilometers traveled were by road. As a result, road transport accounted for 83 percent of transport energy consumed in the EU in 2013.[14] A fresh demand surge is expected from the emerging economies as they adopt motorized transport in larger numbers, and worldwide CO_2 emissions from autos are forecasted to double by 2050.

As suggested by these factors, any blueprint for greener future mobility needs to be comprehensive, far-reaching, and extremely useful to displace a legacy architecture that is tough to beat. This is especially true for the emerging economies, where legacy investments are less entrenched and the opportunity to switch to a more sustainable mobility architecture is very timely.

Mechanisms to lower the impact of mobility on the environment

Mobility and the auto industry have an impact on the environment through three distinct pathways. Each of these pathways has been the subject of regulations to steer the domain toward a more sustainable course. They include (a) reducing toxic and harmful pollutants by lowering tailpipe emissions; (b) improving fuel efficiency, thereby reducing dependence on fossil fuels and lowering CO_2 emissions; and (c) improving the reuse and recycling of the materials used in cars so that demand for virgin raw materials is reduced and discarding of materials in environmentally damaging landfills is slowed.

Reducing toxic and harmful pollutants

The early reaction by environmentalists to unbridled motorization began in the U.S. in the 1950s. The Federal Clean Air Act of 1963 and the Air Quality Act of 1967 established a framework for regulatory mandates. Vehicle emissions, including nitrogen oxides, carbon monoxide, and soot particles, came under comprehensive regulations. Each of these pollutants affected health in different ways. The World Health Organization (WHO), for example, showed that inhalation of very soot particles could lead to cancer.

During the 1960s, as cars got bigger and heavier, automakers adopted high-performance engines. These engines required fuel blends, which were boosted by the addition of trace amounts of lead. One of the early targets of clean air legislation was to ban the use of lead in gasoline, to prevent emission of toxic lead into the environment. By 1996, leaded gasoline had been phased out in most of the Western world. Many of these emissions also depended on the quality and formulation of the fuel used. Over a period of time, other additives or fuel constituents such as sulfur were also regulated. For example, oil refineries were obliged to reduce the level of sulfur in diesel fuel from a level of 500 ppm to less than 15 ppm.

Across the main auto markets of the U.S., Europe, and Japan, designated regulators imposed a set of standards requiring cleaner cars and more sustainable mobility. The U.S. EPA mandated that cars sold in the U.S. reduce NO_x emissions to a fourth between 1994 and 2007. In parallel, between 2004 and 2007, the standard for the level of particulate matter was reduced by 90 percent. The mandates in Europe and Japan were similarly aggressive and were overseen by their own equivalent agencies. By 2012, automakers in Europe had to meet Euro 6 levels of emission requirements. Vehicles meeting these norms emitted less than 3 percent of the particulates emitted by their predecessors from 1990; NO_x emissions were down to 5 percent. This evolution also involved changes imposed on auto-related services. Gasoline stations, for example, had to deploy new-technology dispensers so that evaporative emissions, which could occur at the time of filling up, would be trapped and not released into the environment.

In summary, regulations were sequentially updated as science expanded our knowledge of how autos and mobility were affecting air quality. Over time, this resulted in the adoption of a range of exotic technologies and innovative mobility strategies, as discussed in chapter 5.

Notwithstanding progress in some aspects, the situation remains acute.

Across the U.S., between 1970 and 2016, GDP increased threefold, population grew by 50 percent, vehicle use climbed by 170 percent, and yet emissions in aggregate declined by 70 percent.[15] To take stock of progress that was achieved, it is useful to return to California. This state, which has a combination of unique geography and a large vehicle population, imposed the toughest standards anywhere in the world on autos. According to the American Lung Association's 2016 State of the Air report, there was good news and bad news for Los Angeles.[16] The city recorded its best air quality ever, in the history of the report, in terms of particulates and ozone. Yet Los Angeles also remained the U.S. metro area with the worst ozone pollution. Even in a state with the toughest standards, six of the top seven cities for ozone pollution were in California.

Across the world, despite the imposition of ever tighter regulations, the rapid pace and high density of motorization in both emerging and developed economies has meant that the problems remain serious. In 2016, the WHO concluded that "more than 80% of people living in urban areas that monitor air pollution are exposed to air quality levels that exceed the WHO limits. 98 percent of cities in low- and middle-income countries with more than 100,000 inhabitants do not meet WHO air quality guidelines."[17] According to WHO estimates, outdoor air pollution is linked to more than 3 million deaths each year.

Our current trajectory, though boosted with a lot of technology, still seems inadequate. It appears that a fundamentally new approach to mobility will be required to make any meaningful correction to the course.

Improving fuel efficiency and lowering carbon dioxide emissions

Global efforts to reduce the emission of CO_2 and the consumption of fossil fuels received a boost from an unlikely source. While people could see the pollution debate coming to a boil in the 1960s, the oil crises of the 1970s arrived as a rude shock. The issue was not related to climate change, but it brought into sharp focus the reality that lifestyles, especially in industrialized economies, were being sustained by an ever greater exploitation of the Earth's resources and a vulnerable supply chain stretching to the Middle East. Nations confronted the reality that accessing and securing stable supplies of energy would come with mounting political, economic, and military costs.

Faced with a 60 percent reduction in its oil supplies almost overnight, most of the industrialized world had little time to react. Oil shortages affected daily life. The arrival of fuel rationing just as cars and trucks were becoming indispensable for everyday mobility shook most nations. In the U.S., fuel supplies were rationed and conservation measures such as the 55 mph national speed limit were announced. The spread of affluence, which had seemingly been assured by the expansion of the 1960s, suddenly seemed threatened.

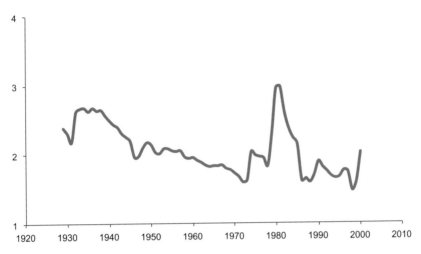

Figure 3.2 Inflation-adjusted average historical annual gasoline pump price (U.S. dollars). The oil crises in the 1970s caused fuel rationing and an abrupt climb in the price of gasoline. This triggered far-reaching changes for regulators, consumers, and automakers.
Source: U.S. Office of Energy Efficiency and Renewable Energy.

The global economy was thrown into turmoil. In many countries around the world, governments scrambled to respond, resorting to a combination of austerity drives, energy rationing, increased taxes on fuels, and a desperate attempt to switch to alternatives. The priority placed on energy conservation benefited the nascent drive to reduce carbon emissions.

Unlike Europe and Japan, where taxes on fuel rose, the U.S., for its own political and social reasons, chose to pursue a different path. Successive administrations were wary of citizens voting out any government that sought to impose additional fuel taxes. This approach would have lasting consequences. By 2016, taxes on auto fuel in Germany approximated 50 percent of the retail price, compared to about 11 percent in the U.S. With this course, the U.S. was forgoing one effective lever that most nations use to implement long-term energy policy and factor both direct and indirect societal costs associated with use of fossil fuels.

Instead, in the U.S., regulations imposed minimum standards on fuel efficiency for car fleets. Each automaker had to meet a mandated national sales-weighted fuel economy target, termed CAFE, for corporate average fuel economy. Administration of the program was entrusted to the U.S. National Highway Traffic Safety Administration (NHTSA). These targets were progressively tightened from the 1970s, and in the early years they worked very well. Between 1974 and 1985, CAFE fuel economy targets for passenger cars in the U.S. mandated very significant improvement, from 12.9 miles per gallon (mpg) to 27.5 mpg.[18] Chapter 5 reviews how these standards were met by automakers, who were forced to revamp their entire product lines. This journey underscores the valuable role that can be played by stable long-term policy and regulations.

The U.S. approach had one shortcoming. It remained an indirect approach to achieving the desired goal of reducing fuel consumption. After impressive gains in the 1980s, when customers still felt the effect of higher fuel costs, in the 1990s fuel prices collapsed. The immediate crisis had passed, and the focus on energy conservation tapered off as the world was once again flush with cheap oil. The pressure to build on the gains made was also eased as successive U.S. administrations watered down fuel economy regulations. For the next decade, technology and features were reoriented to provide customers with bigger and more powerful vehicles, with the result that progress in fuel savings ground to a halt. Considerable momentum that had been gained for energy conservation with great effort was lost.

Not until 2005 was a reduction in carbon emissions once again emphasized in the U.S. The period between 2005 and 2010 saw significant swings in crude oil prices and therefore in the retail price of gasoline. Between the spring of 2007 and the summer of 2008, the U.S. retail cost of a gallon of gas practically doubled. The shock once again led to customers rapidly switching to cars that were more fuel-efficient. Yet in the six short months between June and December 2008, the retail price of a gallon plummeted to almost a third of its peak price. Demand once again swung abruptly to bigger, heavier SUVs, and small cars fell out of favor. Customer's preferences diverged from what the auto industry was federally mandated to produce. Automakers quickly reversed strategies once again, torn between meeting customer demand for bigger cars and meeting federal standards. Such volatility would repeat several times over that decade and the resulting roller-coaster ride for fuel prices led to large swings in customer preferences and thwarted any stable long-term policy for energy conservation. Leaving customers vulnerable to the vagaries of crude oil price fluctuations would also whipsaw the entire industry. Many other developed economies, in which higher taxes constitute a much larger fraction of the retail gasoline price, experienced a more muted whiplash effect from these crude oil price gyrations. Further, with higher taxes they were already embarking on the journey to alter consumption habits and lower carbon emissions.

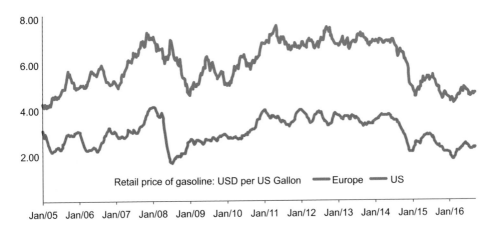

Figure 3.3 The EU policy of placing higher taxes on fuel has helped the drive toward conservation and also damped the impact of sudden swings in oil prices.
Source: U.S. Energy Information Administration.

In response to the increases in crude oil prices, the Obama administration chose to once again prioritize fuel efficiency, calling for higher stepwise targets. Spurred by renewed regulatory pressures, the U.S. industry saw its CAFE standard increase from a level of about 25 mpg in 2002 to almost 32 mpg by 2014.[19] Encouraged by the progress, the U.S. government announced the next wave of U.S. regulations, which were aimed at achieving a CAFE fleet average of 54.5 mpg by 2025.[20] This mandate would require almost a doubling of efficiency once again and set the industry on a new ramp of technological progress.

President Obama had to sell the message of conservation and environmental protection to two audiences. To the global community, he needed to demonstrate that the U.S. as a prominent carbon emitter was serious about lowering its emissions and overall environmental impact. Such a commitment by the U.S. was viewed as critical to convincing other large nations, such as China, to also commit to reducing carbon emissions. The mandate would lead to the U.S. cutting its carbon emissions from cars and light trucks in 2025 by half, and over the course of the program to reducing annual CO_2 emissions by an amount equivalent to the entire quantum of emissions from the U.S. in 2010.

To Congress and his fellow citizens, President Obama emphasized the virtue of conservation on the basis of economics. Sidestepping the challenge of pitching for a cleaner environment, a goal that might fail to stir enthusiasm for many U.S. voters, the administration chose to emphasize the economic benefit. As citizens were reeling under high fuel prices with oil at $140 per barrel, American consumers were urged to see the benefit of having the kind of car that would save them money. The government estimated that the new regulations would save a typical customer buying a 2025 model car, $8,000 at the gas pump over the lifetime of that car.[21] It would also halve the amount of oil imported from OPEC countries by 2025. The austerity many U.S. families were facing in the post-recession economy and a populace tired of involvement in military operations in the Middle East made this approach more appealing. The new regulations also provided incentives to encourage natural gas, electric, hybrid, and fuel-cell vehicles.

The new U.S. targets did make allowances for vehicle size. They sought to enforce an indexed scale of fuel economy standards so that the pressure to improve efficiency would be faced across all classes of products. A relatively small Ford Fiesta would be tasked with meeting a 2016 standard of 40 mpg while a larger Ford Taurus would be set a target of 36 mpg.

To complement the efficiency regulations, the U.S. implemented a trading scheme whereby manufacturers are allowed to bank and trade credits under the overall compliance mandate. This scheme resulted in a trading market-place that assigned a monetary value to achieving these targets. By 2015, according to data released by the EPA, automakers that were not in compli-ance or that feared falling short of compliance, such as Fiat-Chrysler and Mer-cedes-Benz, had already purchased more than 10 million credits from other, compliant automakers, such as Honda, Toyota, Nissan, and Tesla, which had surplus credits.[22] This active marketplace in fuel-efficiency credits is expected to grow, placing greater financial burden on manufacturers that lag the ramp-up of efficiency and rewarding those that move ahead of the plan.

Nudging the U.S. auto market onto a trajectory of higher efficiency and lower greenhouse gas emission will require consistent long-term policy goals, sustained across successive administrations, and backed by regula-tions, and appropriate incentives or penalties. When energy prices move in divergence to policy goals, the sector can face harsh economic outcomes. An industry under pressure to market fuel efficiency in an era when oil prices are dropping faces few palatable options.

Europe's approach to fuel economy and carbon emissions

Europeans embraced the philosophy that over the longer term, energy con-servation would continue to be needed, and their policy sought to moder-ate consumption. Hence, in Europe the retail price of fuel fluctuated more modestly, damped by higher taxes. The more stable movement of retail fuel prices in Europe contributed to a more consistent policy on regulations and fewer shocks to the system.

European vehicles were consequently more compact and lighter than U.S. vehicles and utilized smaller, fuel-efficient engines. Yet to deal with volatility in crude oil prices since the 1970s, European automakers also needed to adopt their own conservation measures. The EU had also ratified the Kyoto Protocol and sought a parallel carbon emissions reduction roadmap.

Whereas the U.S. regulations mandated uniform targets for all automakers, the initial EU approach was to allow the industry association to allocate targets among its members to meet the total fleet obligation. This alternative approach was motivated by a fundamental difference in dynamics among the various industry members. In the U.S., the three main domestic manufacturers each produced a broad range of products, from economy cars to luxury cars. For example, GM made everything from Chevrolets to Cadillacs. Hence regulators could force through a corporate fleet average. In Europe, such a regulation would prove more complicated. The European manufacturers represented a broader cross section of companies, and those that made luxury cars (for example, Mercedes-Benz, BMW, or Jaguar–Land Rover) protested that they could not be asked to meet the same standards as companies that manufactured only small economy cars, which could more readily meet high fuel-efficiency targets (for example, Fiat or Peugeot). It did not help that these manufacturers were distributed across different countries in the EU and that national interests to protect the companies and the jobs they represented also played a role in what agreement could be forged.

In Europe, CO_2 emissions from autos were measured in grams emitted per kilometer of travel (g/km), a measure also used as a surrogate for fuel consumption. Using 1995 as a baseline, the target called for achieving a 25 percent reduction in CO_2 emissions, to a level of 140 g/km by 2008, equivalent to about 39 mpg. The industry missed the voluntary target it had set for itself by almost 10 percent.

In response to the European industry's failure to meet its own goals, the EU Parliament shifted from a policy of voluntary compliance by automakers to one of EU-wide targets applicable to the sales fleets of the major automakers. From the 2015 target of 130 g/km, targets have been further increased by 23 percent to the 2021 level of 95 g/km of CO_2.[23] At this level the EU fleet would meet an average fuel efficiency of over 57 mpg. The European Parliament has further indicated that by 2025, the targets would be further revised to a fleet value of 68 to 78 g/km of CO_2, or better than 70 mpg. As discussed in chapter 5, Europe has had better success driving improvements with this more forceful approach.

Energy conservation in the Asian auto industries

The Japanese auto industry is different again: it evolved in an atmosphere conducive to the conservation of space and energy. In a nation that is very dependent on imported oil and raw materials, fuel is used with care, and in a nation with a high population density, space is at a premium. For these reasons Japanese cars evolved to emphasize compact dimensions and light weight. So, even though the Japanese automakers gained considerable market share as a result of the oil crises of the 1970s, they too were spurred to action by their government, which anticipated tougher times ahead. In 1979, the Japanese government passed the Energy Conservation Law, which was enforced on products sold from 1985 onward. The Japanese government, working through the Ministry for Trade and Industry, ensured that these efficiency standards were subsequently updated periodically to maintain progress toward long-term goals. By 2008, the Japanese market was already demanding the highest fuel efficiency among the large markets, being almost 8 percent more efficient than Europe. Revised targets rolled out for 2020 call for a fleet average of 20 kilometers per liter or approximately 46 mpg, reflecting a further improvement of almost 20 percent compared to fleet fuel efficiency in 2015.

In 2000, China's auto market was insignificant—it sold 0.7 million cars, whereas in the U.S. more than 17 million vehicles were sold. By 2013, China had emerged as the largest global market, selling almost 18 million cars. As a result, China has had to face the challenges of very rapid motorization and the consequences of large-scale environmental impact. Even as the country is still maturing in the auto sector, it is already confronting significant congestion and pollution challenges. The Chinese have had to rapidly advance their fuel efficiency and tailpipe emission laws to keep pace with the explosive growth of the market.

According to the New York–based Institute for Transportation and Development Policy, in 2014, CO_2 emissions from transportation in China were estimated at 190 megatons—a figure that is expected to climb to 1,100 megatons by 2050 in the baseline scenario.[24] For reference, the corresponding figure for the U.S. in 2014 was 670 megatons. China has woken up to the magnitude of the challenge the country will face internally, as well as pose to the rest of the world, as its large economy adapts to consumer desires for higher levels of motorization. The efficacy of their actions will have a major bearing on global carbon emissions in the coming decades.

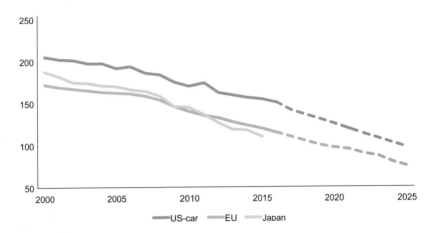

Figure 3.4 Grams of CO_2 per kilometer. Fuel economy improvements in the U.S., Europe, and Japan have been improving and new targets for 2025 promise substantial gains.
Source: International Council on Clean Transportation.

Well-to-wheel analysis: A fuller picture of energy use

The shift from focus on miles per gallon or kilometers per liter to measuring CO_2 emissions has been necessary. It obliges one to take into account a fuller picture of the energy cycle. The ongoing debate over the impact of energy use and carbon emissions has resulted in a number of myths being propagated. In the eagerness to find solutions, there has been a tendency to accept one or more technologies as the answer to the problem. Unfortunately, this complex issue cannot be managed with any single breakthrough. A sound and mature analysis and a framework of solutions are needed to chart a course for the future.

Myth: If everyone shifted to zero-emission vehicles (ZEVs), such as electric cars, the problems of carbon emissions and tailpipe emissions could be solved simultaneously.

Compared to conventional cars, almost all electric or plug-in hybrid vehicles demonstrate impressively low carbon emissions, for two reasons. First, electric motors are inherently more efficient for energy conversion. Second, electrified drivetrains offer the possibility of regeneration of energy during braking. A good fraction of the energy that is lost through the dissipation of heat during braking in a conventional vehicle during stop-and-go city driving can be recovered and used to recharge batteries. These factors improve energy efficiency over a given journey. But this conclusion is based merely on what happens in the vehicle itself.

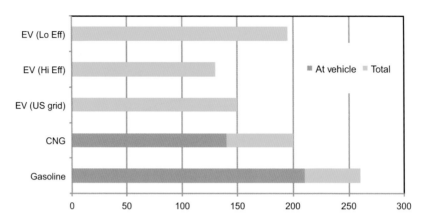

Figure 3.5 Well-to-wheel greenhouse gas emission (g/km CO$_2$ equivalent). While electric vehicles are themselves very efficient, unless the electrical grid supplying the power is also relatively clean (high efficiency), gains at the car will not significantly lower total greenhouse gas emissions. Data shown are based on a typical reference car with typical efficiencies.
Source: Oak Ridge National Laboratory.

Many scientists and researchers rely on a more comprehensive measure that takes into account a fuller set of considerations—the "well-to-wheel" analysis. This approach considers a combination of the cost, energy, and effort expended in producing, storing, and distributing the fuel, in addition to the use of energy in the car itself. In other words, if it takes a lot of effort and carbon emissions to get the fuel into the car in the first place, then that aspect also needs to be considered.

A pure-electric vehicle, such as a Tesla or a Nissan Leaf, whose energy needs are usually met by electrical power from the grid, is considered a ZEV. Yet if the electrical grid that charges the battery in that car is itself powered by high-sulfur coal, as it is in many parts of the world, then the gains of lower carbon emissions from the car are lost at the point of power generation. The overall emissions at the coal-powered electricity-generating plant also need to be factored in when assessing the total impact on the environment. On the other hand, in a nation such as Norway, which has abundant hydroelectric power, a policy of encouraging electric vehicles makes a lot of sense. The electrical power is generated with very low carbon emissions.

In most countries, electrical power is generated from a basket of sources, including hydroelectric, coal, oil, and gas-fired thermal power plants and nuclear reactors. In aggregate, in 2013, more than 67 percent of the world's electricity was generated from fossil fuel sources.[25] For each context, therefore, a more detailed analysis of the quality of grid power is necessary before we can assess how much better they are in terms of greenhouse gas emissions. In figure 3.5, the effect of the quality of the electrical grid on the fuel efficiency of electric vehicles is evident. It also reveals the quantity of emissions that happen even before the fuel (whether compressed natural gas [CNG] or gasoline) goes into the vehicle. Furthermore, an electric vehicle operating in a region with poor-quality electrical grid power (low efficiency) may fare no better than a CNG vehicle.

Myth: An economy that is based on hydrogen rather than carbon is the solution for the future.

As hydrogen powered vehicles would not emit any carbon exhaust, many have considered hydrogen as a fuel to be the sought-after answer for sustainable mobility.

The problem lies in the details. Hydrogen does not occur freely in the atmosphere, to be trapped and used. Like electricity, hydrogen is a carrier of energy but needs to be produced somewhere. There are many ways to do this, but another primary fuel is needed.

For example, hydrogen can be produced by the electrolysis of water. However, electrolysis requires a huge amount of energy, usually electricity, to separate hydrogen molecules from oxygen. Since that same electricity could be put to use directly, taking advantage of the well-established global network for electricity distribution, using electrolysis to produce hydrogen offers minimal promise.

Hydrogen can also be produced from alcohol, natural gas, and similar molecules rich in hydrogen. These processes require the use of "reformers," but their by-products are similar, and so too are their efficiencies. Furthermore, this approach adds another expensive system, the reformer, to an already complex and expensive machine.

Hydrogen has other disadvantages. It has very low energy density by volume and hence needs to be massively compressed or even liquefied for storage and distribution. The process of compression takes further energy. Longer-term storage may also require cryogenics, involving again a significant use of energy just to facilitate storage. An expensive new infrastructure would be required across the regions where hydrogen would be used, and this would ultimately have an adverse impact on its economics. For the longer term, large-scale production of hydrogen would be possible through thermonuclear splitting of the water molecule, although here too, the nuclear reactor might just as well be put to use delivering electricity.

There are specific domains in which hydrogen can be a preferred solution. Hydrogen produced from renewable sources, such as wind and biomass, offers the promise of a good net greenhouse gas impact, even though the economics are still a challenge. Countries with a large surplus of renewable electricity power, such as Norway, may actually use hydrogen as a form of storing energy, if the compression and storage energy is justified. In these cases, the use of electricity directly remains a strong alternative.

If, however, these technologies are supported by updated infrastructure and if our energy sources migrate to cleaner power, there are many attractive pathways to cleaner future mobility.

Mandates and incentives for zero-emission vehicles

Electrification is accepted as a fundamental transformation strategy for the auto industry. We anticipate a number of important issues that nations need to consider as they encourage increased use of all-electric or hybrid-electric vehicles.

Renewables represent a fast-growing fraction of the electrical grid in many nations, and the electrical grid power is rapidly getting cleaner. In 2015, according to the IEA, more than 50 percent of global power generation capacity that was added was from renewable energy sources, mainly wind and solar photovoltaic cells.[26] The capacity of renewable sources is expected to grow further, by 42 percent by 2021. In Germany, renewable energy sources advanced from supplying about 3 percent of grid power in 1990 to supplying 31 percent by 2015. Germany calls for more than 80 percent of power to be generated from renewable sources by 2050.[27] But few nations are on track to match Germany's pace.

This course requires significant capital investments in renewable power generation and infrastructure. Fortunately, with lower-cost solar cells entering the market and incentives to promote energy production across household rooftops available in many nations, communities can quickly follow Germany's lead. The approach to incentivize distributed power generation using solar cells can significantly accelerate progress. Impressively, in 2016, Germany's electricity grid recorded a few days when the entire country's demand was met from renewable energy sources. Sadly, recent changes in the political landscape, especially in the U.S., have dampened hope for faster progress..

As the use of renewable energy sources increase, a significantly larger role for electric or electrified vehicles may be expected. There is growing consensus on this among industry and regulators. Anticipated fuel efficiency mandates demand a considerable stretch from the current status. It seems unlikely that national carbon emission reduction goals can be met with conventional combustion engine technologies alone. A significant fraction of the fleet will have to be pure-electric vehicles or at least plug-in hybrids. In an environment in which the grid power takes a good fraction from renewable sources or even from nuclear sources, such vehicles can significantly accelerate efforts to lower carbon emissions.

ZEVs may also help address air quality in many city centers and high-population areas. Even in countries where the grid power consists of larger fractions of coal-sourced energy, electric vehicles and plug-in hybrids can operate as zero "local" emission vehicles in certain sensitive and congested environments. In other words, they can help protect sensitive areas such as city centers from tailpipe emissions, even if on a total well-to-wheel basis they are no less polluting than some conventional vehicles. The emissions they cause may be far removed from centers of high population, and in some settings, this can be a partial and acceptable solution.

As a result, incentives, tax benefits, and mandates are being rolled out to boost the appeal of electric vehicles. The U.S. state of California has been aggressively rolling out mandates for clean air. As early as 1990, California enacted a set of rules requiring automakers to ensure that 2 percent of their sales fleet by 1998 were ZEVs, increasing to a mandated 10 percent of vehicles sold by 2003. ZEVs were defined as both pure-electric vehicles and hydrogen fuel-cell vehicles. By 1996 these rules had been diluted as a result of protests by the auto industry, which claimed that the requisite technologies were neither ready nor commercially viable to meet these obligations. In response, the regulatory authority, the California Air Resources Board (CARB), broadened the category, including some classes of hybrid-electric vehicles and later even some "ultra-clean gasoline vehicles," which did not conform to the original definition but were seen to contribute to reducing emissions in a practical manner. Even with this dilution the state pushed forward toward achieving lower carbon and tailpipe emissions with a larger basket of vehicular technologies. The U.S. federal government in 2005 enacted the Energy Policy Act of 2005, which included the alternative fuel motor vehicle credit, providing specific incentives for the entire country for a range of low-emission vehicles or ZEVs.

Europe too has adopted incentives and concessions to boost the demand for such cars. Electric vehicle buyers in Europe enjoy exemption from certain vehicle taxes. In the UK, for example, buyers of certain cars also enjoy grants, while in Germany electric vehicle customers were eligible for tax incentives.

Nonfiscal incentives have also been successful in persuading customers to switch to cleaner vehicles. Many progressive employers and organizations, including Google, Microsoft, Apple, SAP, and Mattel, provide incentives for employees who use clean, advanced-technology vehicles. Employee benefits may include free charging in parking lots and preferential parking areas. In California, such vehicles are also eligible to use the less congested high-occupancy vehicle lanes, enabling users of such cars to enjoy a speedier commute.

In Europe, many cities allow electric vehicles to use bus lanes. Some cities have also encouraged the shift to zero-emission mobility through exemption from payment of congestion fees, access to better located and lower-cost parking, and access to recharging support infrastructure. By July 2016, London had already installed more than 850 electric car charging points on its streets.

In China too, interest in such cars has been boosted by nonfiscal incentives. On "red alert" smog days, when conventional vehicles face restrictions, electric vehicles are exempted. This is part of China's national policy of encouraging this class of cars, referred to as "new energy vehicles." China has reportedly set aside a fund of $16 billion to deploy charging infrastructure across highways and cities to boost electric vehicle and partial-electric vehicle popularity with buyers. When such steps are considered together with investments made by Chinese corporations and state-owned enterprises, it is apparent that China is seeking to execute a roadmap aiming for global leadership in electric vehicle use.

In chapter 5 we delve more deeply into technological advances and product innovations.

Contributions of modal shifts

Transit-oriented development (TOD) is an approach that stresses more comprehensive coordination between urban planning and investments in the mobility architecture while aiming for social, economic, and environmental goals. This approach bakes the key transit infrastructure into the master plans of urban development. TOD can be the glue that reinforces the symbiotic nature of that relationship. Transit investments boost the attractiveness of those urban areas, and reciprocally, the urban areas feed transit systems, ensuring economic viability. Such coordinated development reduces the need for movement, and for the mobility that is undertaken, it offers many sustainable options.

The community of Hammarby-Sjöstad in Sweden has undertaken such coordinated development, with impressive results. The carbon footprint for the transportation of the average resident of Hammarby-Sjöstad is about half that of a resident in the neighboring suburbs.[28] Residents have seen personal car use decline by almost half, while the use of public transit has doubled compared to that in neighboring suburbs of comparable affluence.

In Germany, an increased emphasis on TOD principles has resulted in greater use of public transit, from a level of about 105 trips per capita per year in 1990 to 140 in 2010. Anticipating growing demand, and mindful of CO_2 emission obligations, Madrid has increased its public transport capacity by more than 70 percent over the past two decades. Investment in cleaner public transit modes and encouraging the use of these modes over cars has allowed the EU-28 nations to improve the energy intensity of mobility. Carbon emissions have been correspondingly lower. When urban light rail and trams are considered, more than 40 percent of public transit in Europe in 2015 was powered by electricity.

In Asia, high population density and a demand for space-efficient and energy-efficient mobility in urban areas have led to priority being given to public transport and TOD principles. In a representative selection of cities, per capita energy used for private passenger transport in Asia was estimated at 40 percent of that in Europe and 13 percent of that in the U.S.[29] Even cities such as Shanghai that had embarked on a trajectory toward increasing motorization have issued targets to allow public transport to account for 35 percent of travel by 2020.

Energy options

Besides the use of electricity and hydrogen, there are other ways to lower carbon and other tailpipe emissions. Though gasoline and diesel have been the dominant automotive fuels, other fossil fuels offer possibilities for more efficient energy conversion and lower the quantum of emissions. Each fuel comes with its own positive and negative attributes, and many are relevant only in specific contexts or regions.

A common alternate fuel and one used in many urban areas is liquefied petroleum gas (LPG). A major advantage to using LPG is that for cars and buses, the conversion from gasoline use is relatively simple. In addition, LPG has an intrinsically higher octane number, which is conducive to better combustion; compared to gasoline, it results in lower CO_2, emissions; and LPG can result in significantly lower soot and particulate emissions and lower sulfur and nitrogen oxide emissions, thereby avoiding smoke and the visible degradation of the urban atmosphere. For these reasons, in many nations, such as Japan, taxi fleets have switched from diesel to LPG, helped by incentives. The city of Vienna, Austria, operates buses almost exclusively on LPG. However, in most nations LPG is produced from crude oil, and therefore its use does not alleviate dependence on that energy source. Also, most countries have limited LPG distribution infrastructure, and this inhibits applications in rural areas or for long-distance travel.

Natural gas is another alternate fuel that often finds favor with urban transit authorities. Like LPG, it offers many advantages over conventional fuel, most of all in its superior octane number, better combustion characteristics, and lower particulate emissions. In fact, in a vehicle, it may have lower CO_2 emissions than even diesel. However, when the full cycle efficiency is assessed, including production and distribution of the fuel, it loses some of its advantage compared to diesel or gasoline. CNG must be stored at high pressure to make it sufficiently dense for practical use and requires careful management of trace amounts of methane emissions which are very harmful to the ozone layer. Even so, in many cities it is popular for taxi and public transport fleets. Its appeal increases in regions where gas pipeline infrastructure is available. In New Delhi, facing unacceptably high levels of nitrogen oxides and particulates, the local administration banned use of diesel for public transport and forced a large-scale shift to CNG. A 2010 survey of city transit authorities in Europe showed CNG at the top of the list of intended bus fleet acquisitions, with 48 percent preferring this option.[30]

Since 1990, more natural gas fields have been discovered around the globe, giving rise to the hope that the global production capacity of CNG will increase. Between 1973 and 2013, natural gas as a primary energy source grew from 16 percent to over 21 percent.[31] Bernd Bohr, former chairman of the German automotive supplier Bosch, is optimistic regarding the future role for natural gas, saying, "It has the potential to offer up to 25 percent improvement in CO_2 reduction and has better prospects for generation from biomass."[32]

Another alternative is to look for carbon-based biofuels, in which case the biosphere reabsorbs an equivalent amount of carbon, reducing net CO_2 emission into the atmosphere. Many nations eagerly pursued the production and use of biofuels after the oil crises of the 1970s. Imagine growing the fuel a country needed! This was indeed what Brazil, a country with a vast acreage of sugar cane, embarked on, with a fair degree of success. Apart from the geopolitical and economic advantages, it also represents a shorter loop of the carbon cycle. Instead of burning fossil fuels that are the result of thousands of years of trapping carbon, ethanol produced from sugar cane, for example, can circulate the carbon within a harvest cycle. The alcohol produced from sugar cane is formulated into ethanol as a fuel that is combusted in engines. This releases carbon into the atmosphere. The next season's sugar cane crop essentially absorbs a significant amount of carbon from the atmosphere and thus completes the cycle.

Ethanol blends easily with gasoline and so is often used in U.S. pumps as E10 (10 percent ethanol content blended with gasoline) or in Brazilian pumps as E22 (22 percent ethanol). When such a policy is deployed nationally, it allows the replacement of a significant quantum of gasoline, with very little change to vehicles or infrastructure. Ethanol-fueled vehicles offer slight advantages in hydrocarbon emissions but can have more harmful effects through evaporative emissions, which are much more harmful to the ozone layer than CO_2. But biofuels offer the possibilities of custom fuel blends that are chemically reconstituted. Jürgen Dohmen, an engine specialist at FEV, believes "we may expect a range of tailored fuels from bio-mass to address future sustainability goals."[33]

Through the years, the auto industry has also explored the use of biodiesel. Biodiesel is classified as fatty acid methyl ethers produced from a variety of sources, including rapeseed or jatropha seeds. They are commonly blended in small fractions (less than 5 percent) with diesel. In the case of these biofuels, pilot experiments have usually stumbled over a few issues. They must be deployed at sufficiently large scale to be economically viable but, apart from systems for producing ethanol, the production systems have not proved to be robust at large scale.

Fervor and support for biofuels cooled by 2005, when an unexpected problem was encountered. In some cases in which food crops such as corn were used for producing fuels (such as ethanol) in large scale, a complex ethical question arose: the trade-off between food inflation and cheaper energy. Also, in some parts of Asia, large areas of virgin tropical forests, which are significant carbon absorbers, were being cleared so that an environmentally favorable fuel from palm oil could be produced.

Such issues are not insurmountable but must be addressed through a carefully designed policy backed by aligned investments. Finding fuels more appealing than gasoline and diesel is difficult: those established fuels offer exceptionally high energy density, coupled with a well-established infrastructure. Yet the idea of a shorter carbon loop associated with the use of biofuels is attractive. Biofuels can go a long way in complementing a range of initiatives as the world moves toward a more sustainable future. Amory Lovins, cofounder and chairman of the energy think tank Rocky Mountain Institute, is an ardent supporter, remarking, "A move from fossil fuels to renewables is essential for the future of our planet."[34]

Two Princeton University researchers, Robert H. Socolow and Stephen W. Pacala, have advocated that stabilization of the world's carbon emission trajectory could only happen with a portfolio of solutions.[35] Deploying such a portfolio will require orchestration of all available levers including conservation, switching of energy sources, and the use of technologies to improve efficiency. The good news is that almost all components of this portfolio are already available. No specific invention is necessary to effect a change of course. Their conclusions point to the important role for deployment and focused execution.

Validating this viewpoint, where multiple levers are used, progress is visible. In Europe, since 2000, some evidence of the decoupling of the energy consumption of transport and economic growth is evident. The energy consumed in transportation per unit of GDP generated fell by 13 percent between 2000 and 2013.[36] This critical decoupling is a goal that all economies seek. As efficient infrastructure is put in place and technological innovations are employed, the energy intensity of the economy will fall. This is key to achieving sustainable economic growth. As we discuss later in the book, the CHIP mobility framework can help guide the implementation of such an approach, one relevant to both developed and developing economies.

Reuse, recovery, and recycling of vehicles

An important aspect of the sustainability of the mobility architecture we propose and one that warrants more attention has to do with the vast quantities of materials that are used over product life cycles.

A global industry that turns out more than 80 million cars a year will consume in aggregate around 100 million tons of raw materials, mainly steel, aluminum, and plastics. Each year, approximately 27 million cars reach the end of life and are discarded or recycled. The amount of discarded materials can itself cause serious environmental damage. The need to recycle or reuse constituent auto materials has gained urgency since the turn of the twenty-first century.

Fortunately, the auto industry has traditionally found value in recovering and recycling materials, long before it became a subject of regulations. This behavior was motivated by simple economics, which recognized value in the discarded materials. Particularly in Europe and Asia, the war years had bred the instinct for conservation and re-use of materials. Through organic evolution, mostly involving small-scale industries, between 80 and 85 percent of vehicle content have historically been recycled and reused.

In the U.S., the Automotive Recyclers Association has been in existence since 1940. The U.S. auto recycling industry registers annual revenues in excess of $30 billion, aggregated from more than 7,000 recycling centers distributed across the country.[37]

The fact that cars are built with a lot of metals, mainly steel, helps. Steel and aluminum are easily recycled. They are sent to smelters and resupplied to foundries and steel plants as scrap inputs. Plastics, fibers, and foams, mainly from interior parts, are also recovered, although some of these materials are sent to landfills. The use of biodegradable organic inputs such as soy for making the foams used in seats and jute or hemp for the fibers used in interior trims would further improve the ecological footprint.

Until recently, this recycling industry has evolved because of a natural motivation to extract value from scrap, which can sustain businesses. Yet this approach has been inadequate in a world that is simultaneously concerned about sources of new materials and about limiting the spread of landfills. A more focused plan is being put in place to significantly improve end-of-life reuse.

In Europe, for example, approximately 16 to 17 million new cars enter the market annually. The continent operates a fleet estimated at about 230 to 250 million vehicles. It is also estimated that approximately 13 to 14 million vehicles exit the system each year. Of these, roughly half are scrapped, and the other half find their way to markets in Eastern Europe, Africa, and the Middle East. The cars that are scrapped have, over decades, been filling scrap yards and landfills. Even though an informal market existed to recover useful materials and components, it could not stem the scourge of unsightly junkyards littering the rural landscape.

In 2000, the European Parliament issued a directive that the rate of reuse and recovery was to reach 95 percent (measured by weight of scrappage) by 2015. Ensuring the effectiveness of such a policy required a range of actions that were not easy to implement. To start with, some accountability had to be established to be sure that cars to be scrapped got to designated processing centers. Auto design and manufacture had to be conducive to recovery of materials for secondary use. For example, if metal parts are bonded with adhesives to plastic parts, it is not easy to separate them so that the metal and the plastic can be separately processed for recycling. Cars may employ exotic materials, and this means that the recycling center must have adequate information on the inventory of materials in each car so that they may be meaningfully extracted. This has required extensive documentation and follow-up, both for the automaker and for the recycler.

The industry will face even tougher challenges in the future as new materials and technologies are employed. Recyclers must deal with hazardous components such as airbags that are recovered from scrapped vehicles. (Airbags use incendiary devices for firing and gas generation to inflate the airbag.) Catalytic converters include precious metals that are very valuable. Soon, scrap yards will see growing numbers of electric vehicles, which employ very high-voltage (400–800 V) batteries and ultracapacitors. Even passive materials such as carbon fiber require special processing for recovery and reuse in their second cycle.

Just as with vehicle emissions, the industry has faced new regulations on recycling auto parts even as consumer enthusiasm remains mixed at best. Automakers routinely focus on designing products for easier assembly so that manufacturing process costs are minimized. Since automakers see these costs in their profit and loss statements, they are motivated to improve the efficiency of the manufacturing process. For better recycling and reuse, however, products also need to be efficient for disassembly. Designing a product so that materials and parts can be disassembled more easily often increases the price of that product. Such costs add up. Historically, consumers have not always been willing to pay higher prices for a "greener" car. According to a survey in Europe conducted by the German market research corporation GfK in 2008, at the height of the rise in fuel prices, 62 percent of respondents indicated a willingness to pay more for an "eco-car." By 2012, this fraction had sagged to 49 percent, pushed down by the already lower fuel prices.

To ensure that end-of-life mandates are effective, regulators have placed obligations on automakers to ensure that their cars are recycled at the end of their lifetime. By 2010, most European countries had reached a level where reuse, recycling, and recovery accounted for 83–88 percent by weight of the scrapped vehicles. In Germany, the figure actually touched 95 percent.[38]

Many countries and cities have witnessed a remarkable revolution in the management of household waste. Residents have been gradually educated on the value of waste segregation and reducing the amount of waste that ends up in landfills. In a similar manner, governments and automakers need to go beyond just mandating recyclability of vehicles. More effective tools are needed to educate consumers so that materials recyclability gets factored into their choice of car. Society's efforts to improve reuse and recycling will then be more successful.

In closing

Regulations and mandates can have a powerful effect on stimulating and steering technological development and user behavior. The advances in emissions, fuel efficiency, and end-of-life recycling bear testimony to this effect. It is equally important that regulations, policies, incentives, and fees steer the right behaviors and use patterns. The adoption of electric vehicles on the back of financial and nonfinancial incentives is evidence of this form of guidance. The set of targets on the horizon will require substantial further renovation of fundamental propulsion technologies. Efforts to see through this phase must be resolute and capable of absorbing innovations.

New technologies and mandates often involve additional costs and impose additional burdens on users. Enthusiasm for undertaking the extra costs and burdens varies. A sustainable mobility framework for the future must include the customer's perspective. In addition to using incentives and fees as tools, governments and industry will need to engage in customer education about the true impact of various mobility choices and options to truly make a difference. The food and nutrition industry has taken positive steps toward educating customers about the choices they can make to achieve a healthier lifestyle. A similar effort is necessary to guide people toward mobility choices that are faster, smarter, and greener.

4　New Attitudes

Yet all experience is an arch wherethrough
Gleams that untraveled world ...

—*Alfred Lord Tennyson, "Ulysses"*

The romance around cars has been magical. Cars have helped sell everything from Swiss chronographs to women's designer gowns. Fashion shows branded by Mercedes-Benz, luxury luggage branded by Bentley, and designer sunglasses branded by Porsche highlight how autos and auto brands have been used to create image and lend their aura. Autos have defined mobility for most of the developed economies. They offer high-utility, round-the-clock availability, and a way to express personal style and panache. The automobile charmed its way into a special place in human society. A dog may be man's best friend but cars were not too far behind.

Now it appears that the shoe is on the other foot. In many situations, smartphones are supplanting the personal car in people's priorities. Smartphones and connectivity features are being used to promote car brands. Advertisements extolling 4G LTE connectivity are being used to pitch Chevrolets to millennials. Ford, Hyundai, and Chrysler are scrambling to outdo one another in luring future customers by boasting how well they have integrated Google's Android Auto or Apple's CarPlay. Even in a hypercompetitive market there are thousands of eager customers around the world, many who will even brave subzero weather to stand in queues overnight just to be among the first to possess a brand-new smartphone model. A half century ago they did the same for cars, such as when Lee Iacocca launched the first Ford Mustang.

These shifts in consumer interests are motivated by a complex interplay of changing economics, cultural values, and new possibilities in a world of connected products and services. The drift in society's priorities carries

important messages for cities, automakers, technologists, and entrepreneurs. What society expects in the future is a different and complex new
architecture for mobility. In this chapter we attempt to read the tea leaves
and propose directions that will help mobility providers align their offerings
with the interests and preferences of a new tribe of customers.

The car culture

People's love affair with cars blossomed in the post–World War II years. In
the U.S., the rapid conversion of many factories from producing armaments
and military hardware to civilian applications enabled auto production to
grow rapidly. Many soldiers returned home with a familiarity with handling
machines, gained from driving jeeps, fixing tanks, and maintaining aircraft.
The GI Bill also provided them with money in the pocket—to be used for
education, starting a family, and even launching small businesses. The economy was growing rapidly, and peace brought with it unbounded optimism.

In Europe and Japan too, economic growth kicked in, as they set about
rebuilding their nations from the rubble. The Marshall Plan provided a substantial injection of U.S. monetary aid into Western Europe to help the devas-
tated economies get back on their feet and reengage in the global postwar
economy. Road and highway construction was in high gear, and personal
mobility for that generation was as critical as digitization is today.

Cars had become a tool for society as well as a medium of expression for
their owners. Corporate sales forces were more mobile and could range farther, while those engaged in the trades and crafts could expand their businesses using their automobiles as mobile workshops. Families took vacations
by car, while young couples found cars to be an ideal private space for court-
ing. A culture developed around cars, as did a dependence: families got used
to drive-in movies, drive-in diners, and even banks with drive-through teller
windows.

Seizing the opportunity, the auto industry boosted the auto from its utili-
tarian role to a cult object. Cars became the basis of popular global sporting
events such as Formula-1 races; rallies and car clubs sprouted for every possible genre of the product. Numerous Hollywood blockbusters, including
Bullitt, Italian Job, and *The Love Bug,* lent starring roles to cars. Just as fashion
models sashayed down ramps, show cars pirouetted on turntables in auto
salons and at car shows before the admiring gaze of both the cognoscenti
and the lay public. Antique cars became expensive collector items. Blending
rational benefits with emotional joy, the auto industry propelled itself to a
position of prominence as an unparalleled industrial sector.

Figure 4.1 Car culture in America. Cars emerged as central to many forms of social interactions and daily life.
Source: (CC BY 2.0) simon17964.

Postwar optimism and effects on motorization

The postwar years saw an accelerated population growth, creating the baby boom generation in many developed economies. In the second half of the twentieth century, the U.S. population almost doubled, from about 150 million to more than 280 million,[1] while Japan's population grew by 50 percent, to 126 million. Europe saw its population grow by 20 percent. Consequently, more people entered the workforce and consumption grew. In the U.S., for example, the working population more than doubled as workplace participation grew from 59 percent to 67 percent of the adult population. These changes swelled the ranks of mobility consumers. In 1950, about 57 percent of driving-age Americans possessed a driver's license.[2] By 2000, almost 88 percent had one.

The auto industry also helped shrink a hitherto large gender gap in work on both sides of the Atlantic. In many countries the war production effort had inducted a large number of women into factory work for the first time, when labor was scarce. After the war, women's participation in the workforce remained considerably higher than before the war. For many families, this meant additional disposable income. Women also started driving in much greater numbers. In 1950, one out of every two adult women had a driver's license. By 2010, women outnumbered men as licensed drivers in the U.S.[3] In Germany the number of licensed female drivers between the ages of twenty and twenty-nine increased from 65 percent in 1975 to 85 percent by the end of the century.[4] Automobility multiplied an individual's options for work and social activities, expanded her geographic reach, and opened up new vistas of experience for men and women, young and old.

Simultaneously, cars became more affordable, and in the U.S. the vehicle fleet quadrupled between 1950 and 1995, to over 200 million vehicles. Car sales significantly outpaced growth in the number of licensed drivers. Analysts assessing the level of motorization in any country commonly measure the population of cars per thousand persons. Between 1950 and 2006, this figure in the U.S. climbed from about 300 to over 800. This meant there were 1.24 cars for every licensed driver.[5]

In Europe, the 1957 Treaty of Rome fostered cooperation in industrialization and trade across Western Europe. Europeans typically spent a relatively larger share of household income on food and accommodation and a smaller share on autos and mobility than did their U.S. counterparts. European cities had evolved to more compact and mixed-use layouts, lowering the demand for personal transport. U.S.-style suburbs did not take off in Europe, at least not to the same degree. Even so, the lure of personal mobility was strong, and car sales in Europe grew from approximately 3 million to 14 million units per year between 1963 and 2000.[6] In Germany, motorization grew from about 100 to more than 600 between 1960 and 2000.

A car for every household became the norm in these countries.

Winds of change: The skepticism of the 1960s

The winds of optimism that wafted through the auto industry during the 1950s and into the 1960s started to peter out by mid-decade. In the U.S., the sense of optimism and prosperity was pierced by the Vietnam War, which was brought directly into living rooms by that new invention, the television. Many young people began to question what they were fighting for. As surely as the crew-cut GI morphed into the long-haired hippie, the 1960s gave birth to willingness to debate authority and government policy.

Disenchantment with the auto industry also began to set in. Ralph Nader's influential book, *Unsafe at Any Speed*, sharply criticized the auto industry's attempts to seduce buyers with titillating features while skimping on integrity of design and safety features.[7] The honeymoon with the automobile was drawing to a close.

Similar stirrings of reform roiled Europe as well. The summer of 1968 saw huge student protests in Paris that quickly spread through much of France. Teens and young adults were rebelling against postwar paternalism. Students were joined by industrial workers, who had their own grievances against paternalistic industries and their management. France's president Charles de Gaulle faced the ire of his young population in much the same way as President Lyndon Johnson faced protests in the U.S. On both continents, disenchantment also flowed from concern for conservation and the environment. The materialism that had been unleashed and celebrated in the postwar years had turned many of the younger populations against a consumption-focused society and the industries that fed it. Just a decade earlier, GM's CEO Charles Wilson had testified before the U.S. Senate, saying, "For years I thought what was good for our country was good for General Motors, and vice versa."[8] Such confidence suddenly seemed misplaced.

These cold winds of disaffection accompanied a strong skepticism about the benefits of increasingly autocentric societies. Cars were being associated with deteriorating air quality in cities and dependence on foreign oil. Consequently, regulation of the auto industry in domains such as safety, emissions, and fuel efficiency grew significantly in the U.S., Europe, and Japan. The industry surrendered some of its eminence as a vanguard of technology and innovation and was forced to align many elements of its technological roadmap merely to conform to regulations governing safety and environment. As Steve Jobs once said, "Innovation distinguishes between a leader and a follower." The auto industry would find it harder to hold on to its magic while it was following the regulator's agenda.

Peaking of vehicle mobility

With more people, more drivers, and more cars served by more miles of roads and highways, distances traveled in the U.S. grew sixfold between 1950 and 2007, to a total of almost 3 trillion vehicle miles traveled (VMT). Families became more mobile, and the annual distance traveled grew to just over 10,000 miles on a per capita basis in 2004.

At the dawn of the new millennium, that growth stalled. It seemed that a combination of factors had driven the trend to an apparent limit.

Until 1985, the growth in VMT had been remarkably linear, growing at about 3 percent per annum, and interrupted very briefly with short-term dips coinciding with the oil crisis of 1973 and the recession years of 1980–1983. Starting in the mid-1980s, the rate of growth slowed to an average of 2 percent each year.[9] Overall distance peaked in 2007 at about 3 trillion VMT. Thereafter household vehicle ownership rates also declined, by about 4 percent between 2009 and 2014, as did the ratio of cars to licensed drivers.[10]

Travel intensity did not resume in the post-recession recovery as it had on previous occasions.[11] (Some of this may be attributable to the structural changes we examine in the following sections.) Only in 2015 did that figure again see an increase as the U.S. economy started recovering and oil prices collapsed. Even so, the U.S. Department of Transportation forecast projects a much slower increase in VMT for the next three decades, of about 0.9 percent per year.

Similar trends were also evident in Europe. In the UK, the average distance traveled by car each year had peaked, and subsequently declined by 15 percent between 1990 and 2010. In France and Germany the corresponding figures showed declines in use by about 7–8 percent. In Japan the decline was much greater, with 24 percent less travel per car over those two decades.[12]

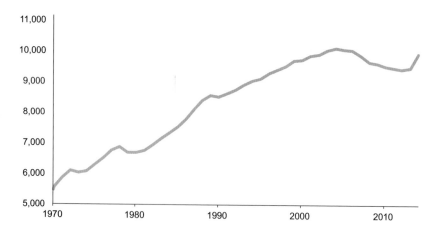

Figure 4.2 After secular growth for decades, per capita distance traveled annually by car (VMT) in the U.S. shows signs of having peaked.

Sources: U.S. Department of Transportation, U.S. Census Bureau.

Factors that changed the trajectory of mobility in the developed economies

Tighter economics suppresses mobility

Mobility is closely linked to how robust the economy is. Globally, notwithstanding emergence of new growth economies, the world has seen a trend toward lower average annual rates of growth over the past five decades. The world economy grew at over 5 percent annually in the 1960s and has since gradually slowed to less than 3 percent. Similarly, the U.S. economy expanded at almost 8 percent in the 1970s, when averaged over the decade, and has since slowed to less than 3 percent.

As economic growth rates slowed, job creation also suffered. In 2013, more than 24 percent of American sixteen- to nineteen-year-olds faced unemployment, a significant increase over the 15 percent figure observed in 2006.[13] Student loans were at an all-time high and repayment loomed ominously for many young adults with diminished job prospects. Between 2007 and 2011, new car sales to people aged eighteen to thirty-four years declined by almost 30 percent.

Mobility was slowly getting more expensive, and this too played an important role. In 1950 the average car sold for about 45 percent of average annual family income. In 2014, the equivalent family had to spend 61 percent of its annual income for the car. The average American family spent almost 50 percent more on transportation—almost $9,000 annually—than they did on food. Even for those comfortably in the middle-income segments, transportation costs accounted for almost a fifth of income.

Economics play a role in other ways as well. In many countries, taxes and other fees related to owning and operating a car have been climbing. As incomes flatten, these costs increasingly form a barrier to many aspiring young families. Japan has a particularly aggressive approach to taxing cars that do not conform to their "mini-car" category. For a midsize family car, taxes could amount to fifty times the amount paid in the U.S. In Europe too, car owners pay well over ten times the level of taxes for car ownership and use than in the U.S.

An era of depressed incomes and climbing costs for car ownership and use does not bode well for mobility with a personal car.

Transitions to the new digital millennium

Digital technologies have changed the meaning of "mobile." Cellular telephones transformed communication and offered an alternative to people moving from one location to another.

Smartphones evolved and expanded in utility very rapidly. At very low cost, they provide a broad spectrum of benefits for productivity, connectivity, and entertainment, combining telephony, email, video chat capability, photography, and on-demand TV and movies. Mobile phones promote constant connectivity and sustain social interactions across geographies. New models with ever greater functionality are launched almost every half year, and existing phones can be upgraded with new software and apps even more frequently. Significantly, these devices, powered by increasingly intelligent apps, allow users to tailor and customize functions to suit their profile. Growing up in the age of Facebook, selfies, and Instagrams, modern users have become accustomed to having products and services catered around their personal tastes and being allowed greater freedom in expressing their personalities.

A U.S. survey by Cisco in 2011 revealed that two-thirds of college students preferred the utility of an Internet connection over the use of a car. Such a transformation in expectations signals a readiness to adopt new forms of mobility and an oncoming upheaval for the auto industry.

At the same time, driving went from being a source of fun to a chore during which the driver's attention had to be focused on mundane duties, often for a large fraction of a commuter's free time. To many, this was valuable time robbed from more productive uses or entertaining engagements with a smartphone.

Familiarity with the automobile had eroded its novelty. When every household could have a car, a certain dilution of the aspirational motive to car ownership set in. According to Michael Sivak, a researcher at the University of Michigan, "Young adults of this generation appear less enamored by the automobile than their parent's generation"—this may be a consequence of the fact that car ownership had become commonplace, and hence the car has waned in its image as a prime possession that was a top priority to their parents.[14]

Millennials and their outlook on life and mobility

Millennials represented approximately a quarter of the population in both the U.S. and Europe by 2015. The attitudes of these "digital natives" toward mobility are shaped by their preference for urban living, familiarity with technology, and their experience of economic headwinds. According to a Nielsen survey, "Millennials are walkers and less interested in the car culture that defined Baby Boomers."[15] Of those surveyed, 62 percent preferred to live in urban, mixed-use communities and to walk to work and shops. In 2007, 77 percent of U.S. adults less than twenty-five years old owned a car. By 2011, this figure had dropped to 66 percent.

Furthermore, faced with a high level of accidents and fatalities involving young drivers, many states in the U.S. enacted graduated driving license laws imposing more restrictions and higher costs on new drivers. Gone were the days of the sixteen-year-old informally indoctrinated into driving by parents or siblings. The more cumbersome process, coupled with the higher costs of acquiring a license and insurance, created further disincentives for many millennials. Similarly, in Japan, new drivers are usually expected to attend driving school, which typically costs the equivalent of $2,000—a lot of money for a young adult who may have infrequent need to own or operate a car. Between 2003 and 2013, more than 100 driving schools in Tokyo went out of business owing to low demand.[16]

A pattern that has repeated across the U.S., Europe, and Japan reveals that fewer of the young populations acquire driver's licenses or have access to a car, and consequently they drive less annually.

Increased role for public transportation
As driving and car ownership rates have declined, the demand for public transit has increased. Public transit allows commuters to remain productive or entertained with their smartphones and social networks while they travel—a highly prized benefit for many.

In Japanese cities, 48 percent of all travel is undertaken using public transit. In European cities the figure is almost 23 percent.[17] In 2014 the average EU citizen took almost three trips per week on public transport, defined as journeys made by bus, trams, or metros.[18] In Germany, for young adults aged twenty to twenty-nine years, use of public transit doubled from 9 percent in 1997 to 18 percent a decade later.

As a car-centric society, outside a few very isolated pockets, U.S. reactions to public transit have historically been lukewarm. Many cities have suffered from a vicious cycle of low service quantity and quality, low expectations, low demand, and low investment. Infrequent service, poorly maintained buses and rail coaches, and poor last-mile connectivity infrastructure, witnessed in many cities, will inevitably lead to nonviable systems. Yet even in the U.S., where the personal car has a very prominent role, some habits are changing, stimulated by newer investments and more modern transit systems. Between 1995 and 2014, ridership on public transit increased by 39 percent, a figure that is greater than the population increase and the increase in highway miles driven.[19] Younger populations, it seems, are more likely to switch from personal to public modes. Between 2001 and 2009, among sixteen-to thirty-four-year-olds, personal car use per capita declined by 23 percent, while at the same time the number of passenger-miles traveled using public modes increased by 40 percent.[20] This correlates with a large increase in light rail and streetcar services that have been added to many cities. However, the U.S. still significantly lags Europe in the use of public transit. On a per capita basis, the average German resident takes almost six times the number of trips on public transit as the average American.[21] A key factor appears to be the significantly better public transit integration with multiple modes that is available in Europe. Trips in Europe also tend to be shorter, and European cities are more compact.

Increasing hassles for car use
Progressively, since the 1990s, for those who were still driving, that experience was becoming increasingly less rewarding and consumed more time. During the suburban boom years, commuting to work was tolerable when a sustained increase in roadway length and capacity meant that lengthier commutes were not badly penalized by unacceptable travel delays. However, after 1990, notwithstanding efforts to improve highway capacity, travel duration started to increase. In 2011 the average American spent 1.17 hours each day in his or her car, and urban commuters alone lost an estimated cumulative 5.5 billion hours annually, or a week's equivalent for each motorist.[22]

In recent years this trend has flattened, apparently indicating that a psychological limit was reached. This fits a pattern that is repeated across the globe: there seems to be a threshold to tolerable distance and time for commuting, after which alternative choices are made. In fact, some cities and communities seem to be counting on this dynamic to influence a shift to public modes of transit. "One way to ease traffic: Let it get so bad that motorists give up" was a headline story in the *Washington Post* referring to urban densification initiatives under way in several cities in South Florida, including Miami and Fort Lauderdale.[23]

However, the frustrations do not stop once the threshold for tolerable time and distance spent commuting has been passed. At the destination, finding affordable parking in many cities is a chore. Overall, there are growing nonfinancial disincentives to use personal transport in cities.

Changing population demographics

Adults in their prime working and child rearing years have greater need for mobility than most other groups. Mobility uses extend beyond commuting to activities of transporting schoolchildren, shopping, recreation and vacations. The post–World War II years ushered in a period of an increase in the working population and an expanding economy. That trend started to peter out toward the end of the twentieth century. Between 1990 and 2014, according to global data from the International Labour Organization, labor force participation declined from 66.3 percent to 63 percent of adult population.

The U.S. has also seen a similar decline as its population has aged. During the latter half of the twentieth century the U.S. economy saw robust expansion and absorbed a lot of people into the workforce, so that the labor force grew until it peaked in 2000 at 67 percent of adults. Since the turn of the twenty-first century, even before the recession of 2008, the U.S. labor force has been contracting, dropping by 2014 to 63 percent, erasing gains made over three decades.[24]

The fastest-growing population segment in the U.S. since 2000 has been those aged sixty-five and older, a segment that has a declining demand for mobility and driving. This segment is expected to double from 11 percent of the population in 1980 to 21 percent by 2040.[25] The dynamics of an aging

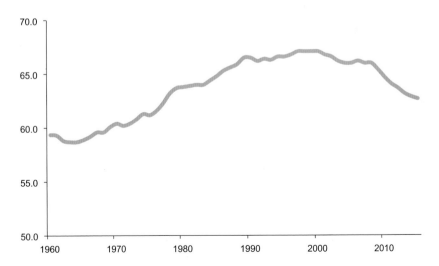

Figure 4.3 The percentage of adults in the U.S. labor force has declined since 2000.
Source: U.S. Department of Labor, Bureau of Labor Statistics.

population and the need for different mobility choices, is acute in Japan, where more than 23 percent of total population is already older than sixty-five and the total population itself is declining.

On the other hand, the demand for mobility is expected to increase in many emerging economies, where working-age populations are growing. As affordability spreads with development, these societies are likely to see many more users of transport.

Growth of e-commerce

For many infrequent drivers, one major use of cars has been for noncommuting activities, such as shopping or entertainment. With the increase in online shopping, the usefulness of a car for shopping has been declining.

The growth of online giants such as Amazon and Alibaba has taken a toll on a spectrum of traditional retailers. Starting from a very low baseline in 2005, online retailing was accounting for almost $1 out of every $6 spent by 2015. Even behemoths like Walmart were not spared. In 2016, Walmart announced it would be closing more than 250 stores worldwide.[26] In certain categories, such as clothing, more than 10 percent of U.S. consumer spending was through an online medium. For books and magazines it was even higher (20 percent), and for computers and electronics online purchases already accounted for a quarter of sales by 2013.

Across Europe too, online retail sales have been growing at over 18 percent per annum, well above the rate of conventional retail sales.[27] The growth may be even more impressive in emerging economies. In terms of fraction of retail sales undertaken online, it is estimated that China overtook the U.S. by 2015, with approximately 11 percent of total retail sales happening online compared to 8 percent in the U.S.[28] And online retailing in China is growing at a blistering 53 percent year over year.[29] In India the volume of online shopping was expected to grow fourfold from 2013 to an estimated $8.5 billion by 2016. During this period the number of active online shoppers was expected to double, from 20 million to 40 million.

Another domain expected to follow suit is online ordering of food for delivery. Deliveroo is an example of a fast-growing enterprise serving customers from their choice of lower-priced eateries. Launched in 2013, it was operating in twelve countries by 2016. Deliveroo's market in London is served by more than 3,000 bicyclists delivering food from more than 2,500 restaurants.[30] Uber too has sensed an opportunity here and has launched UberEats. Uber hopes to leverage its logistical reach and skills in tailoring specific apps to disrupt the smaller players in this domain. Collectively, these services target tech-savvy young professionals who are hard-pressed for time. With no need to stop at a supermarket on the way home, many commuters may actually find public transit a viable alternative. Because of their greater comfort with the Internet, smartphones, and the digital economy, younger consumers are more likely than older ones to shop online.

Entertainment faces a similar outlook. The prime movie-watching segment of twelve- to twenty-four-year-olds is watching fewer movies in theaters according to Nielsen: the figure dropped steadily from an average of 10.3 movies watched in 2008 to 7.1 in 2014.[31] Seven in eight members of this group said they depended on streaming movies and TV shows.

With shopping, dining, and entertainment available with just a few clicks and online applications finding growing adoption, it is no surprise that the role of the car has shrunk.

The sharing economy

In 1971, John Lennon implored a generation of youth to imagine a different future: "Imagine … no possessions." Imagine … no cars to own. It took another generation, but now many consumers seem to have adopted this way of thinking. And it may no longer be necessary to harbor countercultural tendencies to welcome this point of view.

The year 2015 generated a lot of headlines on the emerging sharing economy. That summer, within a few weeks of each other, both the *Economist* and *Time* magazine featured cover stories on the sharing economy.

Airbnb, a poster child of the sharing economy, arranges for people to share apartments or rent out villas or beach houses as an alternative to hotel rooms. By 2016, it was valued at $24 billion and was expected to become bigger than Hyatt and Hilton combined. The idea behind such sharing may seem radical and invasive of privacy to many. But to those "born on the Web," with social media sites as their constant companions, such sharing experiences come more naturally, especially with fellow members of a club or affinity group.

Fundamentally, the concept of what is a tribe has changed, and with it notions of what is appropriate to share. Apps such as Rentez-vous, NeighborGoods, and ShareTheMeal allow clothes, tools, and even food to be shared through online platforms.

Sharing assets and investments can make a lot of sense. For an economist, there is better return on investment: shared assets are put to use for a greater fraction of their useful life. For the ecologist, there is better use of space and material resources: fewer products are needed to serve the same number of customers. And for the consumer, there is a better variety to choose from at lower cost, and perhaps there is a different and more personal experience to go with it.

While for some, a car is a prized asset, to others, car ownership is bondage. Some find liberation in shedding car ownership. Fortunately, we have many options today to retain access to a car without necessarily owning a car. If we can decouple the concepts of owning and use, a new world presents itself.

As the sharing of cars increases, it could have profound implications for automakers, as discussed in chapter 10.

In closing

As society attempts to configure the architecture of future mobility, it is important to comprehend how significantly the mobility needs of people and their communities are changing. Furthermore, all *affairs* need to be sustained by novelty, and people's running love affair with cars shows signs of weariness. These factors, together, demand a transformed mobility architecture and cars will likely play a less prominent role in this future.

A number of analysts have assumed that even as the industrialized economies see their dependence on the automobile flatten or even decline, aspiring millions from emerging economies will seek to fulfil their wishes for personal mobility and sustain the growth of global auto sales. In 2000, for example, sales in China contributed to less than 2 percent of global vehicle sales. By 2013, the Chinese market accounted for a quarter of global sales. Similarly, car sales in India grew fivefold between 2000 and 2013. While there is little doubt these countries and regions will witness accelerated economic growth and therefore expanded mobility needs, their ascendancy will occur in a digitized age. The auto was a major agent of economic growth in the twentieth century. Digitization will play a dominant role in the twenty-first. Indeed, China and India as two examples are already witnessing very rapid digitization of their economies—this is manifested in their rapid adoption of smartphones, the proliferation of e-commerce, and their increasing leverage of the power of connectivity. Further, growth in these countries will occur in a century in which they already will face much higher urban population densities. The specter of the deleterious environmental impact that can be unleashed should their large populations follow the traditional path of industrialization and mobility will also motivate a different course. Mobility, as it serves high density populations in Japan where the centrality of the automobile has been displaced, may offer better insights to the future in these fast growing Asian economies.

Marion King Hubbert triggered a global debate on energy sources and limits to supply when he coined the term "peak oil" in 1956. More recently, discussions of "peak car" have started to appear. Many auto industry analysts postulate that by the next decade, annual global vehicle sales will surpass 100 million, then flatten. These are not just voices inimical to the auto industry and they lead to strategic implications. Bill Ford, chairman of Ford Motor Company, has affirmed that his company is preparing for a future in which fewer cars are sold and people have access to a broader range of mobility solutions.

Box 4.1 Recasting future auto sales outlook

Factors such as congestion, regulations, increasing cost, diminishing ownership prestige, and millennial preference have been considered by many analysts as "weak signals" for the future outlook of car sales.

Phil Gott has served as senior director of long-range planning at IHS Automotive, an organization renowned as one of the leading analysts and forecasters for the auto industry. Based on extensive surveys and studies conducted all over the world, Gott cautions: "Those who have dismissed these signals as inconsequential indicators of future trends have failed to recognize the context in which these are occurring. For the first time in history, there exists a confluence of real need to ensure economic and environmental viability of cities in the context of new social attitudes and many real and virtual solutions that enable change."[32]

Analysis of global light vehicle sales over the past twelve years indicates that once about 80 percent of a country's population live in urban areas, motorization of the country begins to decline. Regions that fit this category include North America, Western Europe, Japan, and Korea. Going forward, urbanization will continue to increase, and the effect of new mobility solutions, such as car sharing or multimodal connectivity, will make the overall impact on motorization levels much more pronounced.

Based on forecasts from the IHS, the magnitude of the impact can be estimated by postulating that motorization in cities with a population above 300,000 or so will be limited naturally by congestion or artificially by regulation, combined with the presence of viable alternatives. Gott suggests that "motorization caps ranging from 250 to 600 cars per thousand people appear reasonable while allowing for a broad range of deviations due to local conditions." By applying these caps to global cities and building up a market forecast, one can calculate that the global light vehicle market could virtually "flat line" at just over 100 to 110 million units a year sometime between 2020 and 2025, as opposed to growing to more than 130 million units by 2035 as some hopeful forecasts propose. In this scenario, many automakers will be forced to drastically revise their plans for future capacity and market share.

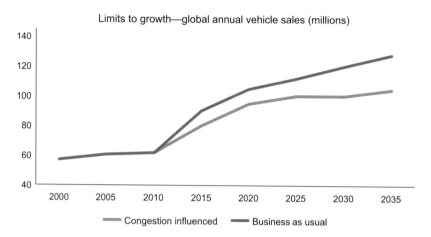

Figure 4.4 A combination of factors is likely to cause global annual sales of vehicles to confront limits to growth sooner than previously estimated.
Source: IHS Automotive.

Yet, cars will not disappear from our streets in the near term. They are too valuable in many functions, and certainly in nonurban settings they will continue to play an important role in mobility. However, cars will be obliged to share the mobility platform with a broad range of products and services, which together will form the tapestry of future mobility. It appears that a new blueprint is needed that knits this adaptable mobility system to suit modern times and new societal attitudes. The CHIP mobility framework we propose will assist this effort.

II The Innovation Response

In part I we examined a changing world. Societal dynamics reveal rapid urbanization and a consequent densification of population that demands changes in mobility options. Further, universal aspiration for an improved quality of life confronts a growing concern for the global environment. Changes in demographics, differences in stage of economic development, and cultural changes exemplified by a tech-savvy generation mean that expectations for mobility around the globe are changing.

Part II begins the discussion of mobility solutions by exploring the penchant of our species to innovate and adapt to solve problems society confronts. It is no surprise that the auto industry continues to drive significant innovations in mobility—after all, for much of the previous century this was a dominant industry. Impressive advances in powertrain technologies have made vehicles more efficient, while innovations in products and services have made travel safer and more comfortable. To serve the mobility needs of a generation of digital natives, innovators have delivered intelligent machines and intelligent mobility agents. The emergence of self-driving cars, also promise an exciting future, one in which mobility might be comprehensively overhauled. However, we go well beyond innovation in the auto industry alone. With parallel innovations in the marketplace and in business models, cars are increasingly complemented by other modes and services, particularly in large cities. These mobility solutions and their service providers have significantly expanded the options available and help reshape how people move about.

We also examine complex outcomes and a multiplication of benefits when these new innovations are effectively harnessed. For example, sustainability problems are not solved by sustainability responses alone. The sharing economy is an outcome of cultural changes and powered by new connectivity technologies, but a consequent outcome such as the emergence of car sharing, can also help address the dual problems of congestion and carbon emissions. Air quality in city centers can be improved by increasing use of public transit, or by limiting access to electric vehicles or by invoking several other solutions individually or in tandem.

Modern society is configuring a multitude of levers, both physical and virtual, to deliver our future vision of faster, smarter, and greener mobility.

5   Innovations for Sustainability

Necessity … the mother of invention.

—*Plato*

In chapter 3 we reviewed the evolution of the environmental debate and the impact of mobility solutions in use today. We had also addressed the topic of reduction of waste material arising from the manufacture, use, and disposal of products.

In this chapter we look at innovations directed toward achieving three goals that should render future mobility more sustainable. They each employ different pathways and harness different technologies. The three goals are to:

a. Lower carbon emissions to reduce global warming and greenhouse gases, and lower potential geopolitical risk to access of fossil fuels;
b. Lower other harmful emissions, including smog-producing particulates, to improve the quality of air we breathe; and
c. Reduce traffic fatalities and injuries to make mobility safer.

Innovations to lower carbon emissions from mobility

In 2011, a study in Europe concluded that a bicyclist's use of energy was measured at 16 grams per kilometer (g/km) of CO_2, after analysis of the energy expended and the calorific content of food intake.[1] In 2015, Volkswagen's high-efficiency experimental plug-in hybrid prototype car, the XL1, was unveiled. Its parsimonious efficiency meant it could stretch a gallon of diesel to travel 310 miles, a figure equivalent to 21 g/km of CO_2 emissions.[2] In other words, the two occupants of an XL1 would produce lower carbon emissions than if they had traveled on bicycles. Granted, for the sake of this experiment, they would be asked to refrain from exhaling over that distance!

When traveling by car produces lower carbon emissions than cycling, we can truly celebrate the innovation in mobility technology.

The journey from the U.S. passenger car fleet fuel consumption average of 13 miles per gallon (mpg) in the 1970s to the 2016 U.S. fleet figure of 31 mpg had taken four decades. The journey from here to 310 mpg may be faster and will be powered by innovations of all sorts.

Figure 5.1 The U.S. passenger car fleet average fuel economy is at about 31 mpg. Some concept plug-in hybrid prototypes have demonstrated the potential for a tenfold improvement . *Source:* Volkswagen.

Teaching an old dog new tricks

Nikolaus Otto was born in Cologne, Germany, in 1832. He lost his father soon after he was born, and had to drop out of school at the age of sixteen. In an era when the Industrial Revolution was giving rise to all kinds of new machines, he was not excited by his first job as a salesman of goods produced in the European colonies, peddling rice, sugar, coffee, and tea. In 1864 he formed NA Otto & Cie in Cologne with the intent of designing and producing what would become the internal combustion engine. The thermodynamic cycle describing the engines we have all come to rely on in our cars and buses every day still goes by the name Otto cycle. Since then, Otto's invention has been employed in almost all forms of mobility starting from Karl Benz's patented motorcar to its widespread and successful use even today. This evolution has been punctuated by numerous technical advances, many of which we review here, as automakers have sought to achieve better efficiency, reduce emissions and improve reliability.

The U.S. and downsizing

During World War II, numerous initiatives were undertaken to conserve fuel. Most were locally deployed based on alternative fuels that could be used. Private ownership of cars was still uncommon. The first occasion requiring the public to confront fuel conservation on a large scale coincided with the oil crisis of the mid-1970s. The fuel economy regulations that were quickly announced demanded rapid and substantial fuel economy improvements. In the 1950s and 1960s, the mantra for car design in the U.S. was longer, lower, wider. This had a further consequence—cars were getting heavier with each passing year. Abruptly facing the prospect of fuel rationing and skyrocketing fuel costs, drivers started looking to smaller and more efficient imported cars, which had hitherto been peripheral products. Companies that had been marginal players in the U.S. market, such as Volkswagen, Toyota, Datsun (now Nissan), and Honda, were suddenly inundated with more demand than they expected.

U.S. automakers had to rush back to the drawing boards to revamp their product strategy and commit huge sums to change course. Out of this effort, a new breed of cars was quickly developed that represented some of the most significant changes to the way U.S. cars were designed and built. The big American sedan gave way to more compact cars. Large station wagons were replaced by more efficient minivans. And heavier rear-wheel-drive architectures were replaced by lighter and more compact front-wheel-drive technology.

These efforts resulted in the weight of a typical American midsize car being slashed by almost 20 percent, to about 2,500 pounds. As a result, engine size could be reduced by 35 percent, and cumulatively these measures boosted fuel efficiency by almost 35 percent, to a figure of 31 mpg for a midsize car like the Chevrolet Citation. By 1990, many large full-size cars, such as the Oldsmobile 98, had been redesigned with front-wheel drive and delivered in excess of 25 mpg. Automakers also sought to project their new products not merely as fuel-efficient but as built with advanced technologies. Ford's Taurus embraced aerodynamics as a statement to project a modern image, even as Ford's engineers significantly improved fuel economy from that of the preceding models.

A second outcome of the oil crisis was that it encouraged globalization of auto technology. Even as U.S. customers gravitated toward Japanese and some European cars, U.S. automakers rushed to leverage their overseas businesses in Europe and Japan, to create new models that were derived from the products they were already building in these parts of the world. These cars were smaller, lighter, and more fuel-efficient than a majority of the traditional U.S. models. They were also significantly more efficient in the use of space and energy. The Chevrolet Chevette, the Ford Escort, and the Plymouth Horizon were all cars that were developed and launched in Europe but were subsequently produced in the U.S. as well.

Motivated by a combination of high fuel costs and regulations mandating fuel efficiency improvements, the U.S. fleet transformed in a remarkable manner. In the decade after 1975, the fuel efficiency of the U.S. fleet more than doubled. If the 1950s were about fins and chrome, the 1980s were about downsizing and efficiency.

Sadly, the focus of innovation in the U.S. shifted in the 1990s. Oil prices collapsed, and with them enthusiasm for energy efficiency. Pressure from the government eased, and customer preferences changed quickly. Relieved of concerns about fuel cost and availability, customers reverted to larger, more powerful vehicles. As Bernard Shaw had prophesied, "Virtue is insufficient temptation."[3] For many, the attraction of green credentials paled in the face of an extra 100 horsepower or a more luxurious ride that one could affordably indulge in. Fuel-efficient subcompacts were replaced by bigger and more powerful sedans. Minivans made way for heavier SUVs. Since trucks and SUVs were governed by different standards than cars, their renewed popularity contributed to lowering the fuel efficiency of the total fleet.

There were important lessons from this journey. First, faced with the crisis, changing customer preferences, and tough regulations, automakers

Figure 5.2 The oil crisis of the 1970s accelerated the efforts of U.S. automakers to downsize their products. The front-drive Chevrolet Citation (lower image), launched in 1980, was significantly lighter, more compact, and more fuel-efficient than the midsize Chevrolet Malibu (upper image), while offering occupants comparable interior space.
Source: General Motors.

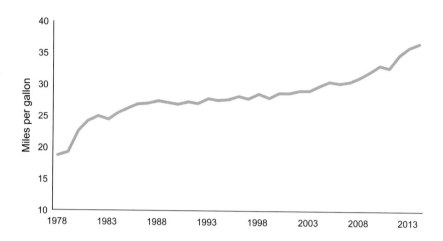

Figure 5.3 Fuel economy of U.S. domestic cars. Under pressure to change, the 1980s saw remarkable progress in the U.S. fleet fuel economy. This would not be sustained in the 1990s as oil prices dropped and political convictions waned.
Source: U.S. National Highway and Safety Administration.

produced remarkable efficiency improvements within a decade. Second, as policy vacillated, valuable momentum toward sustainable mobility was squandered. Technological innovations are steered by long-term priorities. This is what draws innovators and investment to create better solutions. If the long-term course is unclear, motivations for innovation suffer.

Europe bets on the diesel

Europe had been marching to a different drum. Car ownership was lower in Europe than in the U.S. Yet the oil crisis was felt across the world, and Europeans also reacted to the new global view on energy security and environment protection. Regulations to improve fuel economy followed. The Europeans started with one advantage over Americans: their cars were already smaller and more fuel-efficient.

The approach in Europe was also markedly different in another respect. European automakers chose to achieve even better fuel efficiency from their smaller cars through broader adoption of diesel engines. The diesel thermodynamic cycle has intrinsically higher efficiency, and its fuel economy, when driven in city traffic, is inherently better than that of the conventional gasoline engine. Between 1990 and 2010, the diesel share increased fourfold in Europe, accounting for more than 58 percent of annual sales. This strategy contributed to faster improvement of fleet efficiency and lowered related

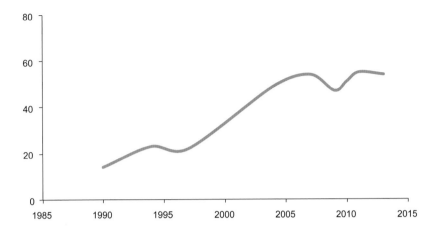

Figure 5.4 Sales of diesel cars in Europe as a percent of sales fleet. Europe's drive for better fuel efficiency was initially boosted by rapid growth in the sales of diesel-powered cars.
Source: International Council on Clean Transportation.

CO_2 emissions by almost 20 percent. But this strategy would prove to be a double-edged sword.

As emission standards became more stringent over time, European auto-makers discovered that diesels had some intrinsic disadvantages. Nitrogen oxide (NO_x) emissions from diesels were typically higher than those from gasoline engines. In addition, diesel exhaust contained a higher quantum of soot or particulate matter. The choice that European society faced was between one technical solution (diesel) that offered better prospects to lower emissions of CO_2, a greenhouse gas, and another technical solution (gasoline) that led to lower NO_x and particulate emissions, which helped lower smog and health risk. The European Community, a signatory to the Kyoto Protocol, faced urgent CO_2 reduction commitments. In the initial push, Europe accelerated CO_2 emission reduction, and this explains the surge in the penetration of diesels in Europe during the 1990s and 2000s. But with the advent of Euro 6 emissions standards around 2012, these cars required more expensive emission technologies to control their higher particulate and NO_x emissions. The advantage had begun to swing the other way, now favoring gasoline-powered vehicles.

Between 2000 and 2016, the fleet fuel economy of cars in Europe improved by 33 percent, from 172 g/km of CO_2 to 115 g/km. There were parallel gains in tailpipe emissions as well.

In summary, Europe discovered that what was gained in the swings could be lost in the roundabouts. But the approach to allow competition between camps of automakers favoring diesels and those favoring gasoline had a positive outcome. Advances in technology for both diesels and gasoline-powered engines were rapid, and customers benefited from better performance and efficiency, no matter which option they chose.

Japan votes for hybrid electrics

While Europe zigged, Japan zagged. Their surprisingly different trajectories were not irrational but were related to their respective economic and environmental conditions. Japan was reluctant to adopt diesel technology for many reasons. The higher traffic density in Japan's crowded cities made Japan wary of diesel emissions and smoke. A large share of the market in Japan was dominated by very small mini-vehicles with engines of less than 660 cubic centimeters, whereas the average European economy car had an engine that was typically twice as large. Scaling down diesel technology to suit the very small engines in Japanese cars posed significant cost challenges. Between 1995 and 2010, the diesel fraction in the Japanese passenger car fleet declined from about 10 percent to less than 2 percent. However, having bet on gasoline engines, Japan's adoption of hybrid-electric powertrains served it well, both for its domestic market and for exports to the U.S. For Japanese automakers, the U.S. market was critical, and their strategies required alignment. Taking the hybrid route not only boosted Japan's fleet fuel economy improvement, it also furthered Japan's market expansion. Toyota's Prius went on to stellar success in the U.S. and several global markets, and demonstrated Japan's prowess at taking very complex technologies and shaping them to become market and business successes. In the process, Toyota gained the reputation of being the most environmentally friendly automaker.

In the Japanese market, automakers were encouraged by government incentives to support the sales of cleaner hybrid-electric vehicles. Hybrids account for over 21 percent of all new car sales in Japan, and, when added to the fuel-efficient mini-car segment, high-efficiency cars account for more than 60 percent of all sales. Between 1995 and 2015, Japan's fleet fuel economy improved 70 percent, to 21 kilometers per liter (km/l) (about 49 mpg). These are very impressive improvements for cars that were already considered efficient two decades ago.

Even though we have showcased downsizing in the U.S., dieselization in Europe, and hybridization in Japan, in reality, the auto market is global, and so these trends have globalized as well. Once technologies are developed, automakers seek the best returns on their investment, and there is a lot of cross fertilization of ideas and approaches. Hybrids are gaining popularity in Europe even as the U.S. has seen more use of diesel engines, especially in light trucks. Collectively, the competitive landscape has accelerated our ability to lower carbon emissions from cars.

Government's role: From enforcer to supporter

Before World War II, the auto industry had been left alone by the respective governments. There were a few cases in which governments sought to establish their nation's auto-manufacturing capabilities, but by and large the industry was left to operate by itself. In the years after the war, governments saw their role as that of investing in new infrastructure and building highway and road networks. These initiatives were needed to foster economic growth, improve the efficiency of logistics, and deliver convenient and affordable mobility to their population.

By the 1970s, several issues had flared up, and many governments were obliged to take on the role of regulator as well. The proliferation of cars and roads was resulting in various social issues. Regulations aimed at improving vehicle and road safety, lowering fuel consumption, and improving air quality were becoming necessary. In this phase, inevitably, a certain adversarial relationship emerged between regulators and the auto industry. The former, led by lawmakers, rolled out a series of regulations and standards, and the latter were obliged to be in compliance with new rules. For the auto industry, this often meant that automakers had to effect internal changes and make fresh investments to comply with the new regulatory norms. Often, most of the product cost increase, caused by adding content to meet regulations especially those related to the environment, could not be recovered from customers, who balked at paying more for mandated equipment. Such content addition usually meant lower profit margins for automakers. Regulators and automakers often found themselves on opposite sides of proposed legislation.

By the 1990s there was a further change in the relationship. The Cold War had ended, and governments increased their focus on economic matters. The Japanese manufacturing industry was making deep inroads into Western markets, and its market share gains in automobiles were highly visible. Governments in the U.S. and Europe turned their attention to shoring up their domestic manufacturing industry and maintaining well-paying industrial jobs. Spending some of the peace dividend to improve the long-term competitiveness of the auto industry became an element of U.S. strategy.

The government redirected some of the impressive R&D talent in its national laboratories as these institutions too looked for newer challenges, knowing that many of the defense-related sources of R&D funding would decline.

The U.S. Consortium for Automotive Research (USCAR) was launched in 1992 including Daimler-Chrysler (now Fiat Chrysler), Ford Motor Company, and General Motors as an umbrella organization for conducting technology research to help the U.S. auto industry remain competitive. The following year USCAR entered into a cooperative research program with the U.S. government, the Partnership for a New Generation of Vehicles, aimed at bringing extremely fuel-efficient vehicles to market by 2003. The target figure of 80 mpg represented a threefold improvement of the Corporate Average Fuel Economy (CAFE) target for 1985. Over the course of this program, which was canceled by the George W. Bush administration in 2001, the federal government spent close to $800 million, while U.S. automakers spent almost $1 billion collectively. R&D was undertaken on such diverse subjects as carbon fiber composites for lightweight structures, materials and configurations for batteries, and advanced simulation methodologies for modeling complex processes such as vehicle crashes and combustion. Prototypes from GM, Ford, and Chrysler were built to demonstrate technologies capable of meeting these "stretch" targets. While none of the prototypes was economically viable, they served as technology demonstrators. Many of the product and process developments would find use in commercially viable future vehicles. At least as far as technological development was concerned, the interests of the auto industry and the government found greater alignment during that decade. And for some time at least, the adversarial relationship had morphed to one of some degree of cooperation to address societal goals.

The vagaries of politics altered priorities as administrations changed. When the Bush administration succeeded the Clinton administration, the preferred topic became the hydrogen economy and the FreedomCAR consortium. FreedomCAR had laudable goals of zero dependence on foreign oil and zero greenhouse gas emissions but failed to comprehend the true complexities of creating and transitioning to a hydrogen-based economy.

Cooperation in Europe

Spurred by developments across the Atlantic, European governments and automakers saw the need for parallel efforts within Europe to ensure long-term competitiveness with Japan.

EUCAR, the European Council for Automotive R&D, involving all the major car and commercial vehicle manufacturers in Europe, was formed in 1994.

Working closely with the auto sector's industry body, the European Automobile Manufacturers' Association (ACEA), it has played an important role in coordinating the roadmaps and R&D challenges faced by the industry. With its members representing annual R&D expenditures in excess of €32 billion, it carries the voice of the largest private spenders of R&D in Europe. EUCAR has contributed to cooperative strategy formulations, bringing consensus on technology roadmaps and fostering standards for medium- to long-term projects.

Just as the Partnership for a New Generation of Vehicles program in the U.S. set bold new standards for fuel efficiency, EUCAR created new fuel efficiency benchmarks, setting the goal at almost three times the figure normally achieved by a contemporary European family car. This goal of 3 liters of fuel per 100 kilometers translated to almost 78 mpg.

Overall, these positive interventions by governments in the U.S. and Europe have been useful in prodding progress. Within the span of a decade, several stretch goals were achieved by some production cars that were salable and practical.

In the auto sector, the pairing of government with automakers had made for strange bedfellows. Through the decades, the auto industry had preferred to remain at arm's length from governments, wary of their inclination to impose new and costly regulations. Yet during this period the convergence of their interests to improve domestic economy and technological competitiveness revealed powerful potential. Future mobility will call for governments to play a similar nurturing role as new and very different infrastructure will require investment, and a more complex role for supervision will evolve. Automakers, technologists, and entrepreneurs are likely to find collaboration with governments helpful and indeed necessary.

Tackling future targets

Globally, for the auto industry, the next decade will demand a very significant push with technology to meet future targets, which call for improving fuel efficiency by a further 40 percent by 2025 compared to 2016.

Across the board, significant improvements in structural design have resulted in cars that are stronger and safer. Vehicles are expected to become even lighter with the use of more aluminum and sometimes even carbon composites. Electrification is being employed to limit parasitic losses in accessories such as the water pump, power steering, and climate control. Aerodynamics is being improved so that cars draw less power while traveling at highway speeds. Turbo-charged, downsized engines further reduce mass and improve efficiency. And electrification of the propulsion system is expected to make significant contributions to improving sustainability.

We now turn to that other aspect of sustainability, tailpipe emissions.

Innovations to lower other harmful emissions

Combustion is a dirty business. One needs to only recall those images from Hollywood movies of dark, acrid smoke billowing from staged explosions. Engineers are obliged to tame such explosions within the engine and harness every possible quantum of energy from combustion while rendering the emissions out of the tailpipe clean enough to not bother the patron at the sidewalk café as the car drives by.

Over the years, automakers have complied with increasingly strict emission norms by (1) addressing the process of combustion inside the engine and (2) subsequently treating the gases in the tailpipe with complex chemical reactors, often referred to as "after-treatment." They have each required different kinds of technologies, and step by step, more complex systems have been added to vehicles to achieve these standards.

Engine design recruits a range of scientific advances in areas such as fluid mechanics, tribology, and chemistry. The combustion chamber, the metaphorical heart of the engine, is a finely engineered piece of sculpture. Within it, pistons accelerate from rest to a speed of 50 mph in 2.5 milliseconds. Valves are choreographed to open and close over 100 times within 1 second, their timing dictated by complex valve control mechanisms. The airflow that rushes into the combustion chamber is designed to swirl and tumble like a gymnast in precise trajectory. In gasoline engines, the spark is accurately timed to occur within a window of 20 microseconds. In modern engines, each cylinder firing is like a mini-explosion within which every infinitesimal characteristic is carefully controlled. It takes all of this to get the kind of fuel efficiency and exhaust emission to meet current standards.

Even then this exhaust cannot be released into a modern city atmosphere. It has to be further processed in after-treatment devices. Catalytic converters fitted to the exhaust system use precious metals such as platinum, palladium, or rhodium to foster chemical reactions with oxygen in the air that convert toxic CO and unburned hydrocarbons to CO_2 and water. Particulate filters eliminate a very large fraction of soot emissions from diesel engines and thereby curtail health risk. Three-way catalytic converters simultaneously also tackle NO_x emissions that are contributors to smog. In some engines, typically diesels, an additional measure to lower NO_x emissions has been the use of exhaust gas recirculation to lower the combustion temperature. As targets for NO_x emissions were lowered again for 2010, a further level of treatment was required. Selective catalytic reduction is a relatively new technology that uses urea in liquid form. Commonly referred to as diesel emission fluid in the U.S. and AdBlue in Europe, this urea is injected into the exhaust gas ahead of another catalytic reactor to reduce the NO_x emissions. The exhaust system of most diesel cars and buses also houses filters that trap soot particles and rid the gas that is emitted out of the tailpipe of a significant quantum of those harmful pollutants.

When smog was identified as a serious issue in California in the 1950s, the exhaust emissions from a typical family car were roughly 3,600 mg/mile of NO_x.[4] In 2015, a family sedan meets standards that limit such emissions to 50 mg/mile. CO emissions have been lowered by almost 95 percent over the same period. Parallel gains have been achieved for the other constituents of exhaust emissions. A similar story unfolded in Europe, where in the last two decades alone, permissible levels of NO_x emission saw a tenfold reduction, from more than 900 milligrams per kilometer (mg/km) to less than 80 mg/km. In that same window, diesel cars lowered particulate emissions from a level of 100 mg/km to 4.5 mg/km.

These tough standards are enforced with increasingly complex rules that are often unique to specific markets. The margins for passing these standards are razor thin. In a world where cars employ sophisticated software to determine their optimal functioning, it has led to a high degree of complexity in vehicle systems and their controlling software. Even as efforts are under way to harmonize standards across the world, to make it easier for both regulators and automakers, there remain many possibilities for failures, which lead to very costly recalls and corrective action. On rare occasions, manufacturers have been caught with systems that violated regulations.

In 2015, the auto industry was rocked by a scandal, dubbed Dieselgate, which reverberated across the world. Investigations launched by the U.S. Environmental Protection Agency uncovered a software code that had been included in a significant number of Volkswagen diesel cars. It appeared that the purpose of the code was to defeat the standard test procedure for emissions. Essentially, those diesel cars fitted with the software would behave in compliance with emission norms when the car's systems sensed it was being tested. In normal everyday driving, the emissions would be significantly worse. A combination of penalties, fines, and remedial repair costs, in addition to lawsuit settlements, in the U.S. and Europe are expected to take the collective cost of that violation to well over $25 billion. In the state of California, an outcome of Volkswagen's Dieselgate scandal resulted in a pointed decree that obliged that automaker to undertake specific actions in addition to the fines and penalties imposed. In that state, Volkswagen was obligated to offer a portfolio of pure electric vehicles for sale to the public and ensure that they would meet certain minimum sales numbers. In addition, Volkswagen was required to participate in several clean air initiatives including the state's Green City initiative by contributing to zero-emission transit applications and promotion of car-sharing services.[5] The scandal led to the dismissal of many people at the helm of Volkswagen. It also led to regulators across the world looking deeper into their test procedures to eliminate loopholes and sniff out suspect software code in the cars being tested.

Many think that the internal combustion engine will require ever increasing bits of technology at escalating cost to remain in compliance with advancing regulations. They point out that we have been pushing that venerable device further than we had ever imagined, and that additional improvements are coming at significantly higher cost. At the same time, a spate of new products such as electric vehicles signals a readiness to take the baton and end the long domination of internal combustion engines. But even as we anticipate an electric vehicle future, and a dirge for engines is heard in many quarters, Dan Hancock, former president of the Society of Automotive Engineers, cautions, "Engineers are capable of creating solutions that meet the anticipated new goals for fuel economy and emissions. The main question is whether these goals and resulting solutions are affordable for customers. Conventional powertrains will be around, perhaps in upgraded or hybrid forms, for the foreseeable future."[6] Wolfgang Bernhart, senior partner at Roland Berger, a global management consultancy with an extensive automotive domain practice, concurs, saying "All major European automakers will place most of their bets on optimized combustion engine technologies, augmented by electrification, to meet the next threshold of fuel economy in Europe of 95 g/km of CO_2."[7]

Nikolaus Otto's contribution to technology, the internal combustion engine, has been with us for more than a century and a half, and chances are it will be with us for quite a bit longer, very likely coexisting with a host of other very competitive technologies.

An electrified future

Most automakers have looked on with envy as companies such as Apple regularly trigger high-voltage consumer and media interest with the launch of every new generation of gadgetry. Steve Jobs developed a cult following, and Apple still knows how to draw a crowd for its new-product announcements.

Product introductions in the auto industry are truly high-priced galas. Glamorous auto shows in Geneva, Paris, and Tokyo and dedicated launch events in exotic locales such as Monaco, Marrakesh, and Malaga serve as the backdrop. Journalists are flown in from all over the world to meet top executives and perhaps take a few laps around a test track or a jaunt through scenic mountain passes. Yet the format has grown stale, the innovations are usually incremental, and most journalists return quite jaded. Very rarely does the hype live up to its billing. When Ford launched the first Mustang at the 1964 World Fair, eager customers thronged to dealer showrooms, and the deposits that poured in for bookings would take care of the planned production for a full year. It even got Lee Iacocca on the cover of both *Time* and *Newsweek*. When Ratan Tata, chairman of the Tata Group, launched the low-cost people's car, the Tata Nano, in New Delhi in 2008, public euphoria and interest in the product transcended what the auto industry normally witnesses and bookings overwhelmed the company's business plans. But such commanding performances are few and far between.

If Silicon Valley had not found an Elon Musk, it may have needed to invent one. The Valley needed a Musk as badly as Musk needed that ecosystem. Musk, who went on to found Tesla, which has made waves in the auto industry, packs some truly impressive credentials to be a disruptor in autos—vision, style, wit, and a good dose of swagger. Fueled by funds from the sale of his startup PayPal, he set his sights on spectacular goals—transforming mobility, the colonization of Mars, the development of renewable energy sources, and even intercontinental travel at hyperspeeds. In his biography, Ashlee Vance observes, "Where Mark Zuckerberg wants to help you share baby photos, Musk wants to ... well ... save the human race from self-imposed or accidental annihilation."[8]

For his endeavor to transform mobility, Musk had chosen electric vehicles. He applied the Silicon Valley ethos of innovation, hard work, and a degree of irreverence for tradition. While most automakers had launched electric vehicles targeted at the compact segment of the market, Tesla's entry at the premium end of the scale forced the industry to reexamine the entire business proposition. Musk had concluded that the business model would be more robust by appealing to wealthy buyers who still cherished the idea of a more ecological way of life. Tesla vehicles came with swoopy styling, a gigantic battery, and supercar performance. With the Tesla Model

Figure 5.5 Tesla's bold strategy of targeting the luxury electric vehicle segment has met with impressive success. Tesla has positioned the product more as a tech toy than as an auto. *Source:* Tesla.

S, he was attempting to show that indulgence could be virtuous, debunking the stereotype reinforced by Ferraris, Lamborghinis, and Bentleys. Tesla also announced a plan to roll out a nationwide network of charging stations that could provide a significant fraction of a full charge in just 20 minutes. Tesla hoped that these two factors would be sufficient to allay customers' "range" anxiety.

On March 31, 2016, the auto industry found the answer to a question many automakers were asking: Can the auto industry still create the kind of waves that a company like Apple had made a habit of while launching a product? Elon Musk launched Tesla's new Model 3, following the acclaim bestowed on that company's luxury Model S. For this follow-on product, Musk was answering critics of electric vehicles with two simple claims. The Model 3 would be priced at $35,000 and so would be affordable to many middle-class families. And it would travel up to 215 miles on a charge, erasing concerns of limited range that had plagued electric cars. Before the month was out, the car had drawn more than 400,000 bookings from all over the world, backed by a $1,000 deposit each, almost two years before customers would be able to get their hands on one. Musk was proving that cars still have that magic pull. The right product with the right pitch could still draw in the crowds.

The auto industry is characterized by large capital commitments, complex supply chains, and a global market reach. This structure means that even high-flying business ventures can collapse in a matter of decades. In that sense, it is too early to pronounce Tesla's impressive but short history a success. Musk and Tesla must be credited with a bold and different approach to electric vehicles, targeting premium segment products and delivering impressive product results, even if the company's financial viability remains in question. To a jaded audience, Tesla has made cars sexy again.

Hybrids and electrified options

Electric vehicles were with us at the dawn of motoring. Even Ferdinand Porsche experimented with electric vehicles well before he was inspired to create the Volkswagen Beetle. While they had much going for them, they were burdened by one factor, their Achilles' heel. Batteries remained woefully inefficient as energy storage devices. Batteries that conform to "appropriate" cost, weight, and size for an automobile do not let one travel very far. In 1996, anticipating zero-emissions mandates in California, GM had invested a fortune to bring a modern electric vehicle to market, the EV1. It was a technological tour de force, offering high-efficiency motors and controllers, low drag aerodynamics, low-resistance tires, and so on. Yet it could not overcome the battery deficiency. Business innovations to get around this limitation were also experimented with. In 2007 a high-profile venture, Better Place, backed by Renault, attempted to have banks of charged batteries available at service stations that could swap the empty batteries in the car within a short period of time—essentially similar to replacing a cylinder of LPG gas. The venture failed for a combination of technical and business reasons.[9]

Notwithstanding decades of research on modern storage technologies, the best of current batteries today are still too big, too heavy, and too expensive. As a result, compared to recent evolutions in communication, the pace of progress with electric vehicles has been glacial. To satisfy customers, automakers must add either a heavy and expensive battery or an on-board charging system with a combustion engine or perhaps a fuel cell. These additional components add to a car's cost and complexity.

Pragmatism, characteristic of the Japanese auto industry, helped it race to a commanding global leadership position for hybrid-electric vehicles. Hybrids represent a logical compromise that overcomes the range limitation of electric vehicles. Hybrids employ both a conventional, usually less powerful engine, which is augmented by an electric motor fed by batteries. This configuration is best represented by the Toyota Prius, the world's best-selling hybrid. By 2016, Toyota accounted for 80 percent of global hybrid vehicles sales and had more than 9 million vehicles on the road.[10] But once one adds both an electric drive and a conventional drive to a vehicle, it is possible to conceive of a large number of very different kinds of electrified cars. Some employ a small battery just to augment engine efficiency under specific conditions, while others, often referred to as "plug-ins," can run off the larger battery exclusively for a limited range. The trade-offs are cost, range, and efficiency.

For many years, European manufacturers were skeptical as to the value of hybrid-electric vehicles and preferred the diesel alternative. Equipped with a full range of high-efficiency diesel vehicles, they felt they were already ahead of many gasoline passenger car fleets produced in other parts of the world. However, with the relentless advance of emission standards, the diesel advantage is being handicapped by growing cost. Simultaneously, the cost of batteries for electric vehicles has been declining very rapidly and already there are viable options for electric vehicles to deliver a range of 300 kilometers or more. Finally, as much of Europe is seeing increased electricity generation from renewables, electric vehicles offer an excellent opportunity to soak up power at night, when other loads are low. As a result, modern plug-in hybrids from European automakers offer remarkable fuel efficiency and are boosted by incentives and credits to make them an even sweeter deal for consumers.

The product range of electric vehicles and hybrids continues to grow as more of the industry anticipates further advances in storage technologies and increased demand for zero-emission vehicles (ZEVs). Electric vehicles and hybrids come in different flavors, to suit a wide spectrum of customers with very different needs. The Nissan Leaf, BMW i3, and Chevrolet Volt are city cars built to be affordable with a range of 80 to 120 miles (130 to 200 kilometers), although the latter two can use the optional range extender to travel farther. A Tesla Model S is a luxury electric vehicle and provides the range desired by its users with a very large and expensive battery. As battery technology progressed, by 2016 both Tesla's Model 3 and the Chevrolet Bolt, a newer sister product to the Volt, could claim a 200-mile (320-kilometer) range on a single charge, making electric vehicles more appealing to mainstream buyers. For its hybrid performance car, the i8, BMW uses a parallel hybrid configuration with an on-board 240 horsepower engine.

Each of these cars is tailored to a different set of customers and offers a different blend of virtues and constraints. Automakers have taken to heart the old saying, "There are horses for courses." Our CHIP mobility thesis depends on such a variety of solutions to address the broad spectrum of the market.

Figure 5.6 The main challenge for electric vehicles is to go farther on a single charge. For this, a breakthrough in battery technology is necessary. Fortunately, newer products are delivering better range with bigger and more efficient batteries and on-board chargers.
Source: BMW.

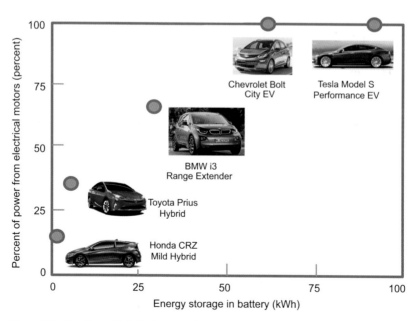

Figure 5.7 Electric and hybrid-electric vehicles come in various shapes and configurations, recognizing very different needs for users.

As more automakers explore variations on the theme, momentum is accelerating for broader adoption of electrified vehicles in the auto industry, pushing it past the cusp for maturation. In 2016, annual sales of hybrid vehicles crossed the million mark, and more than 11 million hybrids were operating in the world. Globally, sales of electric vehicles (excluding hybrids) are expected to grow fivefold, from about 0.5 million in 2015 to about 2.5 million by 2020, by which time they will account for approximately 3 percent of global vehicle sales.

When the premier European auto show opened in Paris in October 2016, the limelight was dominated by a series of announcements from Volkswagen, Daimler, and Renault, among many others, unveiling a range of significant new electric vehicle products. While the regulars at such motor shows are accustomed to rhetoric, this time the promises were sharper. Volkswagen's CEO, Matthias Mueller, announced the group's 2025 strategy, promising multi-billion euro investments in "an electrification initiative, second to none in the industry."[11] Volkswagen brand CEO Herbert Diess assured the public that "in 2020 we will begin to introduce an entire family of electric vehicles in the market. All of them will be based on a new vehicle architecture which was specially and exclusively developed for all-electric vehicles."[12] As proof, Volkswagen rolled out a brand-new product, the I.D. Volkswagen's leadership appeared to count on the I.D. family of electric vehicles to save Volkswagen from the aftermath of the Dieselgate scandal and, just as the Beetle and the Golf did in the past, power it back to a position of market leadership.

Across the glamorous Salon halls, rival Dieter Zetsche, the chief executive of Daimler, promised, "We're now flipping the switch. We're ready for the launch of an electric product offensive that will cover all vehicle segments, from the compact to the luxury class."[13] Daimler also announced that the car it unveiled, called EQ, claimed to invoke the image of electric intelligence, would be not just a single model but the basis for a new brand of products.

Impressive as these initiatives are, they pale in significance when compared to the plans that appear to be under way in China. A newcomer to the problems of the developed world, China has also responded with several bold initiatives. It is already home to the largest battery manufacturers in the world, and it has created a class of "new energy vehicles," many of which are pure-electric or hybrid-electric, that will benefit from a significant injection of incentives. These measures in China are expected to change buying habits and cause customers to favor new energy vehicles even as the wave of motorization in that country gathers speed. By 2016, even as vehicle sales in China breached the level of 24 million units, vehicles classified as New Energy Vehicles found growing popularity and registered sales in excess of 500,000.[14] More importantly, China hopes to use electric cars to leapfrog the developed economies in mobility technology.

Batteries and energy storage

Battery technology is the primary constraint standing in the way of faster adoption of electric vehicles. The battery is simply an energy storage device. But it faces a formidable incumbent, a tankful of gasoline or diesel, which puts up a staunch defense against this expected disruption. There is a reason conventional fuels have proved so tough to displace.

Liquid fuels that are commonly used, such as gasoline and diesel, pack a lot of energy into a compact and light fuel tank. A typical compact car, such as a Ford Focus, weighing about 2,900 pounds (1,300 kg), would carry a fuel tank of 13 gallons (about 50 liters) to deliver a range of over 350 miles (560 kilometers). That volume of fuel, if it was gasoline, would weigh about 75 pounds (35 kilograms). If the same car employed contemporary batteries, as used in the Tesla Model S, to carry the same quantum of energy, the batteries alone would weigh more than 3,700 pounds (1,700 kilograms), significantly more than the weight of the car. And the cost of a battery carrying that quantum of energy in 2016 was prohibitive—over $125,000. Without affordable higher-capacity batteries, we need to devise smarter ways to use energy. A lot of sophisticated driving strategies are employed in electric vehicles to make the limited energy they carry on-board go farther.

Progress continues to accelerate and new investments continue to flow to R&D in this domain. Numerous alternative chemistries and materials are being evaluated to deliver compact and light batteries that can pack a lot of energy, deliver a lot of power, and still have stable and safe operating characteristics. EV batteries are not simple solid state devices but rather a complex arrangement of numerous cells whose internal connections and thermal environment need to be managed very carefully. The best commercial lithium ion batteries in 2015 could offer an energy density of about 0.25 kWh/kg—a figure that continues to see improvement every year. The cost barrier is also being tackled and lithium ion battery costs have been dropping almost 14 percent per annum since 2000. Yet current batteries remain expensive for widespread use. Effective packaged battery cost was estimated at approximately $300 per kilowatt-hour for products like the Chevrolet Bolt, launched in 2016. This means that for a Chevy Bolt, the batteries alone would cost almost $18,000. For a Tesla Model S, a comparable estimate would be $27,000.

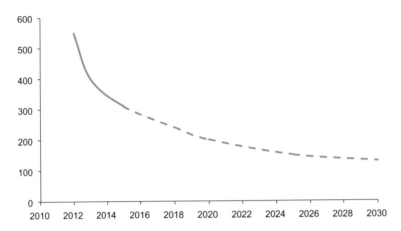

Figure 5.8 The costs of lithium ion battery packs are expected to decline over the next two decades, rendering them commercially viable.

Looking to the future, Mark Reuss, GM's executive vice president in charge of product development, estimates costs to almost halve, to levels of $145 per kilowatt-hour in the near term, and to less than $100 per kilowatt-hour by 2020.[15] By that time, a 30 kWh battery pack suitable for a small city car would cost about $3,000, greatly expanding the practicality of the solution. At that level electric vehicles will become comparable to conventional cars on the basis of cost performance.

There is every reason to anticipate faster innovation in this domain and when we advance to the next level of battery capability, the disruption of conventional cars will likely be very rapid.

Time and tide wait for no man

As we anticipate the industry passing the inflection point, many recognize that the transition will be painful to incumbents. Ford Motor Company, Toyota Motor Corporation, General Motors, and Bavarian Motor Works (BMW) have all retained "motor," referring to the internal combustion engine, in their corporate name to define their core identity. The internal combustion engine remains a cornerstone of their competitive advantage, honed and sharpened for more than a century. A shift to electric drives will erase much of this relative advantage. Factories that manufacture engines also house a lot of expensive equipment, which will be rendered obsolete with a rapid transformation, creating a massive burden on their balance sheet.

There is an elegant simplicity about electric motors. They contain far fewer parts than the average combustion engine. There are no expensive pistons and valves and no complex fuel injection or after-treatment systems. They are easier to build and assemble and will require fewer workers. According to a member of its management board, Volkswagen predicted that a significant migration to electric vehicles could result in a "five figure" drop in the number of jobs across their global operations.[16] Labor unions are concerned about such outcomes. There will also be serious ramifications for industry economics and for a large fraction of the auto industry's supply chain.

There will be other challenges to address as well. Electric vehicle batteries consume a significant amount of lithium, a material of limited availability. Electric motors and their magnets use rare earth metals, which are also limited in supply. Their mining and extraction can be environmentally damaging and cause high carbon emissions. At the end of their lives, these electric vehicles will require different approaches to manage the high-voltage electronics and the recovery of many exotic materials. It is important to take a macroeconomic view of total system cost and environmental impact while assessing the various solutions offered for the future. Yet, over decades we have learned to cope with similar issues relating to conventional cars, and so these issues for electric vehicles are not insurmountable.

Time and tide wait for no man, and no company or country can defy the onset of such change as it happens. A positive view would be that such a shift will increase the genetic pool of the mobility industry. It will favor new players who come with a new set of skills. Large corporations such as Panasonic, LG, Samsung, and Siemens, which are not considered auto industry players, are gravitating toward this domain. Competition has been responsible for improving the genetic pool of any species. As electrification muscles into the auto industry, we are set for a period of vibrant competition between technologies and business cultures that will improve future mobility.

Fuel cells

In chapter 2 we addressed the energy issue around hydrogen. Here we examine how this is being harnessed in cars.

As daunting a transformation to a hydrogen-based economy may be, there are many reasons why automakers and even some governments have been very eager to pursue fuel-cell technology. We need only consider the image proffered by its proponents: a man walks up to the rear of his car, places a cup beneath the tailpipe, and traps the water and water vapor that constitute the emissions and proceeds to drink it. What more dramatic proof

Figure 5.9 Toyota has packed a lot of technology into its hydrogen fuel-cell car, the Mirai. As a pioneer in the field, the technology remains expensive, and the initial plans call for modest sales. *Source:* Toyota Motor Corporation.

of clean mobility could one ask for? A fuel cell typically consumes stored hydrogen to generate electrical power, and the by-products are essentially water vapor. The fuel cell, instead of a battery, powers the electric motors that drive the car. Cars powered by fuel cells offer many advantages. Unlike electric vehicles, they can carry sufficient fuel on board to achieve a range of more than 400 miles (640 kilometers), and refueling takes not much more time than for a conventional car—around three to four minutes. Unlike a hybrid, they can travel into some city center areas that are restricted to ZEVs. In a sense, they offer an attractive alternative to both electric vehicles and hybrids.

Buoyed by its success with the Prius, Toyota was eager to win the fuel-cell race as well. Toyota's innovative product, the Mirai (meaning "future" in Japanese), was offered to the public in 2015, though in very limited numbers, with sales restricted to California, where a small number of hydrogen fueling stations are operational. This too is not an inexpensive solution, with the Mirai being a midsize car selling for the price of a Cadillac or a Lexus. As with the Prius, this early generation of cars is probably more expensive than even these elevated street prices would indicate. They typically enjoy massive subsidies while the automaker tests the water with this new technology. Honda was not far behind with its rival fuel-cell product named Clarity. Both automakers have disclosed very modest volume ambitions with these pilot experiments.

When the first-generation Toyota Prius was launched, many analysts questioned Toyota's strategy. Toyota was perceived as bringing very risky and complex technology to market, backed by very heavy financial subsidies. Toyota persevered with that technology and has reaped the advantage of being seen as an innovator. This time around, even as the challenges seem as formidable, fewer voices are expressing reservations. Placing bets against human ingenuity must have unfavorable odds. Over the next decade, fuel cells will join the race alongside electric vehicles and hybrids for green mobility.

Propulsion for future mobility

After decades of dabbling with electric cars, hybrids, and even some fuel-cells, most pundits concur that the electrification of mobility will accelerate significantly in the coming decade. The pressure has been building on all fronts—technology, economics, environment, and consumer attitudes.

We have noted that the dual challenge of lower tailpipe as well as CO_2 emissions is getting extremely difficult to manage with conventional engines. Further improvements are rendering this solution very complex and expensive. At the same time, battery costs fall every year, and the benefits of scale work to the advantage of electric drive components, boosting their claim to be ready to disrupt conventional engines. Tesla has shown that cars can benefit from a fresh wave of customer enthusiasm if they are seen as modern, clean, and innovative.

As these variations of electrified propulsion take the next steps toward wider acceptance, their challenges will be as much related to business economics and the environment as they are to technology. Carlos Ghosn believes that "technology is not going to stop us getting even better. However, affordability will be the challenge to conquer."[17]

Modal shifts to lower carbon emissions

In this chapter we have noted innovations that have packed a lot of technology to improve efficiency and lower emissions from cars. Almost all of those technologies, including electrification, alternative fuels, and connectivity, can and are being applied to minivans, mini-buses and buses. Often, buses can afford to adopt even more technology, thereby ensuring that public modes are rendered even more competitive than personal cars. So, separate from the issue of congestion, shifting to public modes can also generate benefits for the environment. Data from the European Commission show that public transit uses less than 30 percent of the energy per passenger-kilometer used by a personal automobile. While buses are still predominantly diesel-powered, most cities are rapidly switching to hybrids, natural gas, or biogas.

When we also consider metro rail systems, the gains are even more impressive. For the average trip by metro rail, the energy use is estimated at 0.12 kilowatt-hour per person-kilometer. Travel by personal car averages seven times that level of energy. In Europe, when metros and trams are also included, 40 percent of travel by public modes is electrified already, contributing significantly to lowering emissions.

Comparing energy efficiency of public modes with personal cars is not always easy. Both are highly dependent on degree of occupancy. In some cities, low levels of ridership on public modes can give rise to situations where use of a personal car may be more efficient. We deal with the topic of public transit in greater detail in chapter 9.

Innovations to improve traffic safety

Motoring was introduced in the UK in 1895 with the import of the first car. The first motoring-related fatality, that of a young woman pedestrian, occurred in Surrey in 1896. The coroner reviewing the accident hoped "such a thing would never happen again." Sadly, ever since, the risks of operating powerful and increasingly rapid machinery in our cities and highways have only grown.

Road injuries are the ninth leading cause of death in the world, with 1.25 million fatalities in 2013.[18] In Europe, road transport accounted for 97 percent of all transport fatalities in 2008.[19] Young populations are particularly vulnerable—in the age group of fifteen to twenty-nine years, it was the leading cause of death. Inevitably, this leads to a very high emotional and economic cost—the latter alone was assessed at approximately $2.25 trillion, or 3 percent of global GDP.[20] Extrapolating this data, it is estimated that if current trends continue, by 2030 traffic fatalities will be the fifth leading cause of deaths around the world. If one adds the impact of injuries, the magnitude of the problem increases.

If Rachel Carson woke up the world to the dangers of environmental degradation, it was Ralph Nader who raised the clarion call for auto safety. He galvanized opinion across citizens, governments, and the auto industry. In 1959, GM had launched the Chevrolet Corvair, a radical new product developed under the stewardship of the talented Ed Cole, who would later become GM's president. It was intended to signal a new direction in automotive design. Yet the Corvair gained fame for the wrong reasons. It withered under fire from Ralph Nader's attack in his book, *Unsafe at Any Speed*.[21] In fact, his criticism went beyond the Corvair. It was directed at the entire U.S. auto industry for its casual treatment of a subject he considered vital—safety. He charged the industry with adding meaningless design changes each year while neglecting to address fundamental improvements in design for safety and durability. The book was hugely influential and set in motion the role of government in regulating auto safety.

Bob Lutz, an experienced and colorful industry leader who also served many decades later as GM's vice chairman, offered grudging but honest credit to Nader. "The book had a seminal effect, and it created a deserved role for government in automotive safety. It leveled the playing field among automakers."[22] From then on, many of the technologies and features we have come to expect in everyday cars would be mandated by regulations. Airbags to limit injury, and anti-lock brakes (ABS) and electronic stability programs (ESP) to avoid crashes are just some examples. Rigorous tests by government labs were obligatory to certify vehicles, and later a system of star-based ratings helped educate customers on the relative safety performance of competitor products. These test results forced automakers to improve the design of vehicle structures to be safer in crashes.

From the 1980s, safety performance got a big boost as cars began to employ more electronics. With more sensors and more on-board processors, it was possible to improve safety performance not only by improving chances for avoiding accidents but also to mitigate injury when collisions occurred. According to the National Highway Traffic Safety Administration (NHTSA), the combination of ABS and ESP has contributed to a decline in single-vehicle crashes by almost 35 percent for passenger cars and as much as 67 percent for SUVs.[23] Further, it is estimated that in the U.S., between 1960 and 2012, safety equipment in cars saved more than 610,000 lives.

Looking to the future, both automakers and regulators have logically increased the focus on the range of electronics and software that increasingly dominate a car's function. Modern cars may employ well in excess of sixty processors with electronics used across systems for safety, stability, accident avoidance, and injury mitigation.

Adaptive cruise control was another application of machine intelligence to make driving less of a chore. Early cruise control systems could do little more than hold a constant speed, making minute adjustments to the throttle. Soon cruise control was augmented with better sensing capabilities whereby the vehicle monitors the car ahead and reacts if the car ahead slows down, essentially adding a layer of protection and reducing stress and workload for the driver. Advanced versions of this hardware not only maintain a desired speed but can also intervene and automatically slow or even stop the vehicle if it "senses" that the vehicle ahead is braking and that a collision could occur.

Leveraging advances in communication, we are on the threshold of an era when cars and traffic lights will talk to each other. Vehicle-to-vehicle (V2V) and vehicle-to-infrastructure (V2I) communication, which we anticipate will be mandated in some form or other, opens many possibilities. For example, if the car in front could "communicate" to the car following that the brakes were being applied even before the car had started to slow down, a possible collision could be avoided. The trailing car would gain valuable reaction time, which, in the domain of safety, makes all the difference between a crash and avoidance of a collision. Similarly, critical infrastructure, such as traffic signals, might communicate to a car when the light is about to turn red, allowing more reaction time to brake safely to a halt. Many fatalities occur at traffic intersections, so technologies like these are strong contributors to the safety agenda. With some developments, there may even come a time when traffic lights are rendered obsolete. Much as people crossing paths in a busy mall make small adjustments to avoid running into each other, if cars could actively sense the presence and trajectories of other cars in the vicinity, they could make adjustments to pass each other safely.

Going forward, consumers will expect that advances that have led to semi-autonomous driving or autonomous driving will lead to the avoidance of all accidents. The technology at this stage is not ready for this utopian goal, but rapid strides are being made. Societal perspectives have rapidly swung from viewing autonomous driving as a threat, to viewing this technology as a tool for improved safety. The rationale is that human beings can get fatigued or distracted and make mistakes, while computers will not. Sensor technologies will allow better detection of pedestrians and bicyclists. We delve deeper into autonomous driving in chapter 8.

As cars became safer and as occupants were better protected, the situation outside the car demanded attention. It became apparent that improvements to traffic safety would require additional focus on pedestrians and bicyclists, the more vulnerable road users. In Europe, it was noted that the risk of fatality for pedestrians per kilometer of travel was higher than that for motorists by a factor of nine; for cyclists it was higher by a factor of seven.[24] This perspective also led to regulations to ensure that cars were not only designed to improve occupant safety; they also needed to be designed to be less "aggressive" to pedestrians or bicyclists.

Similarly, it was not adequate to focus only on vehicular technologies. Some countries, especially a few in Europe, had maintained a similar pace in attending to road infrastructure, including improving design standards, road surface adhesion, water drainage characteristics, more visible lane markings and the redesign of intersections. Many cities replaced street intersections with roundabouts, reducing the risk of side collisions. Sensors were fitted to city streets and highways to monitor traffic and coordinate with signals. Video cameras monitor congested intersections. Importantly, the nonmotorized modes were separated from the motorized ones. Dedicated bike lanes, sidewalks, and improved pedestrian cross-walks all contributed to lowering the number and severity of accidents.

The most gratifying outcomes are visible in Europe where vehicular technologies have been harnessed in tandem with improved road infrastructure, better driver education and enhanced focus on ensuring compliance to regulations. As a result, compliance with laws such as those governing seat-belt use is high. Very harsh penalties are applied to drivers who are under the influence of alcohol or other substances. Helmet laws for motorcycles are widespread and enforced rigorously.

In 1998, many of the EU governments articulated a roadmap to support their Vision Zero initiative. Simply stated, the EU roadmap called for achieving an ideal situation of zero traffic fatalities in the respective nations. It was understood that this vision could only be achieved by a combination of roadway and highway design, intelligent cars with appropriate safety technologies, and better driver training and education. Sweden's role in taking a lead with this approach has found many admirers around the world. Sweden's implementation is decidedly comprehensive. The country's two automakers at the time, Volvo and SAAB, made safety a cornerstone of their brands. Many vehicles, including all school buses, government vehicles, and many taxis, are fitted with breathalyzer kits and will not start if the driver is found to be impaired. Legal levels of blood alcohol are a quarter of those in the U.S. More than 1,100 speed cameras deployed across highways and cities deal with speeding violations. Since penalties for speeding and drunk driving are harsh, Sweden has induced better driving behavior—fewer than 0.24 percent of drivers were found to have blood alcohol levels in excess of the law in a recent survey.[25]

In 1990, the European nations together recorded about 76,000 fatalities.[26] By 2013, this figure had fallen to about 26,000. These results were achieved even though the number of cars and total travel increased. The progress made was encouraging enough to validate the approach, and in 2010, a challenge to reduce fatalities by a further 60 percent was put in place.

Japan too has implemented a comprehensive set of initiatives backed by regulations to improve safety performance. In 1970, Japan recorded about 16,700 fatalities; by 2014, this figure had fallen to just over 4,000.

The position of the U.S. as the car capital of the world translates into a lot more vehicle use and many more fatalities. In 2015, 35,092 people lost their lives on roads—a worrying 8 percent increase over the prior year.[27] An additional 2.3 million people were injured in accidents. Cars sold in the U.S. employ some of the most comprehensive safety equipment, yet progress has been slower than in Europe or Japan. Indeed, as cars and roads get safer through technology, the spotlight is bound to fall on behavioral issues. Based on data pertaining to the U.S. from NHTSA for 2014, a third of the fatalities recorded that year were related to drunk drivers. And almost half of the occupants who died were not restrained with seat belts, even though seat-belt use was mandated in most states.[28]

The experience in Europe and Japan is revealing. Significant improvements in safety record emerge from a combination of (1) road and infrastructure investments, (2) vehicular standards and technologies, (3) driver training, and (4) enforcement of traffic laws.

A far greater problem looms as large populations in emerging economies such as China, India, Brazil, and Russia achieve higher levels of motorization. Estimates for 2013 from the World Health Organization (WHO) suggest that in China, up to 261,000 people lost their lives in traffic accidents.[29] Most fatalities involved pedestrians, bicyclists, and motorcyclists. While China has adopted newer vehicular technologies such as airbags and ABS and is quickly catching up with Western standards of safety technology in cars, enforcement remains weak. Hence compliance with laws requiring motorcyclists to wear helmets or car occupants to fasten their seat belts is poor. In addition, large fractions are new drivers in a country where car ownership is relatively recent. Poor driver training and indifferent adherence to traffic rules also contribute to a high number of accidents.

India is another hot spot for high levels of traffic-related deaths. WHO estimates that in 2013, almost 230,000 people lost their lives on Indian roads.[30] Indian conditions are complicated by a high mix of heterogeneous traffic in urban areas. This leads to large speed variations between pedestrians and the cars they share road space with. Many of the issues noted in China also apply to India, including large numbers of new drivers, poor driver training and licensing, and low rates of compliance with safety regulations.

These nations are witnessing very rapid motorization. They are also investing huge sums to create a lot of new infrastructure and even smart cities. They are presented with a unique opportunity to embed within this new infrastructure many of the elements that will contribute to safer mobility. They can attempt to harness the next generations of technology to avoid retracing the same path taken by the developed nations half a century ago. Yet if the opportunity over the next decade is lost, humanity in those countries will pay an unnecessary and unacceptably high cost for mobility.

The ills of progress: Driver distraction

Through history we have observed that adding technology is not the same as achieving desired results. In 1997, a report examined the effect of addition of ABS brakes on traffic accidents.[31] The study involved the same models of cars and compared those fitted with ABS with those that did not have the system. It observed no difference in the rates of accidents. In fact, cars fitted with ABS actually had a slightly higher rate of fatalities for its occupants than cars without ABS. Many researchers have postulated that human psychology often compensates for the additional margin of safety provided by these systems.[32] They have observed that drivers of cars with ABS brakes actually drive faster on slippery roads, placing their faith in the ABS system to save them from harm. There appears to be a subconscious human correction factor at play that defines and accepts a tolerable level of risk. As technologies reduce risk, it appears that behavior compensates perversely, to assume additional risk. Driver education and training, not only at the stage of licensing but also with the rollout of any new technology, are important to manage this dynamic and sustain measurable improvements in safety.

As driver aids multiply in cars, many systems such as adaptive cruise control, lane-tracking technologies and the emerging autonomous and semi-autonomous functions are intended to reduce driver workload. Navigation and guidance tools likewise should add convenience and lower stress. Connectivity and telematics functions can even summon medical assistance in the event of a crash. Collectively, they should help render driving safer. Yet,

Figure 5.10 Emerging safety technology in cars will monitor drivers for drowsiness using imaging and software, and provide alerts whenever it is deemed necessary.
Source: ©Continental AG.

increases in connectivity have caused an alarming increase in driver distraction. The driver's seat has become a sort of a pilot's cockpit, requiring managing more complex vehicles with more complex functions. But airplane pilots are highly trained professionals who undergo long periods of instruction, training, and preparation. Cars are driven by people of all ages, experience levels, and competency. With more interfaces to monitor, drivers get distracted. Often, a lack of awareness of the limitations of the electronic driver aids allows some drivers to turn their attention to matters other than safe driving, placing unwarranted confidence in these vehicle systems. When one adds the juggling of smartphones and temptations to text or respond to alerts or calls, the result is an environment that can significantly lower driver alertness and performance. Distracted drivers are involved in a disproportionately large number of accidents.

Some technologies can compensate for human behavior. Advances in cameras and artificial intelligence enable many cars to monitor a driver's eyes and detect drowsiness. They can sound an alert to refresh the driver's attention to the task of driving.

In all these situations, beyond the addition of more technology, the complexities of the human-machine interface and interactions need to be studied. Improvements are needed to ensure that drivers are able to manage the range of tasks they undertake while in a car. The ambiguity arising from what the electronic systems can do and functions that require the driver's oversight and control will need to be managed with better education, awareness, and enforcement of acceptable rules of operation.

In closing

As societies have evolved their mobility architectures, and harnessed a range of technologies to make travel more comfortable and efficient, they have involuntarily introduced elements of risk. The solutions pose threats not only to the planet's environment, but to many drivers and passengers as well. Over the years, awareness and sensitivity to these risks have grown.

Unless the trajectory of human mobility is rendered less dangerous and less harmful to the planet, we will encounter more aggressive curtailment of that fundamental aspect of life – the right to personal mobility. Fortunately, human creativity remains vibrant and active, churning out new ideas and making improvements to individual products as well as to mobility systems. With these developments, we are multiplying the options available to us to change course. There is every reason to believe that we have the tools and the solutions to adopt a mobility framework that will be sustainable.

6 Innovations to Support Mass Customization

To know what you prefer instead of humbly saying Amen to what the world tells you, you ought to prefer, is to have kept your soul alive.

—*Robert Louis Stevenson,* An Inland Voyage

In chapter 4 we discussed how the "digital natives" have come to expect very different mobility solutions than the traditional pattern of car-dependent mobility. They have also grown up as consumers who expect products and services to be uniquely personalized to each individual. As we configure a new architecture for mobility, this expectation of personalization will play an important role.

The canvas for crafting such personalization is vast. Modern consumers have seen their operating environments customized, whether it is their smartphone, their online banking screens, or even their news feeds. They expect that any product or service that seeks their patronage should make the effort to deal with them in a personalized manner. To serve them, product and service providers are expected to acquire a deep understanding of their preferences, even as their privacy is respected. This identification of preferences can be approached in two distinct ways. Some products and services allow customers to configure preferred solutions or services through explicit instructions. For example, customers individually and consciously choose the jingle they want to use for their mobile phone ringtone. A complementary approach, possible in today's world of analytics, offers a tailored solution or service, which is designed after observation and analysis of that customer's preferences in prior interactions, without specific instructions from the user. Imagine hurrying down a drugstore aisle at the end of a trying workweek only to see a discount coupon of your favorite antacid pop up on your smartphone!

Equally, consumers today expect their environments to be adaptable to sharing their personal experiences and expressing their individual character. More and more people are getting used to Instagram, Flickr, and Facebook, which allow them a platform to express themselves and be recognized for their unique values, tastes, and preferences.

In the 1930s, one had to be a Rothschild or a Rockefeller to get a car custom-made to one's desires. Technology is a great leveler, and in this millennium, a custom-made car is available to millions more. Similarly, in the services domain, a Rothschild could expect a chauffeur at his or her beck and call. A modern traveler can summon an Uber ride and have the driver pull up when she is ready to leave. A Rothschild could expect his personal butler to know when he would be seated for breakfast and how well he liked his eggs done. Technology can pamper a modern customer with similar care and indulgence.

Mobility that is flexible enough to suit each individual in the manner he or she wishes to be served will be a part of our future mobility architecture.

In this chapter we explore innovations in product personalization and customization. We have deliberately reserved the elaboration of mobility services and how they may be personalized to chapter 11, where personalization appears as an intrinsic component of the CHIP framework.

The psychology of personalization

Psychology suggests that there are many reasons why customization and personalization work. First, no human being is fully devoid of ego. When the maître d'hôtel welcomes a guest by name and adds a personal greeting, there is a strong reward stimulus for the guest's ego. Similarly, the idea that one's car or smartphone offers a canvas for self-expression enhances the reward experience of the individual's subconscious.

The reward experience can also be enhanced because customization can result in better performance. For example, one tool or machine may be better suited to the physique or ergonomics of the user than another. A customized pair of shoes can be more comfortable than a standard-size pair. It has been observed that people who make the effort to achieve a more customized configuration of a mobile phone, for example, end up using the device more often and over a wider range of applications.[1]

A study of worker productivity in the United Kingdom found that employees who were permitted to personalize their workspace with family pictures and personal curios were up to 25 percent more productive than those whose workspaces had to conform to sterile standards. According to Craig Knight, a psychologist who led the research, "When we can enrich our space we're happier. And we work better when we're happier."[2]

At a deeper level, personalization may preferentially stimulate the reticular activation system in the brain.[3] While this pathway primarily deals with sleep-wake status, it is also responsible for hastening the transition from relaxed wakefulness to heightened alertness. This promotes greater attention to preferred stimuli.

For example, it is not uncommon for a fan watching a football game on television to pay more attention to a specific player, even though all the players are engaged in active movement across the screen. While the brain continues to register the full range of activities, additional neural resources are assigned to track the preferred player. Similarly, at a crowded reception, amid high-decibel chatter, people are able to lock on to a specific conversation on an interesting subject. In these examples, the reticular activation system is stimulated and the target conversation benefits from the preferential attention of the individual. To a marketer, personalization and customization offer that inside track to a customer's neural core. Marketing's personalized advertisements or messages are more keenly perceived by the target's sharpened receptors.

Personalization of products and services to enhance performance and user experience

Any system that seeks to enhance performance through personalization must be capable of:

1. Sensing user needs and the user context with high fidelity;
2. Tailoring responses accurately to user needs; and
3. Monitoring user reaction and responding quickly to user feedback.

Highly digitized service companies have begun to exploit the capabilities of personalization and often serve as role models. As any visit to Amazon's website to browse for new books makes evident, the customer is prompted with information on the basis of prior searches or topics of interest and presented with suggestions of new titles or products that fit the pattern of use by similar customers. Many media sites are now equipped to tailor their interface to enhance value to the customer by personalizing their news and entertainment experience.

Personalization in financial services has been used to good effect to improve user performance and experience. Banks and investment firms deal with a cross section of customers who have varying degrees of familiarity with banking and investing. Customer interfaces and portals need to be configurable to suit novice users and expert users individually. The range of information that can be presented is vast and needs to be filtered based on customer profiles that are both defined by the customer and deduced by the system. These portals are effective only if they are seen as nonintimidating by a novice user while at the same time providing the expert user with the expected analysis of complex investment products, markets, and currencies. Much like smartphone screens, these portals also allow customers to tailor screens to prioritize specific information they are interested in.

The emerging field of personalized medicine is making considerable progress. Approaches that are individualized can enhance efficacy. Personalized medicine aims to create unique drugs based not only on the diagnosed ailment but also on the specific characteristics, nature, and constitution of specific classes of patients.[4] Personalized medicine could, for example, be based on the genetic makeup of the individual at the molecular level, which may be used to select the approach taken for remedy.

The approach is now being extended to diets and nutrition. Although the science is in its infancy, scientists have identified thirty-eight genes linked to human metabolism whose variants are expected to help or hinder absorption of nutrients in foods. The Weizmann Institute in Israel has adopted this approach to assess responses to various diets. Based on individual patient characteristics—lifestyle, family history, medication taken, and even gut bacteria characteristics—they have developed algorithms that can predict blood sugar responses to foods that the individual has not yet consumed. "The algorithm is similar to what Amazon uses to tell you which books you want to read," reports Eran Segal, a computer scientist at the Weizmann Institute and co-author of the study. "We just do it with food."[5]

In a world rapidly adopting wearable technologies for monitoring health and well-being, medical service providers will soon have more accurate personal and temporal measures of moods, alertness, stress, and activity. These signals could enable a whole range of helpful interventions, and possibly, if the user's stress levels are high, even avoidance of stimuli.

Enterprises that offer a personalized array of mobility products and services to customers will enjoy better patronage, and that may lead to better economic outcomes, especially when the technology allows for personalization at minimal or no additional cost.

Personalization in autos

Let us examine how this may be deployed in cars and mobility. Many auto-makers are seeking to ensure that the range of human interactions inside the car (commonly referred to as the human-machine interface) can be tailored to a combination of user-specified and system-deduced context. Cars are becoming increasingly sophisticated in sensing operating conditions so that their performance can be adjusted to suit the driver and occupants. With this, driving or travelling by car can be safer, more productive and more satisfying.

Something as routine as tracking minor inputs to steering or monitoring the driver's eye movements can help determine whether the driver is nervous, anxious, or drowsy. In such situations the software systems in modern cars can provide guidance or modify a response by suitably varying some vehicle parameters. We have noted the higher probability of distracted drivers to be involved in crashes. Cars may be able to sense when the driver is distracted and suitably limit nonessential information in overly complex driver environments.

In modern cars, very sophisticated strategies in the use of airbags to prevent injury are called into play. Airbags must deploy rapidly and with great force to fully inflate within a few milliseconds so that they can effectively cushion the occupants and avoid injury. If a child or a person of slight build is the occupant, the force with which the airbag deploys could itself lead to injury. Modern airbags have seat sensors that can distinguish between empty seats, infants, and adults to calibrate the force of deployment and reduce risk. Newer airbags also monitor occupant posture and position. If an occupant is leaning forward or resting her head against one side, sensors and algorithms factor in this information and adjust the appropriate force deployment characteristics of the airbag.

As vehicles become increasingly configurable, they offer a wider canvas for personalization to enhance user experience. Cars can be switched between economy mode and sport mode depending on driver expectations or mood. In some cars, the vehicle's computer "learns" how the driver likes to drive and can adapt transmission shift points accordingly. Traveling over potholed city streets may call for a cosseting ride, while charging up a mountain road may call for firmer suspension settings. A new frontier for cars is the use of reconfigurable screens in place of an expensive cluster of instruments. Reconfigurable screens allow configurations to be changed for different users and in response to changes in driving conditions. A husband and wife couple, for example, can configure different views as presets, and the system recognizes the user based on whose key fob is used. In addition, seat position, climate control preferences, and driving mode can be customized to suit either husband or wife. Some cars have a cool green display when driven in ecomode and the display morphs into aggressive orange when the driver switches to sport mode. Many new premium cars have added the option of configurable mood lighting to amplify the desired ambience.

Customization in the auto industry: Historical evolution

At the dawn of the motoring age, cars were personalized. They were typically commissioned by wealthy individuals and were built to order. Purchasers could dictate the kind of body they wanted, choose materials and trimmings, and even specify unique hardware. Cars were an expensive conveyance, affordable by a only a few.

Henry Ford changed this with his revolutionary Model T Ford—the world's first high-production-volume car. The statement Henry Ford is renowned for, "Any customer can have a car painted any color that he wants so long as it is black,"[6] came to represent the philosophy of mass manufacturing and standardization. Cars were made affordable for the masses, and production scales quickly grew.

Alfred Sloan, who became chairman of the cross-town rival, General Motors, provided the next inflection point to the growth trajectory of automobiles. Sloan stated that GM would build "a car for every purse and every purpose," and launched the practice that would dominate marketing and sales for over half a century. For him, a standardized product held all the allure of a Mao jacket. He grasped the need for people to differentiate themselves from their neighbors. He dissected the market and emphasized differentiation based on attitudes, preferences, and demographics. The offer of product variety is the first step companies can take toward fulfilling their customers' desires for customization. Alfred Sloan's staircase of brands was fine-tuned to appeal to different audiences. Sporty young drivers would race to a Pontiac store while doctors and lawyers would gravitate to the Oldsmobile and Buick. And while many aspire to a Cadillac, only the wealthy few could afford one. This strategy started the industry down the path to product differentiation with products tailored to well-identified market segments.

One challenge with Sloan's business model was the cost and complexity of keeping the dealership inventories appropriately stocked and refreshed with new models. With five hungry brands to feed—Chevrolet, Pontiac,

Oldsmobile, Buick, and Cadillac—the financials would have been severely strained had GM chosen to develop a full range of products for each brand. Sloan needed a hybrid strategy that would blend his brand specificity with Ford's mass production.

The key to executing this hybrid strategy was to impose a common car foundation for all the brands. Often dubbed "platforms" since they were typically the underpinnings of the vehicle, these foundations defined the components and interfaces that could be shared based on specific and precise rules. Gradually, in the postwar years, the platforms of the different brands converged and the cars themselves were differentiated only by superficial changes to appearance and interiors. Many of the expensive investments were shared, such as dies and tools for crafting the body, engine, and transmission. Differentiation was achieved with a few carefully chosen brand enhancers—for example, high-performance engines for Pontiacs and luxury and refined features for Cadillacs. Sloan's strategy was to get GM's engineers to don the conjurer's robes and, out of more or less a similar set of parts, deliver a Chevrolet for the family, a Pontiac for the sportsman, and a Buick for the doctor. Through the postwar years this practice grew among U.S. automakers. By the 1930s, Ford too found that its standardization strategy no longer worked as car populations grew and Sloan's instinct that people would seek differentiation was validated. Ford followed suit and used the platform-sharing approach to create differentiated products among its brands (Ford, Mercury, and Lincoln), while Chrysler did the same with its range of products.

As with all strategies, a deft hand was required to manage its deployment. Standardization worked well for economics but offered limited market appeal. Product differentiation worked wonders in the market but could ruin economics. Henry Ford and Alfred Sloan had advanced theories that occupied opposite ends of the pendulum's course. Many automakers found that the golden mean was elusive. Often the large automakers oscillated between phases. For some, economics dictated that cars shared so much commonality that all the sister brands looked alike. For others, cost savings were squandered on excessive differentiation. The bottom line, however, was simple: customers wanted variety so that their cars were different from the ones their neighbors owned, but customers also wanted affordable cars. Variety and economy were both important.

How much variety is necessary?

C. K. Prahalad, a visionary management professor who co-authored the influential book *The New Age of Innovation,* proposed the concept of $N = 1$ in business strategy.[7] He underscored the need for contemporary enterprises to pay attention to differences among individual customers and deal with them one at a time; hence $N = 1$. Such business strategies could get customers involved in the process of configuring their own products and services. To accomplish this vision, a company would need to go well beyond the degree of segmentation achieved by Sloan at GM. Where Sloan stopped with products aimed at classes of buyers (for example, Buicks aimed at doctors and lawyers), the strategy of $N = 1$ required understanding each doctor or lawyer and aligning products with their individual needs.

The hierarchy of brands that various large global auto companies have built provide a variety of products differentiated on the basis of size, price, and configuration. Sibling products from the same platform may be offered, for example, from both Ford and Lincoln, differentiated by the level of premium features and brand image. From the Ford stable alone one may choose a Focus, a compact car, or a Fusion, a family car. One may choose among hatchbacks, sedans, wagons, and crossovers. These vehicles are further differentiated by their engines and trim. Just from the Ford offerings it is evident that automakers have attempted to cater to increasingly smaller customer segments. For example, in 2007 a Ford Mustang with a V6 engine could be ordered in more than 16,000 combinations of different options and colors. When other engine combinations are added in, the variety on offer is staggering. Insofar as Ford produced a total of just over 158,000 Mustangs in 2007, it is theoretically possible, though unlikely, that each one was unique.

In the U.S., well over 80 percent of cars sold are retailed directly from the dealer's lot. Customers expect to walk out of the dealer showroom with their new car after a visit, and dealers are very eager to get a car sold with each customer footfall. This implies that dealers are obliged to hold a representative inventory, after factoring in fast-selling models and colors of choice, among the large variety that automakers offer. On the other hand, in Germany, a majority of cars are made to order, a process that may take three to four months. A large number of German buyers expect to be able to look through the specification sheet and more or less configure the vehicle of his or her choice, within the constraints placed by the manufacturer.

Either system triggers its own levels of complexity. The U.S. model requires dealers to stock a large inventory so that each customer has a good selection from which to find a car close to his or her ideal configuration. Automakers have to be good at anticipating customer preference so that they can efficiently manage inventory. This stock-to-sell approach often results in a finished goods inventory that might account for more than three months of sales, across the entire distribution chain. For large automakers, those that record annual revenues of more than $100 billion, this level of inventory locks up a large amount of funds and represents an inefficient use of capital.

The German practice also triggers huge complexity. The German make-to-order system requires an organization to prepare for the millions or billions of possible combinations that may be chosen by customers and to orchestrate the process of building exactly the car they order. In this build-to-order approach, premium German manufacturers are required to manage potential build combinations that can number up to 10^{24}, or a trillion trillion possible options, for just one car model such as an E-class Mercedes. Orchestrating a global supply chain and production system to accomplish such an extremely challenging task often results in order lead times of three to five months to get a specific car custom-built.

Thus we see two very different mass customization strategies on display: most U.S. manufacturers gear their enterprise toward efficient management of inventory (a cost emphasis), whereas German automakers, particularly the makers of premium brands, endure the additional costs of managing greater production complexity, which needs to be recovered through higher pricing. Neither situation is easy to manage, yet each advances the effort to make sure that a customer's wishes are addressed as comprehensively as possible.

In these cases, product variety and product standardization stem from conflicting motivations. Marketing functions in an organization typically urge increases in product variety so that each customer can find among the offerings, the car that best approximates his or her ideal configuration. Yet rampant expansion in variety rapidly leads to difficult-to-manage complexity, which drives up cost. Equilibrium is of course sought, but this equilibrium can be altered by either (1) amplifying differentiation through creative designs or (2) lowering the cost of offering variety, usually with platform strategies.

We will now look at how these two approaches may be realized.

Amplifying differentiation

To understand the kind of customization that happens with smartphones, we can start with the more trivial exterior options. A variety of covers, plastic cases, and monogrammed panels can be used to dress up the average smartphone. Visual personalization and differentiation are easy. A Mickey Mouse theme can be swapped for a candy-pink cover, in case someone wishes a color-coordinated accessory. The form, in this case the cover, is decoupled from the function of the smartphone, which is based on what is inside. Deeper customization occurs in the selection of the contents and apps that are used. A company like Apple or Samsung may ship millions of identical phones from their factories, but each one ends up uniquely customized through the selection of apps used by the individual user. As of mid-2016, Apple and Android each offered more than two million different apps that customers could download to their mobile devices. The number of possible combinations of phone configurations is astronomical.

Beyond the offer of wide product variety, automakers have learned the importance of customization of cars. When Justin Bieber stepped out of his matte black customized smart Mini car in April 2012, the paparazzi blasted images of him and the car all over the Internet.[8] To be shown off by an idol of the millennial generation was the kind of jackpot Mercedes-Benz must have wanted when the company made the decision, early in the development of its Smart Fortwo city car, that the vehicle had to be amenable to the emerging trend of customization. The car was designed with an aluminum space-frame—the structural skeleton of the car—over which composite panels were fastened. This construction allowed, for example, a customer to create an asymmetric look using panels of different color, something not easily done in a large-scale paint shop in a manufacturing plant. It allowed easy changes of color, shape, and texture, just as one might choose to reconfigure a smartphone with a different pattern on the snap-on covers. Not only did this allow customized looks to draw attention to or express the purchaser's personal style, it also allowed the car's looks to be freshened up after, say, two years.

BMW's Mini was another product designed for customization by users. The manufacturer anticipated that its target market would include a healthy share of millennials. Apart from the various options available from the manufacturer that can alter the looks of the car dramatically, a number of after-market suppliers provide special parts that enhance performance and appearance. The Mini is frequently ordered with unique roof colors and decals and has made a statement for being funky in the midst of a number of rather serious-looking rivals.

In a previous era, expressions of personality were limited to bumper stickers used to proclaim favorite causes, political affiliations, and personal interests, such as dogs. Successive generations have been pushing the boundaries for expression. As of 2015, approximately 20 percent of Americans sported a tattoo, and 40 percent of those were millennials. As noted by Chris Weller, "Modernity compels us to declare our identity with conviction, whether we have found it or not."[9] So for those seeking a larger canvas, tattoo painting their cars is a logical target. Predictably, an industry is emerging to cater to these demands.

Another brand in mobility that has parlayed its popularity with tattoos and customization is Harley-Davidson. The company has demonstrated the power of customer-centric product portfolio and personalization options for its range of higher-priced motorcycles. Yet because the tools of the industry advance at a very rapid pace, it will need to employ a whole new set of approaches to respond to customer wishes for products and services.

Figure 6.1 The smart car from Mercedes-Benz is amenable to customization by its users. In an age of growing popularity for tattoos, it is no surprise that cars are getting to sport tattoos as well, perhaps matching that of their owners.
Source: (CC BY-SA 2.0) Kristin Ausk.

Platforms: Lowering the cost of variety

Exterior auto body customization might be considered somewhat superficial. To reach the level of customization exhibited by consumer electronics, car designs will need to change fundamentally. With laptops, for example, discrete parts such as the touch screen, processor, memory, and software may be chosen by the user. In most cases each may be changed independently, multiplying the options to reconfigure products with lower investment.

For more than half a century, the auto industry has been working toward such a goal. But despite advances in engineering and product design, many constraints remain. Highly optimized conventional cars do not allow such decoupling of core product from modular add-ons for customization. Separating form from function is not easy. The external skin is part of the car's structure and is optimized for such functions as structural rigidity, safety, and aerodynamics—for example, engine shapes and layout dictate the form of the front vehicle structure. Furthermore, the software architecture and applications in the vehicle have typically been locked away from user tampering. Products are also closely matched with legacy components and legacy manufacturing facilities, which limits the degree to which those main components of the vehicle may be radically changed. In sum, the flexibility of plug-and-play touted by consumer electronics is not easily realized in autos.

Yet automakers keep searching for ways to craft easily achievable differentiation.

The traditional approach of automakers has been to carve out partitions of the vehicle so that many invisible parts could remain unchanged. This strategy provided some economies of scale since those parts could be produced in large numbers across brands and even models.

The differentiation is achieved effectively by add-on bits that are designed deliberately to look very dissimilar. An economical Volkswagen Golf, aimed at a young family, may share more than 80 percent of its parts with an upscale Audi A3. Yet each product appears carefully tailored to its respective set of clients and emphasizes all the design and styling cues aligned with those respective market segments.

Platforms need to offer economic advantages not only by sharing parts they share but also by keeping the costs low. A lot of attention is therefore devoted not only to the parts but also to how they are manufactured. It is not uncommon for a manufacturing line to be producing at the same time products for Volkswagen and Audi. Automakers sharing an expensive facility investment helps each manufacturer offer customers differentiated products without destroying the economics of their business.

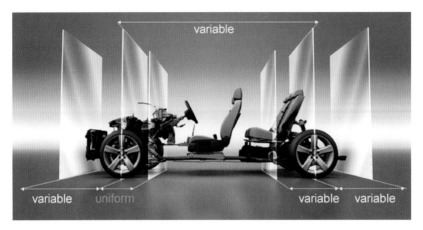

Figure 6.2 Automakers have refined their platform strategies, carefully defining partitions and interfaces. This allows them to create a wider diversity of products, changing only selected variable parameters, while keeping investment and development costs within limits. The example here refers to the Volkswagen MQB platform.
Source: Volkswagen.

The opportunity for revolutionary change is at hand as automakers look forward to a new generation of electric and fuel-cell cars. In 2005, GM unveiled a futuristic concept, the Hy-wire, a car powered by a hydrogen fuel cell. The concept was unique in that the vehicle was designed to be built in two halves—a lower half containing the fuel cell, motor, and the chassis and drive systems, dubbed the "skateboard," because it looked like one, and an upper half comprising the body shell, the shape, and the occupant volume. The idea was that by partitioning the vehicle in this manner, GM could build different configurations of the upper half for different customer segments without incurring fresh investment for the lower half, which would remain the same. It helped that the cars were essentially controlled with drive-by-wire technology. Mechanical links between the steering wheel and the wheels, for example, were replaced by electronic connections, essentially like a gaming console. This meant that changing a car from left-side drive to right-side drive to suit different markets would be as simple as plugging in the controls on the other side of the vehicle. Similarly, a sports coupé and a family wagon could both be produced with less expense and effort by limiting changes to the upper half alone. These fundamental changes in the architecture of the vehicle afforded more possibilities for customization and differentiation. To many in the auto industry, this was a case of "back to the

Figure 6.3a The GM Hy-wire was created using a "skateboard" lower platform (shown on the right) that would accommodate various upper configurations (shown on left) enabling easier differentiation.
Source: General Motors.

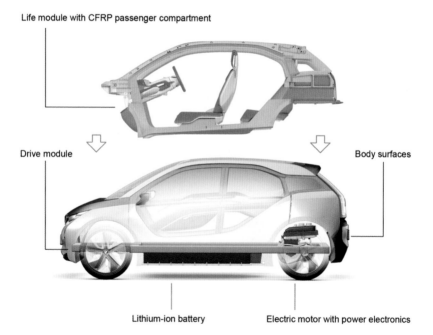

Figure 6.3b BMW has taken such a concept to market with their i3 car, separating the "Drive" module from the "Life" module.
Source: BMW.

future." Cars used to be built on a separate platform until the 1950s when decoupling of the occupant volume and the mechanical bits was easier. The pursuit of improved performance, lighter weight, and better efficiency led to a more integral architecture. The market need to offer variety is taking the industry back to an earlier era.

Though the GM Hy-wire remained a concept vehicle, BMW took the next step to bring such an architecture to market. Its i3 city electric car is built in two halves, labeled by BMW the "Drive" module for the lower part and the "Life" module for the occupant volume. As the first in what is expected to be a series of electric vehicles designed to appeal to different kinds of customers, this architecture protects the flexibility BMW anticipates needing.

In the end, automakers and mobility providers must tune in to the deep desire of the current generation to reject broad classification. The ability to satisfy individual personalization and expression will emerge as an important differentiator to acquire customer patronage. This will apply not only to products but also to mobility services, discussed in chapter 10.

Cocreation

Providing customized solutions based on assessment of individual or segment needs can create significant value for customers and automobile providers. A much greater leap, however, is achieved when customers can be enticed into configuring their own solutions. In an age when reality television and theatrical productions use audience feedback to steer the course of the story and the plot, the tools for interaction and feedback have grown impressively. Many customers expect to participate in the definition and creation of what they buy or use. Some customer-centric organizations have learned to harness the power of information technology to gather such user inputs and to ensure that when they undertake the personalization of products and services, the approaches are based on reliable sources of customer inputs. In *The Power of Co-creation*, Venkat Ramaswamy asserts that "co-creation will be propelled by a new role played by individuals and networks, both of which will be powered by a combination of technology, economics and self-motivation."[10] In some cases, customers will expect to dynamically determine features and attributes of the product or services based on up-to-the-minute personal preferences.

Historically, such technological approaches have often been deployed in high-tech industries. Yet some rather less complex economic sectors also seem to employ sophisticated tools to involve customers in cocreation, with an effectiveness that would shame many large automakers. Women's shoes, for example, are products that are highly personalized and differentiated. Shopping for women's shoes typically involves visiting favorite stores, checking out choices with peers, and, increasingly, looking for suitable designs online. The online retailer Shoes of Prey allows online customization of shoes. Using a sophisticated product configurator and smart graphics, the purchaser can navigate the design process online, choosing from among various basic styles and then tailoring the product with specific choices of material, color, proportion, shape, and embellishment. It would be possible to create a unique design, never to be used by any other wearer. This would be utopia for many users.

Certain enabling features make this customization exercise rewarding. First, the configurator is easy to use. Most customers are not intimidated by the interface and hence happily participate in the creative exercise. Second, at each step, the customer is provided an indication of the price, so there is a level of transparency that allows her to steer the design without fear of being surprised in the last stage by the resulting price. Finally, at every step, the way the image of the design pirouettes on the screen allows visual confirmation and validation by the user. One no longer needs to be a Jennifer Lopez

Figure 6.4 A digital generation demands a seat at the drawing board to create its own unique products and express its own personality. Certain product categories have successfully involved customers in custom-designing the products they purchase.
Source: Shoes of Prey.

to create one's own personal line of shoes. This is the power of customization technology. Behind the scenes, this functionality requires the sophisticated use of technologies covering design principles, product visual rendering, supply chain assessment, logistics estimation, product costing, and pricing. All in all, the system is designed to make the customer feel rewarded for creativity and for getting a unique product.

Automakers and mobility providers may take inspiration from the use of sophisticated yet effective technology for a relatively low-tech product. Interestingly, a similar evaluation exercise, assessing both the opportunity for customer participation and ease of use of several automaker websites, revealed that most were primitive compared to several examples in the non-automotive space. The mobility industry must reckon on future customers being much more demanding of the customization options they seek and the role they expect to play in "developing" their car or their travel options.

Some automakers have begun this journey. Efforts to gain customer intimacy by means of a range of sensing and social media analytics technologies have gained momentum over the past decade. While respecting the privacy of customers, manufacturers and retailers have begun piecing together a comprehensive picture of the profiles and predilections of their customers.

To enrich intimacy with the customer, automakers will need connectivity both with the vehicle and with the owner. Already companies such as Tesla are sending software and operating system updates while the car is safely parked in the owner's garage at night. Smaller versions of black boxes like those in airplanes are being installed in many vehicles, after authorization by the owner, to track and monitor driving habits and patterns of use. Vehicle software upgrades can soon be customized to observe and adapt to the driving behavior of individuals (again, with the permission of the owner). This arrangement can lead to many benefits for the car owner, such as a discount from the insurance provider, and a performance that is better tuned to user expectations. Automakers, when allowed the use of the analytics, can learn a lot more about their products, how they are used, and their customers.

Most automakers recognize that many modern customers are more concerned about the interior and the functionality of their cars than they are about engine performance. For cocreation, some automakers are increasingly looking to customizable interiors and sometimes even exteriors. Products such as Toyota's Vii and Nissan's Teatro for Dayz blend the opportunities of personalization and cocreation. Most of the vehicle's interior is reconfigurable for image, theme, and ambience. Customers can create their own environment and change it even weekly if they so desire.

Figure 6.5 Facebook on wheels: interiors designed for customization. Customers increasingly favor interiors that allow them to express their unique styles. The example shown is Nissan's Teatro for Dayz concept car.
Source: Nissan Motor Company.

Of course, enthusiastic consumers must accept the limits of such technology. Before assuming that everyone can design his or her own bespoke car, they will have to understand that many elements baked into car design are intended to meet safety and regulatory requirements. For example, every automaker must ensure that there are no sharp edges in the interior that may pose a threat of injury in the event of a crash. Customizing trim and interiors will need to stop short of violating these regulations. There are literally thousands of such design guidelines that limit the widespread use of design tools by untrained designers. There will be limits to opportunities for the cocreation of such a complex and regulated product as a car.

Yet we may anticipate greater participation, along with some hand-holding and guidance, in creating unique individual car designs. Styling studios have traditionally used customer focus groups to evaluate alternative car designs. Newer tools and more powerful software mean that such customer involvement can lead to relatively spontaneous redesigns and restyling by auto company designers. More widespread use of 3D printing may soon

Figure 6.6 Building and bonding. Automakers are betting that some of that passion for cars can be sustained when customers are involved in building their own cars.
Source: General Motors.

allow interior trim or other parts to be more personalized by individual users. One U.S. company, Local Motors, is already experimenting with this.

To deepen engagement with customers, Volkswagen, BMW, and Daimler often invite their customers to the factory on the day that "their" car is due to be built. This walk along the assembly line as one's car takes shape seems to create a stronger bond between customer and automaker. Customers feel a sense of involvement as the car is put together. Chevrolet has gone a step further, inviting some customers to actually help assemble the engine that will go in their Corvette sportscar, under the supervision of an authorized inspector. New owners are likely to feel a special bond with the car they have helped build, and such customer intimacy is priceless.

Customizing mobility services

This chapter has dealt at length with the customization of products. However, as services start to play a more central role in delivering every aspect of mobility, more opportunities will appear to tailor services and mobility solutions to suit customers' needs.

Mobility services need to align with the needs of a vast population of users whose priorities vary considerably. Even within customer segments, we have noted that the modern customer has a heightened sense of individualism. Preferences in travel depend on a host of parameters, ranging from the cost and speed of travel to its carbon footprint, the degree of privacy, the level of comfort, and even the ambience. Mobility services must be available and configurable to meet customer selection, whether the occasion is a commute to work, travel for pleasure, or dinner out. Bespoke services will be key to generating customer delight and build customer affinity.

In many industries, the increased service orientation of customer interactions that were historically product-centric has gone hand-in-hand with the expansion of Internet use and smartphones across the globe. Online and smartphone apps are well suited to absorbing and monitoring customer needs and use and, with those inputs, to tailor the way customers are served. Airlines and hotel chains recognize the individual likes of their frequent travelers on the basis of both prespecified preferences and from information gathered about their recent travel patterns. So even before one needs to specify anything, a booking may automatically assign a reservation to a window seat, with a special meal and perhaps access to the executive lounge in the hotel of choice.

As urban mobility begins to make use of multiple modes, city travel apps will integrate information about local weather conditions, travel congestion, the commuter's discretionary travel budget, and even the carbon footprint of the journey. Such data will feed analytics engines that will recommend modes of travel and routing.

As urban travel allows linking several modes, the opportunities for personalization expand even more. Each segment of travel may be optimized differently. Such tailored solutions appeal to all travelers across age groups and further enhance the appeal of alternatives to the personal car. Thankfully, advances in technology and information management have allowed better management and use of the consequent data explosion. We will resume discussion on this subject as it is interwoven into the tapestry of a personalized CHIP mobility architecture in chapter 11.

7 Innovations to Stay "Always Connected"

If you want to go fast, go alone. If you want to go far, go with others.

—*Old African proverb*

It could have been just another showcar framed by spotlights and draped with bored-looking models in one more of the many auto shows that fill the annual calendar. Yet, this one created a special buzz, as if the journalists and visitors sensed the crossing of a new milestone. With a Cadillac show car in the GM pavilion at the 1996 Chicago Auto Show, GM's former CEO, Rick Wagoner, ushered in the era of automotive telematics. GM's OnStar service would herald the age in which people would expect to be "always connected," even in their cars.

In a very short time, modern society has come to expect being connected as a basic need. In 1996 this was a lofty expectation. Until then, a family traveling in a car had broadcast radio for entertainment but few bidirectional connectivity options. Pay phones at gas stations were the primary communication tools for salesmen traveling the highways. The cell phone was in its infancy, and usage costs were very high for connectivity that was often poor or nonexistent.

At the show, GM was offering travelers some of the features they had started to enjoy with their personal computers at home. OnStar allowed users to connect with the external world for such functions as navigation and email access. It added a special round-the-clock concierge service so that travelers could have a personal valet take care of everything from guidance to the nearest drugstore to determining what movies were playing at nearby cinemas. And, most important, for some families, the service included an emergency alert system that either could be triggered by the occupants or would be automatically triggered if an accident had caused the airbags to deploy. Promoted as a service to augment safety and driver assistance, it was a pioneering innovation that was soon adopted by most manufacturers.

Figure 7.1 GM's OnStar pioneered telematics functionality in cars and paved the way for a broad suite of functions arising from connectivity.
Source: General Motors.

Cars used to be self-contained cocoons of privacy and security. The reassuring automated clicks of the door locks as a car started moving used to provide occupants with a subliminal sense of safety and isolation. Yet since the start of the new millennium, drivers and passengers no longer expect the car to provide an experience of isolation. It was not long before the full range of functions, features, and applications available on the smartphone and the home computer was also expected to be available in the car. In-car connectivity was expected to facilitate communication, productivity, entertainment, and safety.

Staying in touch

Many people place a high premium on being able to reach and be reachable by family, friends, and colleagues. For a society that lives at a constantly increasing clock speed, the time spent while on the move is valuable. Moreover, the advance of technology has amplified these demands. Consumers now expect voice, data, and video channels for communication with the external world. Email and a fast-growing assortment of messaging apps make a variety of communication modes available. As the car has come to extend the function of the living room or den, customers have come to expect the seamless use of all these channels while on the move. Though smartphones can keep people connected, the car as a mobile platform can and must do much more. Compared to a smartphone, cars have the advantage of space and size. They can accommodate large-format screens and surround-sound audio speakers, which can enhance the user's experience of reading and interacting with menus, listening to music, or watching movies. Powerful multiband antennae also enhance connectivity performance.

Enhancing productivity

The simple fact that the car is connected and benefits from a communication link contributes to productivity improvement.

Such functions as navigation and dynamic route guidance to avoid traffic congestion have become valuable tools for drivers. Paper maps have become obsolete, replaced by apps. Digital map applications not only enable route planning, they also provide guidance for shopping, dining, and other activities. Already in many cities, urban traffic planners and traffic police dynamically route traffic to reduce pressure on bottlenecks and push information in real time to cars in the vicinity. At the systems level, real-time video feeds from traffic intersections augment alerts of congestion, allowing drivers to assess how bad the congestion is before deciding on an alternative route. Connectivity also helps fleet managers track and improve the productivity of their assets, whether they are taxis, shared cars, or even buses and trucks.

A society on the move expects vehicles to serve many additional roles. For many professionals, the car doubles as a mobile workplace and supports getting work done while on the move. The range of applications keeps growing. Cisco Systems has identified a host of unique applications possible with connectivity in vehicles. In some emerging markets, vans are used for mobile health clinics, and telemedicine has become an important use of connected mobility platforms to serve rural areas. With the advent of platforms such as Apple CarPlay and Android Auto, interfaces and functions are becoming standardized. Users will be able to seamlessly transition from their home to phone to car, further contributing to productivity. The news podcast in progress at breakfast can continue streaming as the commuter starts the journey to work. There is a major incentive for automakers to align with these standard platforms.

It is quite likely that in the future, a car will operate as a networked node in a larger system that includes infrastructure, highways, and other cars. Cars will autonomously connect with electronic stations to pay tolls, be alerted by traffic lights, and recognize speed limits. Roland Berger estimates that better synchronization with traffic lights would reduce unnecessary stops by 40 percent, travel time by 25 percent, and fuel consumption by 10 percent.[1]

Traditional automobiles must be serviced at specific intervals at a dealer's or service center. With an increasing share of the vehicle's performance determined by software, such servicing events are also used to install software upgrades. Tesla shook up this status quo by providing customers the opportunity to download the latest software updates from home, reducing the time taken up by service center visits while allowing Tesla to offer more frequent upgrades. To exploit this capability, however, automakers will need to exercise extreme care since some of the software upgrades relate to safety-critical functions and cannot risk any errors in the download. Such capabilities also, when carefully deployed, improve productivity.

Making journeys safer

A carrot for many early adopters of car-based telematics was the possibility of enhancing safety. The idea that elderly or vulnerable drivers could summon assistance as needed from their cars was a big motivator for many buyers of GM's early OnStar systems. By 2015, OnStar had recorded over a billion customer interactions and had dispatched over 5.5 million emergency services to stricken vehicles and their occupants.[2] The security services they provided included simple roadside assistance and tracing stolen vehicles.

In April 2015, the European Parliament voted to mandate installation of the eCall emergency system for all cars to be sold in Europe beginning in April 2018.[3] This system will transmit vital rescue-relevant information. It is estimated that the eCall system will shorten the time to rescue by 50 percent in urban areas and 40 percent in rural areas. Response enabled by such technologies can significantly enhance road safety.

A new frontier that is being rapidly harnessed is voice commands. In chapter 5, we had noted the concern surrounding proliferation of driver interfaces and the increased risk for driver distraction and stress. Voice recognition technology is rapidly evolving and offers significant promise for a "natural" communication medium between human and machine and this is expected to reduce driver workload and improve safety. It is expected that the power of connectivity will be better and more safely utilized for a wider range of functions as cars adopt this technology.

Technology of connectivity

The technological foundations of connectivity in cars are paced by two trends:

a. The communication channels external to the vehicle. This includes the evolution of cellular network technology, in which significant progress has been made from 3G (the third generation of cellular networks), to 4G LTE, and, it is expected, even more with 5G. In addition, the emergence of dedicated short-range communication channels will augment high bandwidth, safety-critical communication to other vehicles and infrastructure.
b. The pace of upgrading in-vehicle electronics architecture to support the galloping demand for external connectivity.

Advances in cellular networks
Across the globe, there is an insatiable appetite for more data transmission at greater speed. Voice, pictures, video, and movies have characterized the rapid evolution in what people have come to expect from wireless connectivity. In 2015, analysis of the use of downstream bandwidth in the U.S. showed that a single application, Netflix, consumed more than 35 percent of U.S. bandwidth in peak hours, streaming movies and videos. When all forms of video and audio streaming were combined, these services accounted for more than 70 percent of bandwidth.

By 2015, almost 40 percent of global cellular connections were supported by 3G or better, and this figure was expected to grow to 62 percent by 2016, connecting more than 6 billion devices.[4] In 2016, GM announced that its entire range of cars would advance to the next stage and be equipped with 4G LTE and several rival automakers were not far behind. Automakers used to depend on horsepower advantage and faster acceleration to 60 mph for bragging rights. Now they tout faster data transmission speeds to promote their products over those of their rivals. According to a study by McKinsey, almost 20 percent of new car buyers surveyed expected they would alter their choice of car based on connectivity performance.[5]

With the inevitable growth in demand for more and faster data, most automakers expect a wave of improvements will accompany the rollout of 5G communications. According to Christoph Grote, senior vice president for electronics at BMW, "In a world supported by the Internet of Things, 5G communications, with its more centralized infrastructure is necessary to maintain connections in a robust manner. This is critical for functions dependent on dynamic hazard alerts to cars."[6] This view is echoed by Dirk Hoheisel, a board member at supplier Bosch: "With 5G infrastructure, we anticipate stable and adequate communication to support anticipated vehicle-to-vehicle and related communications with a car."[7]

That advance too will offer a temporary solution until the frontiers of technology push further.

Connectivity architecture in the vehicle

Even as the communication bandwidth and speed continue to increase, automakers have found it challenging to keep pace. According to Venkatesh Prasad at Ford, "People have come to expect omnipresent Wi-Fi connectivity in their daily lives and hence the car is no exception. They expect *built-in*, *brought-in* and *beamed-in* services across a spectrum of functions. Hence the automobile has to be configured as an information services platform, delivering communications and computing as services."[8]

The development of cars and connectivity has had to deal with these three very different platforms of technology. With regard to built-in connectivity, all modern cars employ a comprehensive array of equipment and functions for driving, safety, and comfort. These functions have seen considerable electrification, and it is not uncommon for a modern premium automobile to have more than a hundred electronic control units on-board, each with its own operating software linked to the vehicle's main controller. The in-car screen can be used to control air conditioning, view the image from the rear-view camera, or display diagnostics from the car.

At the next level are "nomadic" gadgets and information that are brought in by users. A cell phone in a car brings along the user's portfolio of vital information, which may include contact lists, calendar and meeting schedules, music playlists, and preferred navigation destinations. Paired to the car's internal network by Bluetooth technology, they complement the car's connectivity and functionality.

A third layer of functions that will also have to be managed relates to data delivered or beamed in through the connectivity channels. These include satellite radio, telematics functions, roadside emergency communication, and perhaps even concierge services.

These three layers operate with widely differing generational refresh cycles. Many smartphone users expect a superior level of performance delivered through a combination of chipset technology and operating system upgrades every year. For example, the Android operating system has been upgraded at least once annually, and similarly for the chipsets from suppliers such as Qualcomm. Yet traditionally, a car's built-in hardware does

Built-in functions

Brought-in functions

Beamed-in functions

Figure 7.2 Cars must accommodate a range of devices and services, that may communicate using a range of protocols, and be compatible with a range of standards.
Sources: Delphi, Apple, Spotify.

not change so rapidly, if at all, over the useful lifetime of the vehicle. Prasad points to "the need to coordinate between developments that occur at three different clock speeds. We have one clock speed for the *car platform*, one for *electronics hardware* and one for *software*." Like a multiplug adapter, a specification platform has been used as a standard to aggregate bundles of services as and when needed by infrastructure in an attempt to reconcile this clock speed difference.[9] This provides a practical if not ideal way to keep three different kinds of platforms synchronized.

Service reliability and duty cycles are also very different in the auto industry than in the consumer electronics industry. An interesting example, highlighted by Prasad, refers to the humble USB connector—a ubiquitous piece of hardware familiar to every user of tablets and laptops. Applications in consumer electronics typically require that the connector survive at least 2,000 inserts. Above this level of use, there is likely to be poor contact and some degradation in reliability. Most laptops or devices do not reach this level of use in their lifetime. Yet automotive applications for similar hardware typically require more than 10,000 duty cycles, reflecting the longer active life expected of a car. A USB connector built to this duty cycle would require much more robust specification. It was estimated that this simple change in specification could cause a piece of hardware, normally costing about a third of a dollar for consumer electronics, to soar to several dollars when designed to meet these tougher specs. In the actual case, Ford resorted to a simple design change whereby the connecter could be replaced in service, much as a wiper blade is replaced. With this design change, the cheaper commercial grade connector could be used.

This is not always the case across a wider range of critical systems. Automakers and mobility service providers will continue to confront this challenge of managing customer expectations across the spectrum of built-in, brought-in, and beamed-in technologies. In the following section, we will review how the industry is going about managing this complex task.

Adopting standards for automotive electronics and software

Modern cars use a substantial amount of electronics and software to take care of a growing range of functions. Most automakers also offer a wide variety of products. To ensure that all of them benefit from advances in technology demands a great deal of coordination. Unless their operating hardware and software enjoy a high degree of standard or common elements, this task becomes unmanageable. Software increasingly determines the performance of the vehicle and hence the experience of users. Automakers are also eager to ensure that their signature algorithms are deployed across multiple vehicles to convey a uniform experience. It is useful to consider a parallel example more familiar to smartphone users. Google, Apple, and Amazon each invest in unique ways to respond to human voice inputs. These are replicated across their multiple proprietary platforms. Similarly, having invested in a set of capabilities for one model, automakers wish to deploy the same set across several models, spread over several development cycles.

AUTOSAR (Automotive Open System Architecture) was started as a consortium of multiple automakers and several prominent suppliers in 2003. AUTOSAR is basically a set of requirements and standards that automakers and suppliers have to adhere to. It stratifies the software into three layers. The lowermost layer deals with instruction to the hardware, such as the various chipsets. The middle layer controls the various processors according to instructions from multiple applications. The top application layer embodies the desired performance algorithms. As a result, AUTOSAR allows multiple pieces of hardware to perform exactly as the automaker's application engineers intend them to perform, even if the hardware is procured from various sources.

For an analogy, we can think of the Android operating system. A host of manufacturers (for example, Samsung, htc, and Motorola) across various platforms (such as Whatsapp, Facebook, and Skype) are able to interoperate as long as they conform to the standards and basic software protocols prescribed by Android. As a result, there has been a proliferation of smart-phones, tablets, PCs, and even household appliances that can easily interoperate with one another and can use a standard set of hardware parts.

AUTOSAR has provided the auto industry with a much-needed standard platform. This platform is expected to unleash faster innovation and rollout of products, features, and services across automakers and suppliers. When Android was adopted as a standard platform across multiple smartphone and tablet manufacturers, it opened the floodgates to new features, functions, and apps. Entry barriers were dramatically lowered, and many new manufacturers were able to enter the fray and offer competitive wares using that platform. There is every reason to believe that AUTOSAR may serve a similar disruptive role for the auto industry.

The induction of a new supply chain

The annual Consumer Electronics Show is traditionally held in January in glitzy Las Vegas as industries around the world resume work after the holiday hiatus. The show tries its best to get the new year off to a start with a bang. Enthusiastic entrepreneurs, startups, and tech giants jostle to trumpet new product launches and jaw-dropping new technology demonstrators. Over the years, everything from Fitbit to curved-screen TVs, virtual reality headsets to personal robots, were positioned in the spotlight, to the awe of the faithful band of tech geeks and venture fund analysts who make the pilgrimage each year. Not all the hyped innovations make a successful transition to market. Yet many do, and the exposure they receive at the beginning of the year sends them off with a brisk tailwind.

Since 2010, automakers and auto suppliers have been joining the pilgrimage in ever greater numbers. The Consumer Electronics Show has now seen a parade of auto CEOs as keynote speakers, including Dieter Zetsche of Daimler, Carlos Ghosn of Renault-Nissan, Mark Fields of Ford, GM's Mary Barra, and Herbert Diess of Volkswagen. Indeed, according to Jeff Owens, the chief technology officer at supplier Delphi, "It's really become an auto-show!"[10]

Automakers and their traditional suppliers are hopeful that the sparks of innovation in consumer electronics may just be what their auto customers want to see in their cars. Customers increasingly expect their cars to provide a flexible environment in which built-in devices and systems not only coexist but also interoperate with those that are brought-in and beamed-in. The resulting domain of overlap of automotive content and consumer electronics for both hardware and software is highly coveted for its future potential,

Figure 7.3 Even as electronics are invading cars, the auto industry is invading the annual Consumer Electronics Show. The convergence of these two streams is expected to accelerate the pace of innovation for motorists.
Source: (CC BY 2.0) Chris.

and is beginning to see a rush of suppliers in consumer electronics hoping to tap into the opportunity. Google with Android Auto and Apple with Car-Play have indicated their eagerness to play a strong role in managing software interfaces, standards, and content, hoping to leverage the wealth of customer data and apps they already host outside the car. For hardware too, the numbers of suppliers crossing the boundary from consumer electronics to autos is increasing. In 2015, Hyundai announced its intention to retire the CD player from most of its new cars. It was to be replaced by an infotainment system called Display Audio that was essentially constructed on the platforms of CarPlay and Android Auto. Apart from aligning with users' existing devices, this move is expected to save an automaker like Hyundai both cost and space.

The increased socializing between these two distinct communities has benefited consumers. Lateral transfers of technologies have been accelerated and progress in areas such as the user interface including voice commands and seamless interoperability with a user's own personal devices suggests how the intersection of these two domains of engineering can benefit mobility users.

For automakers, the newly evolving supplier landscape offers many advantages. To start with, suppliers of consumer electronics bring with them the ability to deal with faster product cycles and accelerated obsolescence. Their speed of development in taking an idea to market will enable the auto industry address a long-held gripe by customers. Suppliers' investment planning typically tends to be more flexible. Some consumer products may capture critical acclaim in the market within the first few weeks, in which case production capacity needs to be rapidly increased. For others, a poor launch may result in withdrawal from the market in less than six months. Automakers would welcome such flexibility from their suppliers. They also bring with them a typically lower cost structure. Designed for a useful life of less than two to three years, many consumer products are also built to less rigorous standards and are inherently less expensive, as we saw with the example of the USB connector. For some replaceable automotive subsystems, this approach is acceptable and hence eagerly sought by automakers. Finally, the consumer electronics industry is not intimidated by the scale typically demanded in the auto industry. Annual volumes of 3 to 5 million units are well within the scope of this industry.

At the same time, Jeff Owens cautions against writing off the traditional auto supply chain. As he points out, "Delphi ships out more computers each day than even a company like Dell, along with about 20 billion lines of software code. We are not strangers to the world of computers and software."[11] Traditional suppliers have evolved through decades of dealing with automakers and auto customers. They understand both stated and unstated product requirements from this experience. Years of working in the domain have taught them the importance of design validation and quality assurance, something that could otherwise lead to expensive product liability issues and recalls. Their products may appear overengineered, but they are built so for a purpose.

Automakers are convinced that they will benefit from using both communities to accelerate the flow of innovation to their customers. In the process, how automakers and suppliers work with one another may move into new, unconventional arrangements. When Ford developed its Sync in-car communications and entertainment system, it drew on products from Continental (an auto supplier), Microsoft (a software giant), and Flextronics (a supplier in consumer electronics). This arrangement is very different from the traditional one in which an automaker contracts a tier one supplier, who assigns subtasks to a tier two supplier. Working with these newer structures and relationships will cause automakers to redefine what each party is to do and at the same time redefine the manner in which requirements for the final product are stated.

A course with many challenges

Apart from the fact that communication in vehicles has to embrace three very different clock speeds, many other challenges need to be managed.

Big data is getting very big

All of this connectivity means there will be a large quantum of data flowing into and out of cars. To take the smartphone evolution as a reference, in 2016 it was estimated that each smartphone on average would be generating 2.6 gigabytes of two-way data flow each month—a figure that represented a greater than tenfold increase over just a five-year period.[12] In the U.S., mobile data consumption tripled from about 3.2 trillion megabytes in 2013 to 9.6 trillion megabytes in just two short years.[13] And much of the data growth will happen in mobile applications, using cellular connectivity, which is expected to climb from 6 percent of global Internet traffic in 2015 to 16 percent by 2020. As the world embraces the Internet of Things, the volume of data being communicated is expected to grow several fold.[14] Cisco Systems expects that more than 50 billion entities will be communicating in a world powered by the Internet of Things by 2020. Half of that number would have been added between 2017 and 2020. That works out to an average of almost seven devices per person.

In the world of cars, BMW alone could boast of having a million connected cars on the road by 2013; it estimates that figure will increase to more than 10 million by 2018. The resulting connectivity would require BMW to handle more than 100 million data requests each day. To do so the company would need system capacity to manage one terabyte of data per day. And that includes only vehicle information related to the car. When the data for other activities such as navigation, music, and podcasts are included, the amount of data produced by and within each vehicle would pose a formidable task for information management.

In many ways, Formula-1, a pinnacle of motorsport, is both a sport and a technology laboratory. The cars employ very advanced technologies, typically unhindered by cost constraints. Contemporary Formula-1 cars have sophisticated hybrid engines and electronics installed to monitor and control a vast number of performance parameters. At trackside, engineers pore over banks of computers that spit out, in real time, reams of data based on every corner and every bump the race car experiences on the track. For some it remains the ultimate computer game—one that also involves a driver who places his life at risk. In 2014, it was estimated that the twelve teams participating in a typical race weekend generated and transmitted more than 243 terabytes of data over a three-day weekend. That volume of 243 terabytes in a weekend compares with the 235 terabytes of data representing the entire repository of data at the time in the U.S. Library of Congress.[15]

This phase of innovation will drive some automakers to resemble data giants like Google and Amazon, with data centers and private data clouds to service demands from their customers. Yet to be faced by the industry are the anticipated "data traffic jams" that may arise as a large number of users and vehicles target specific cell sites during peak use.

Boosting data security

As cars have become more connected electronically to the external world, they have also become more vulnerable to data theft, data corruption, infection with viruses, and malicious hacking.

In the summer of 2015, as a publicity stunt, a team of hackers took remote control of a targeted Jeep vehicle while it was being driven by a journalist along a highway in St. Louis in the U.S.[16] Working from their home computers, the team managed to activate various functions, including washers and wipers in the car, culminating in shutting down the car. This "friendly" attack, undertaken with the cooperation of the journalist driver, was intended to send a message to automakers. While this team cooperated with the automaker in generating a patch to plug the loophole immediately thereafter, others may not be so cooperative.

The proliferation of software, interfaces, and connections places modern cars at high risk. In response, individual automakers, their suppliers, and industry associations have encouraged controlled hackathons and have invited hackers to test their prototype systems and security. Learning from the experience of banks and defense establishments, automakers will need to allocate significant resources to safeguard their vehicles and customers. In 2016, Volkswagen announced it was teaming up with a former head of Israel's internal security agency Shin Bet to create a joint venture, Cymotive Technologies, to develop cyber security systems for connected and autonomous cars, leveraging Shin Bet's considerable experience in cyber intelligence.

With many safety-critical systems now installed in autos, malfunctions can result in serious accidents and fatalities. As a result, the validation and certification of technologies used in a car need to be subjected to strict review. Certification, both internally by companies and externally by regulators such as the National Highway Traffic Safety Administration (NHTSA) in the U.S. and its counterparts in other countries, needs to scale up to match the fast-growing system complexity. In 2016, the NHTSA announced a high-level set of guidelines addressing highly automated and connected vehicles. Prominently, it has identified steps the industry needs to take to safeguard data security, system integrity, and access controls.[17]

Who owns the data, and how may the data be used?

The view that in this digitized world, "data is the new oil," has found wide currency.[18] Giants like Google and Amazon are building exceptional value for their enterprises through the smart use of data from a large community of users. When GM launched the OnStar telematics services in 1996, the company was strongly motivated by the opportunity to capture the exclusive attention of drivers and occupants while they were in the vehicle. The value of data and knowledge that could be generated through that exclusive interaction was expected to be very high. GM had anticipated providing a bouquet of services to these customers, who are engaged with their vehicle in one form or another for an average of fifty-five minutes a day.

Understandably, automakers have faced competition from other non-auto rivals who have eyed this valuable relationship with customers with equal interest. The evolution of mobile devices brought into the vehicle, with eyeball capture by numerous other corporate players, has negated the exclusivity that automakers such as GM sought. This situation has given rise to competition between multiple industry sectors, all of which claim some form of affinity with car drivers and occupants.

Google's mastery in adding layer on layer of data to render it an invaluable partner across many aspects of daily life has not been lost on the auto industry. Despite consumer inclinations to prefer a favorite mobile operating system, many automakers have been wary of embracing applications such as Apple's CarPlay and Android Auto. If these systems control the user interface, they will have the inside track to revenues from that relationship with customers. In 2016, the German premium auto manufacturers Audi, BMW, and Daimler pooled their resources to acquire the mapping division of Nokia for more than €3 billion.[19] The acquisition was not motivated merely by gaining access to maps. Rather, the auto companies sought to protect a future value stream that would come from retailing, infrastructure management, smart-city operations, and, of course, mobility. They also recognized that future connected cars, autonomous driving capability, and shared-mobility businesses will all be very dependent on the rich data layers built on top of map data. They were eager to ensure that control and ownership of these critical mobility developments would remain in their hands.

But even in the auto industry, there are contrary viewpoints on the matter. Numerous automakers have concluded they cannot fight platforms that are already well established in the smartphones of their customers. Over the years, GM and OnStar have switched to this path. According to Phil Abram at OnStar, "It's really hard for us to differentiate on any of those (functions commonly found in smartphones). So if I'm not going to differentiate, I can create a better experience for the customer and then invest in areas where we can do things that can't be done with the phone."[20]

In public statements, senior auto executives politely talk about the modern era in which one is obliged to both compete and cooperate with rivals. In private, they fear they will have a battle on their hands to retain affinity with "their" customers.

But even as this switch to proprietary in-car connectivity is progressing rapidly, there is growing concern on the part of individuals and society as to who owns the data generated from their activities and how such data may be used. Some of the concern has resulted from negative experiences. In the early applications of automotive telematics, service providers collected location data as well as vehicle diagnostic information, which they shared with their partners. As the issue of data privacy gained wider awareness, automakers have clarified that they will sanitize the data and make the user and the vehicle anonymous.[21] We are treading warily in a world in which the proliferation of personal data demands tight safeguards to protect privacy. At the same time, the wider use of such data and its analytics can unleash exceptional utility for the individual and commercial value for the sellers of products and services.

As new systems and protocols are being planned for vehicle-to-vehicle and vehicle-to-infrastructure communication, ground rules are emerging. A user may not be identified or tracked along his or her journey without specific authorization. In the U.S., both domestic and import automakers have compiled a list of privacy principles that serve as guidelines for the industry. These principles are in turn based on landmark privacy frameworks.[22] NHTSA has also codified rules on transparency and what may be offered to customers. It prescribes what data may be gathered and how it may be used, limiting data use to context and mandating compliance with deidentification standards. Similarly, in Europe, Article 8 of the EU's Charter of Fundamental Rights safeguards one's rights to personal data protection. Anticipating much wider use and collection of data in a world of connected cars and things, the EU has rolled out data protection reforms with both regulations and directives to ensure compliance. These include the "right to be forgotten" and provisions for stronger enforcement by member states.

Looking ahead: Cars communicating with cars and with infrastructure

The philosophy underlying our thesis is that the focus must shift from individual cars to mobility as a system. Connectivity is a critical enabler to network, configure, and improve the larger system, including such elements as traffic flows, fleet management, road safety, and environment protection.

Automakers have started considering faster and more reliable data links between cars and the environment to be integral to their operation. We have noted the role that such communication between cars and road infrastructure can play to improving safety. This domain of vehicle-to-vehicle and vehicle-to-infrastructure communication is one more critical pillar of future mobility. Communications of this sort require a combination of latency and reliability that cannot be left to current cellular networks. Anyone who has experienced dropped calls or slow connections will appreciate that such cellular channels cannot serve critical communication functions designed to keep cars from crashing into one another. To ensure dynamic and error-free data links for such functions, U.S. authorities have allocated use of the dedicated short-range communications (5.9 GHz) frequency band within the unlicensed Wi-Fi spectrum.

Improved latency and reliability of such communication open the door to many new possibilities to enhance safety and productivity. A city planner watching a congested highway full of cars separated by eight car lengths sees a lot of wasted space. Planners have been looking for ways to increase the throughput of city highways safely without expensive additional investment in new infrastructure. Shortening the separation to, say, four car lengths would almost double the capacity of that highway. Yet this could be dangerous since drivers are limited by human reaction time. With vehicle-to-vehicle communication, semi-autonomous cars on highways could be electronically tethered in chains or platoons, allowing for a much shorter intervehicle distance. As the political and economic costs of building new

Figure 7.4 Vehicles and infrastructure communicating with each other will be a necessity in future mobility.
Source: U.S. NHTSA, U.S. Department of Transportation.

Figure 7.5 The era of cars communicating with other cars and with road and city infrastructure is expected to deliver a new level of functionality, safety, and efficiency.
Source: © Continental AG.

highways continue to skyrocket, intelligent solutions like this can free up more capacity for existing infrastructure. A few decades ago, air traffic controllers were obliged to do the same thing—reduce separation between aircraft so that the productivity of existing airports and runways could be improved without the need to go through painful approval procedures and making a costly investment to build additional runways.

A second benefit could be fuel efficiency. Cars communicating with traffic signals can move smoothly through busy intersections and reduce the time spent and fuel wasted on idling. Every bicycle race demonstrates the principle behind platoons. Riders try to stay in the wake of the lead rider, so that the trailing rider experiences less wind resistance. So too, in tests on U.S. interstates in the state of Utah, with platoons of closely following trucks, the fuel efficiency of the trailing trucks improved by 4 to 10 percent.[23] When this method is tried on a larger scale, even when the platoons involve no more than four or five trucks, the energy savings and carbon emission reduction over a full year can be substantial.

A third benefit that can be derived from the same connectivity technologies, particularly in a military context, is fewer drivers needed overall for a convoy of trucks. One driver might be used in the lead vehicle while the rest of the vehicles in the platoon follow the leader, in synchronized mode. In military applications, this change could limit the number of servicemen exposed to dangerous operations. Many believe that the use of semi-autonomous technologies will first see deployment in truck platoons for both commercial and military applications. The implication for cars is faster development of the core technology for the large car-using population.

In an effort to evaluate critical issues that stand in the way of deployment, in 2012, under a pilot evaluation program launched by the U.S. Department of Transportation, 2,800 vehicles were tested in a limited area around Ann Arbor, Michigan.[24] As a part of the experiment, 73 miles of roadway were fitted with twenty-nine roadside equipment installations. These vehicles employed a combination of vehicle-to-vehicle and vehicle-to-infrastructure connectivity to monitor functional requirements and system performance. This large-scale effort, which also involved many U.S. and import automakers, as well as infrastructure electronics, has advanced understanding as to how such communication may function in real-world conditions in all seasons.

In 2016, the European Union launched the Truck Platooning Challenge. Six major commercial vehicle manufacturers, automakers, and their suppliers are engaged in research on such topics as the security of data communications, system integrity, and system robustness under varied environmental and traffic conditions.

As cars acquire additional capabilities, including direct communication with other cars and road infrastructure, even greater benefits to safety are anticipated. According to the U.S. Department of Transportation, such communication has the potential to help avoid 80 percent of accidents involving impaired drivers.

In closing

The manner in which global society has taken to smartphone connectivity hints at the value it places on this technology. Connected vehicles have a lot to offer to car users: they enhance productivity, safety, and overall user experience. They help city and traffic systems operate more efficiently and can help lower carbon emissions. For these reasons, connectivity is expected to be one of the game-changing technologies in the world of cars and mobility.

According to Phil Gott of IHS, "Within 10 years it is conceivable that every new car will have some form of vehicle-to-vehicle or vehicle-to-infrastructure connectivity."[25] Because of the high cost of these systems, premium and luxury car makers have been the first to deploy the technology. Based on an analysis of life-cycle revenue related to car ownership, it was estimated that in 2015, an average premium car owner spent about 6 percent on maintenance and 4 percent on connectivity services over the life-cycle of use.[26] By 2020, the study predicts, revenues from connectivity services will exceed those from maintenance. According to a study by KPMG, by 2020, more than 20 percent of cars in the UK fleet will qualify as "connected" cars.

8   Innovations for Intelligent Cars and Autonomy

Intelligence is the ability to adapt to change.

—*Stephen Hawking, Oxford University graduation speech, 1962*

Gartner's Hype Cycle of Emerging Technologies is a well-accepted chart that chronicles the lifecycle of modern innovations such as virtual reality, Internet of Things, and quantum computing, tracing their maturation through stages from idea to hype to practical use.[1] In August 2015, autonomous cars landed at the top of this list. Going by typical patterns of innovation, what usually follows this phase of *peaking of inflated expectations* is the *trough of disillusionment* before the entrepreneur progresses to the *slope of enlightenment* on the road to the *plateau of productivity*. To fans of self-driving cars eagerly awaiting their launch in the market, this outlook can be a bucket of cold water. To wizened sages of technology, it can be irrefutable proof of progress. Widespread adoption of new technologies is seldom a linear process. There are twists and turns along the way. In the process, whether product or service, bugs are eliminated, quality is honed and finally rendered fit for use.

Human fascination with autonomous mobility can be traced as far back as ancient mythology. Across cultures, Aladdin, King Solomon, and Prince Rama have all been mystically transported across lands in autonomous modes. In the fifteenth century, Leonardo da Vinci sketched proposals for a self-propelled cart driven by powerful wind-up springs. During the glory years of motoring, in the 1950s, futurists imagined families engaged in board games even as the car ferried them safely along highways. The persistence of this vision of driverless vehicles lends a certain inevitability to the outcome. It seems more a matter of when and not if.

This chapter relates the story of how the building blocks were systematically assembled to achieve this outcome followed by an assessment of how this technology and its uses will serve future mobility.

Figure 8.1 Innovations typically traverse a roller-coaster ride between ideation and commercial application.
Source: Gartner.

Growth of electronics

The road to intelligence in cars and subsequently to autonomous driving was paved by the evolution of electronics in cars over the past half century. Electronics first entered cars to take care of entertainment functions typically within early transistor radios and music systems. They were more widely harnessed from the 1960s as regulations demanded cleaner and more efficient engines and improved vehicle safety. From those early systems, capabilities and complexity grew. Along with the electronics hardware came software to manage the controllers. As functions multiplied and complex interactions had to be coordinated, the amount of hardware and software in a car grew rapidly.

The increased performance required from on-board computers and controllers resulted in growth in the number and sophistication of electronics, such as moving from about a dozen 8-bit processors in the 1980s to over 100 64-bit processors by 2010. Electronics, which constituted about 10 percent of a car's value in 1980, rose to more than 30 percent in 2010. Most experts believe that the curve is steepening again with the advent of vehicle communication, connectivity, and some form of partial autonomy. These changes have caused the complexity of engineering and development to increase. Michael Ruf of Continental believes that "the value of electronics and software in cars will easily breach the threshold of 50 percent, very likely before 2030."[2] In the process, global auto electronics will grow from about $160 billion in 2010 to about $240 billion by 2020.[3]

Intelligent cars

The evolution of intelligent systems in cars has taken a course similar to that of automotive electronics. While innovators have been dreaming of that ultimate goal, the driverless car, they have also been making progress the old-fashioned way, step by step. The approach has involved automating specific tasks that relieve drivers of some workload or provide them some elements of delight. At each step along the way, sensors, system intelligence, and intervention are getting more capable. Broadly these steps have involved:

a. *Automation of tasks that many drivers considered to be chores.* The automatic transmission was an early innovation that spared drivers of the tedium, effort and dexterity of managing a manual clutch. There are several other more recent examples. Traditionally, student drivers taking their driving tests detested the requirement to parallel park on a city street. This maneuver required good judgment and precision, and most drivers found the task difficult. Thus the maneuver was an ideal candidate for automation, to provide drivers some relief. Many recent models offer an automated self-parking feature. Sensors, usually cameras backed by ultrasound, provide spatial inputs that are computed by the car's "brain" for an optimum trajectory, based on which the car is steered, to be safely parked. The driver's actions are limited to following on-screen instructions. A lot of the judgment that is normally required is rendered unnecessary.

b. *Improving the driving experience.* Taking advantage of the on-board computing power as well as newer and better sensors, engineers can dynamically improve the driving experience. Some systems are designed to make driving safer while others are intended to make driving more enjoyable and comfortable. Adaptive systems use intelligent algorithms to tailor responses to the local context. Adaptive cruise control, often referred to as advanced driver assistance systems, can enable the car to follow the car ahead, maintaining a safe distance. Similar capabilities have also found application in adaptive climate control and adaptive ride and handling. Many luxury cars employ adaptive acoustics to lower cabin noise, with active noise cancellation contributing to a calmer, lower-stress environment.

c. *Expanding the driver's personal performance envelope.* Many high-performance cars can overwhelm the skill of even experienced drivers. In such cars a sophisticated suite of functions and software allows the driver to extract a fuller measure of the car's performance without endangering the occupants. Vehicle dynamics control coupled with features such as torque vectoring and traction control can flatter the skills of even a novice driver on a treacherous icy road.

d. *Improving uptime and reducing maintenance cost and effort.* Significant progress is also being made in diagnostics and prognostics. Periodic service and maintenance are necessary for every car to keep it operating as intended. For most car owners, this is an intrusion on time. For fleet operators, downtime for maintenance reduces the usable time of the asset. Furthermore, a spate of recalls announced by practically every manufacturer over the past decade obliges users to respond to notices from automakers and get the problem corrected. A new scenario is beginning to unfold. Cars are expected to increasingly monitor themselves using a lot more data than was used in the past. For most cars, an oil change after 10,000 miles was typical. With newer technologies, cars are "aware" of how and where they have been used. Hence, for a gentle driver, the on-board monitoring may indicate that the car is doing well and that the oil change may be deferred to 15,000 miles. Features of this sort reduce inconvenience to customers and lower operating costs. Some cars are outfitted with electronics to monitor the manufacturer's bulletins and automatically download software and system upgrades, making some service visits unnecessary. The future car will do far better at looking after itself, saving the owner time, effort, and cost.

e. *Intelligent systems to alleviate stress.* Driver distraction poses safety issues. In contemporary cars, drivers may be trying to pay attention simultaneously to unfamiliar roads and instructions from navigation even as the car's telephone is ringing. The driver needs to be protected from distraction and the environment needs to be managed for stress. Lane-tracking assist makes small steering corrections to safely position the car in the middle of the designated lane. Many modern cars add a layer of intelligence to sense such situations to limit nonessential inputs and prevent

excessive driver workload and avoidable stress. These systems are powered by intelligent algorithms that factor in human psychology, the
nature of the inputs, and the driver's stress levels.

Each of these steps is a building block that has expanded the domain
of sensing, endowing systems with better intelligence under a wider set of
conditions and enabling intervention across a wider range of vehicle actions.

Growth of software complexity

A Cadillac of 1970 operated with about 100,000 lines of software code to
control all of its functions. By 1990, this figure had grown to about 1 million
lines of code to deal with CAFE mandates and emission and safety regulations, as well as to keep customers comfortable and entertained. By 2015,
cars were getting connected and gaining limited driver-assisting functions,
and many premium cars were operating with up to 200 million lines of code.

It is useful to compare these figures against those of other well-known
technical products. Manned space missions typically involve a level of complexity that is an order of magnitude greater than unmanned missions, since
they incorporate many additional safety and environmental systems. The
manned Apollo 8 mission of 1968 probably made do with about 10,000 lines
of code. By 1980, the Space Shuttle managed with about 500,000 lines of
code. The 1989 International Space Station was designed to operate with
about 1.5 million lines of code, or roughly about the level of software complexity of a Cadillac one could buy in 1990.

Closer to Earth, advanced aircraft have often set the benchmarks for
sophistication. Even for supersonic front-line fighter aircraft where on-board
computers play a role not only in aircraft performance but also in functions
such as radar and weapon systems, the comparisons are interesting. By 1982
the fly-by-wire F-16 from General Dynamics was designed to be aerody-
namically unstable for achieving maximum maneuverability and hence had
about 45 percent of its performance managed by its on-board computers.
These aircraft were practically not controllable without the flight computers. By 2000, the F22 Raptor from Boeing was further advanced in allowing
stealth operation and super-cruise capability, and depended on its computers to some extent for almost 80 percent of its performance. Yet even
the Raptor managed with about 2 million lines of code.[4] A Mercedes-Benz
S-Class sedan that one could buy from a local dealer in 2015 had almost
eighty times that level of software complexity. Such evolution has prompted

Stanford professor Chris Gerdes to observe that "cars, these days, are reaching biological levels of complexity."[5]

Step-by-step innovations and advances in electronics, software, and embedded intelligence have paved the way for cars that can increasingly move in to assist or even take over from the driver under a limited set of conditions.

An embodiment of state-of-the-art technology

This section examines how this accumulation of capability is expressed in a typical luxury car one can buy from a dealership in most countries—this is no longer the realm of experiments and concepts. These advances have served as stepping-stones to taking the next strides toward future mobility.

The powertrain is usually one of the most technologically rich components of a modern vehicle. Contemporary luxury cars not only have to meet very stringent fuel economy mandates, they also have to satisfy hedonistic performance enthusiasts. They can be specified with small, efficient four-cylinder hybrid powertrains that can achieve impressive fuel efficiency (more than 50 miles per gallon or 4.5 liters/100 km) or a twelve-cylinder powerhouse capable of producing over 500 kW or almost 700 horsepower. Transmissions with eight, nine, or even ten speeds constantly optimize the gear being used to achieve the best balance of performance demanded by the driver and the best fuel efficiency. Some cars also employ cylinder deactivation so that when not all the power is needed, some of the cylinders will temporarily disengage, ready to come back to life at the next instant of demand from the driver. Such measures further contribute to fuel savings.

Technologies we have discussed, such as adaptive cruise control and lane-following, are usually standard. Sensors monitor the surroundings of the car and alert drivers when other cars or objects are obscured in the driver's blind spots. Stop-start systems bring the engine to a stop when the car halts, say for a traffic light, to temporarily stop tailpipe emissions and will start again practically instantaneously when the driver presses the accelerator. Other systems scan for unexpected situations, including pedestrians stepping off curbs, and can automatically bring the car to a stop in an emergency.

The lighting systems, usually LED, dynamically adjust to road conditions and offer an optimum beam pattern depending on whether the environment is a city with intersections or a poorly marked country road. These systems also detect oncoming traffic and can smartly adjust the beam pattern to avoid blinding the oncoming driver. Night vision systems enhance the

Figure 8.2 A modern luxury car packs a lot of technology controlled by 200 million lines of software code in order to ensure its safe functioning.
Source: Daimler AG.

image of the road on a screen in the driver's field of view to improve visibility in rain or night driving conditions. Pedestrians and animals are displayed with highlighted images to caution the driver. At the same time, these cars can monitor the driver's eye movement to detect any hint of drowsiness, at which stage the car provides an alert signal.

To provide the occupants with the proverbial magic carpet ride, camera systems can scan the road ahead to detect the road profile and adjust the dampers in anticipation of bumps so that the car's occupants enjoy a fully cosseted ride. Active body control systems are capable of preparing the suspension before the car hits the bump so that the occupants hardly feel the disturbance. Climate control systems employ active purification to eliminate pollen and other irritants and can switch to recirculation mode when the car senses that it has entered a tunnel so that the occupants are isolated from any smoke from vehicles ahead. To improve vehicle dynamics and aerodynamics, these cars lower themselves on their suspension when driven at high speeds.

Aerodynamic louvers are programmed to adjust their position to allow the optimal amount of air into the cooling system. Too much will lead to unnecessary aerodynamic drag while too little could lead to the engine overheating. These cars are offered with a suite of telematics and navigation, information, and entertainment systems offering full connectivity with the mobile communication devices used by the driver. The instrument clusters in front of the driver are increasingly large screens, replacing the traditional gauges; the screens can reconfigure themselves in specific situations or allow the user to personalize the display within certain limits.

The recent crop of luxury cars also offers limited autonomous driving capability. Harnessing multiple cameras, ultrasonic sensors, and radars, these cars are designed to operate in semi-autonomous mode when crawling in city traffic. Under these conditions, the car manages the function of steering, accelerating, and braking all by itself.

All of these features, this sophistication, and this functionality explain why 200 million lines of software code are needed to ensure their safe operation. Through the incorporation of so many intelligent and adaptive driver assistance systems, such vehicles have already employed many of the building blocks that will be needed to take the next step—driverless cars.

The holy grail of autonomy

The task of driving has seemingly been codified and simplified over a hundred years so that even a sixteen-year-old can maneuver a 4,000-pound SUV in dense city traffic. In reality, the combination of senses, skills, and coordination, coupled with knowledge of traffic rules required for the task, is deceptively complex. It is a tribute to human faculties that we are able to treat driving as a trivial activity. For a machine, executing this task demands accurate sensing, powerful information processing, and very fast and precise reactions.

The U.S. Defense Advanced Research Projects Agency (DARPA) has earned tremendous respect and credibility for fostering many innovations that have become part of our daily lives. The graphical user interfaces on smartphones, the Internet, and global positioning systems are all examples of pathbreaking developments fostered by that agency.

In 2004, DARPA turned its attention to autonomous driving. The agency's approach to harnessing a wide talent pool to tackle the problem was to issue a challenge to universities and industry. The competition required participants to build an autonomous vehicle to traverse a course that was kept confidential until a couple of hours before the start. The course involved 130 miles of terrain, including desert roads, lake beds, mountain roads, and even a couple of tunnels. Vehicles had to be operated in fully autonomous mode with no human assistance once the race started. The performance was judged, and the winner was to be selected based on a combination of speed and adherence to the route defined.

The first running of this competition revealed the complexity of the task. None of the highly regarded technical teams could finish the course. The leading entry traveled a mere seven miles. The prize of $1 million for the winning team went unclaimed. Undeterred, the DARPA issued a fresh invitation for 2005, eighteen months later.

This time the competition attracted more than 195 applicants, from which twenty-three were selected. The entrants were an interesting combination of universities (including Stanford, Carnegie-Mellon, Princeton, Cornell, and Caltech) and industry members, many of which were partnered with a university team. The industry participants included Volkswagen, Caterpillar, and Oshkosh. The latter two clearly had their eye on future off-highway and military applications, which were also a motivation for such a challenge.

The event was an overwhelming success. The winning team of Stanford University and its VW Toureg beat its closest rival, the Carnegie Mellon team, backed by Caterpillar, by a small margin. Apart from the heat, dust storms, and limited visibility, a section of narrow mountain road required precision in positioning, navigating, and steering. Five vehicles finished the arduous course.

Even more impressive were the overall outcomes of the competition. By bringing together such a wide range of specialists and experts with a focus on innovation aimed at autonomous driving, the competition afforded the technical community a huge amount of learning. The media interest surrounding such a high-profile race promoted a spirit of competition among university students and industry R&D specialists. The buzz from the event ensured that these technologies would soon be built on for various applications. Sebastian Thrun, team leader of the Stanford entry, would later go on to become the head of Google's much advertised project for autonomous driving.

The natural next step was to attempt an even more difficult problem. In 2007, DARPA announced the Urban Challenge. This time, instead of navigating their way through a sparsely populated desert environment, participants would have to navigate through 60 miles of urban streets with road intersections and merging traffic, executing such tasks as overtaking other vehicles and parking. The prize money was upped to $2 million for the winner. With eleven final contestants, three teams finished the course. The winning team was from Carnegie-Mellon University with consortium partners GM, Continental, and Caterpillar.

These two challenges, staged in succession, gave a huge boost to research on autonomous driving. DARPA can claim a fair share of credit for motivating the large population of young students and technologists that took on the

Figure 8.3 The crucible for autonomous cars, the 2005 DARPA Grand Challenge. This competition proved to be pivotal in accelerating the development of autonomous driving technology. *Source:* DARPA.

challenge and the progress that was achieved in a very short time. The competitions also promoted development of critical sensors (lidar, radar, vision, and precision GPS) and algorithms for perception and trajectory planning. The pace at which this technology is being incorporated into commercial applications by companies ranging from Amazon to Google to Uber is striking. In a very short time, the U.S. established an impressive lead over other nations in autonomous vehicle technology.

Science of autonomy

Autonomous cars must perform three distinct and critical functions in replacing or augmenting human actions. They need to (1) sense the environment, (2) make decisions, and (3) take specific actions.

Semi-autonomous or autonomous cars will understandably require many more sensors than conventional ones. Based on developments since 2000 and the impetus provided by the DARPA challenges, parallel advances have occurred in several critical areas.

Just as a driver relies extensively on seeing the road ahead, autonomous systems place a high degree of dependence on vision systems. They leverage the rapidly decreasing cost of more powerful digital cameras. With multiple cameras, an adequate field of vision is captured, allowing for all-around views. Advanced vision processing chips, with faster on-board computing, help lower cost and improve system functionality. Traditional systems used stereo vision, although some developers, such as the Israel-based autonomy innovator Mobileye, have bet on lower-cost monocular cameras. Their technology essentially relies on visual inputs to make decisions for the vehicle.

Developers of the precursor to autonomous driving, the advanced driver assistance systems, relied on augmenting vision with radar. Radar output was used to estimate the distance to the object in front of the car and hence provided a better fix for the autonomy algorithm. Many experts in the field, though, remain wary because sensing with radar is vulnerable to errors. In some cases ghost images may cause the system to "see" objects that do not exist, and often, radar signals need to be disregarded because of unwanted reflections from the scenery, such as roadside railings or gantries for signage.

Google's approach has therefore been quite different. The company has eschewed the incremental approach to autonomy. In Google's view, a comprehensive redesign of system architecture would be necessary for this technology to work. Google's approach augments radar and vision with lidar. Lidar "paints" the environment around the car with laser light and from the reflected light creates a three-dimensional data map of the objects around the car. Hence the car can distinguish a curb even in poor-visibility conditions. The data so obtained are coupled with input from other sensors, such as radar and cameras, to create a composite picture of the environment. A drawback of the Google system is that it is a more sophisticated approach, employing more hardware, and hence will be more expensive. Google seems to be betting on a more challenging approach but one the company believes will deliver more robust capability in the long term. Google is also betting that Moore's law, whereby processing density doubles practically every year, will remain applicable to these devices, increasing power and lowering cost with every generation. Already companies such as Cruise Automation are using commercial grade, lower-cost lidar sensors, demonstrating that this approach has merit. At the 2016 Consumer Electronics Show, new innovators were displaying solid-state lidar that promised to lower costs even more rapidly.

User acceptance of autonomous cars is expected to be highly dependent on how "humanlike" the riding experience is. An overly cautious driving strategy will turn off potential users just as much as an overly aggressive one. Deep learning and very high speed processing are key to observing, training, and calibrating systems so that they mimic the behavior of a good human driver.

Artificial intelligence systems employ neural networks that are trained using very large data sets generated from observations from many drivers and situations. Google's ambitious approach is well suited to their deep technical resources and extensive data access. Its technology augments information from on-board sensors with machine learning created from a composite of data sources, including very detailed and dynamically updated maps.

Nvidia is another of the tech suppliers from consumer electronics that seeks to broaden application of their deep learning hardware computation platform to support autonomous driving. The trained algorithms need to be computed in super-fast processors to allow split-second judgment and decision making. Nvidia is hoping to offer its hardware as an open platform to be used by automakers and their suppliers.

Imagine the last time you drove to an unfamiliar destination. The stress levels are higher for the simple reason that many visual inputs are being processed for the very first time. Contrast this with driving your usual commute. The lower effort and reduced stress are attributable to a higher degree of familiarity of what you might expect. One way to lessen the stress of driving in a new region is again by using technology. When additional information such as a picture from Google's Street View is added to visual observations, the driver is better prepared to tackle a road before actually reaching it.

Autonomy solutions that rely on contemporary inputs such as vision, radar, or lidar alone will be handicapped. Most automakers are depending on the fact that future autonomous driving will be strongly enabled by the overlap of numerous data sets, generated from multiple experiences along any stretch of roadway. If these data are aggregated not only from the driver's trips but from the trips made by literally thousands of drivers who have traveled that same road, the underlying data set gets massively rich. Google, for example, with the company's vast access to such data globally, could have a significant advantage in systems that "know" the road well. It is for this reason that Audi, BMW, and Daimler have jointly attempted to retain proprietary ownership of the underlying data sets through their acquisition of Nokia's mapping service provider, Here. They are hoping to groom a powerful alternative to Google's data and thereby avoid commercial dependence on Google to serve their customers.

Staircase in levels of autonomy

The Society of Automotive Engineers (SAE) International has defined five levels of autonomy that are widely accepted across the industry. The levels start at 0, representing the state of conventional cars, at which the driver undertakes all actions. At the opposite end of the scale, level 5 is represented by a podcar, like the ones demonstrated by Google. These vehicles have no controls, steering wheel, or pedals, so there is no possibility for any input from a driver other than an emergency stop button. The levels in between range from cars with some semi-autonomous capabilities (levels 2 and 3) to cars that mostly drive themselves but may allow a driver to override their controls (level 4). In 2016, cars available to the public, including the Tesla Model S and the Mercedes-Benz S-Class, were classified as level 2+. These cars are capable of operating with some degree of autonomy but require constant driver supervision. They are also likely to be overwhelmed in certain road situations, and the human driver must be prepared to take over in an emergency. Drivers therefore need to be familiar with the kind of situations, such as eroded lane markings, in which the car's capabilities are likely to be diminished. Over time, system capabilities are expected to get better as vehicle-to-vehicle and vehicle-to-infrastructure communication improves and becomes more widespread.

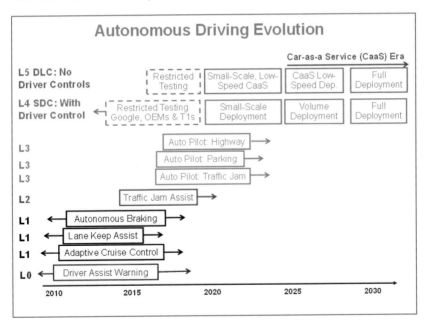

Figure 8.4 The degree of autonomous capability has been formally classified by the SAE. Parallel activities are under way across almost all the functions. Their deployment is expected to be phased in over the next decade.
Source: IHS Automotive.

Figure 8.5 Google has been betting on reaching SAE level 5 autonomy to avoid dealing with ambiguous human interfaces. While this remains a challenging goal, the company is betting that once this is mastered, its system will carry less risk.
Source: Google

Regulations and autonomy

Even as technological prowess gallops ahead, society will still have to deal with the parallel evolution of regulations and the legal framework that will govern this new mode of mobility. Some apprehension in any society is only natural when new disruptions are unleashed on public roads. On the other hand, many nations are aware that this technology can be the basis of major disruptions of mobility and recognize that an early advantage can have very long-term benefits for their industries.

The scope for regulations in the field is not limited to ensuring safe operation of a vehicle. Regulations also extend to issues such as the expected skill levels across a broad swath of drivers and issues such as liability and accountability. Already in Germany lawmakers are calling for the mandatory inclusion of "black boxes" in cars that offer some degree of autonomous driving. Regulators are obliged to walk a narrow line between protecting citizens from dangerous trials and allowing creativity and entrepreneurship to flourish in a community. Over time, increased technological capability and the removal of some of the risk should see many of these constraints dismantled.

Many countries across the world are signatories to the Vienna Convention, which requires the presence in the car of a driver "who shall at all times be in control" of the car. The UK, which is not a signatory to the Vienna Convention, is eager to position itself as an incubator for this technology. The UK's strong manufacturing competence in the motor industry was severely dented when most of its manufacturers foundered one after another. Many administrators in the UK hope that this autonomy revolution can help their economy regain some of its global relevance in the mobility industry. The issue has made for good political messaging. If the UK had thwarted development at the dawn of motoring, when the Commonwealth required a man to walk ahead of every motorcar waving a red-flag, it now hopes its green-lighting of the testing of autonomous cars without the burden of the Vienna Convention will provide it an advantage over its European industrial rivals.

Expensive autonomous driving technologies are expected to see first application in premium brands. As home to a majority of the premium manufacturers, the German industry is watching these developments very closely. In particular, it is concerned about losing this new battle to the fast-moving technology brigade from Silicon Valley which displays less aversion to risk. These cultural differences, can serve as disadvantages to some and advantages to others. Audi's CEO Rupert Stadler is blunt on this issue. "In Europe, everything is forbidden until it is allowed. In America, everything is allowed until someone says, 'It's a little bit dangerous, so let's regulate'. This is a cultural element we have to confront."[6]

Challenges in development

In May 2016 a Tesla car crashed into a tractor-trailer while being driven in the prototype autonomy mode branded Autopilot. Tragically, the driver, a technology-savvy electronics engineer, perished in the crash. The driver had apparently ignored the advisory from Tesla as to when and how Autopilot may be used. The crash reignited the debate over the readiness of the technology and the safety of cars while being driven in autonomous mode. One of the challenges facing the broader application of the technology is the complex interplay between growing machine intelligence and a human driver's vastly better ability to handle challenging and ambiguous situations.

This unfortunate accident has highlighted many issues related to technology, regulations, and manner of deployment, all of which need to be addressed urgently so that similar accidents are avoided and there can be safer adoption of disruptive technology.

The ambiguity intrinsic in the definition of semi-autonomous functions
The value of semi-autonomous systems appears to lie in their offering the driver an opportunity to relax and lower stress. Yet drivers are also expected to be alert and ready to take over when the car's systems encounter a situation they cannot manage. As such, semi-autonomous systems place unreasonable demands on a human's ability to grasp a situation quickly enough to intervene and take appropriate action. Basically, some semi-autonomous systems are still undergoing beta testing. They are likely to have been untested in many of the real-world situations they could be subjected to with even a limited population of customers. This explains the advisory issued by the respective manufacturers who offer these systems. Yet, in dealing with safety-critical technologies, it may not be sufficient just to tell customers to download the latest upgrade. The fact that these cars are on public roads and can pose a danger to the driver and other road users means the risks are unacceptably high when premature deployment is authorized or drivers are not fully sensitized to the risks involved.

Communication of system capabilities and limitations
Technologists and automakers need to be concerned about communicating system capabilities to drivers and customers. Gartner's report—"hype cycle for emerging technologies"—is labeled so for good reason. Public eagerness to accept the hype surrounding new innovations often significantly anticipates their fully validated deployment, often by many years. A system touted as "autopilot" and one described as "driver assistance" may embody similar levels of technical capability yet convey a very different set of expectations to users. In an era when many capabilities are rapidly advancing from the science fiction stage to being the season's "must-have" feature, the hyperbole and license used by advertisers need to be managed carefully. In 2016 the German Transport Ministry formally required Tesla to stop using the term "autopilot" to describe its system, to avoid any chance of misleading users.[7] It is in the industry's own best interests if these technologies are rolled out along with additional training of and familiarization for drivers. Manufacturers of light recreational aircraft are used to such processes: they make new pilots familiar with the aircraft's performance and electronics interfaces.

As the hype of autonomous driving gives way to a sober assessment of the tasks ahead, many industry leaders have been at pains to clarify what they mean when they speak about autonomous cars. Striking a balance between exuding confidence that they are abreast of the latest developments and ratcheting back society's unrealistic expectations is important.

Tardy regulations and gaps in regulatory oversight

Regulations in the rapidly advancing field of automotive electronics need to catch up faster. Unlike in aviation, where regulators stay ahead of deployment, in the automotive industry the lag is significant. Regulators are obliged to balance their role of fostering innovation while protecting customers and road users. Many functions have already been entrained, such as autonomous valet, summon features, and self-parking, and yet regulations do not comprehend the full range of their functions and safety. As more cars employ elaborate and complex software to define their functions, the burden on regulators to catch up will only increase. Apart from technical issues, governments also have to address the societal concerns voiced by many prominent scientists as they anticipate a world in which robots and intelligent machines replace human beings. Without halting technological progress, the right policies can help smooth the integration of automation and intelligent machines in people's lives.

Ambiguities in responsibility, accountability and liability

There are many who feel that over the next decade, the deployment of autonomous driving technologies will be paced by changes in the legal framework. As systems see more widespread deployment, the principles for allocation of responsibility and liability must be clearly understood. With self-driving cars, situations will arise in which accountability may be apportioned among the human driver, the manufacturer of the cars, the car-share owner, or even a third party in the accident. Accident reconstruction and analysis will require deciphering a maze of software and perhaps a complex black box. And a new domain of ethics behind decisions made while the car is in autonomous mode remains poorly studied. Programmed logic can embody both explicit and implicit judgment, which may have a bearing on the ethics of decision making. These are complex topics to manage when a loss of human life is involved.

It has taken a tragic loss of life to alert us to the challenges we face as this much anticipated technology gains maturity. Progress is vital and inevitable. A comprehensive plan to address the issues noted above, spanning technology, communication, regulations, and the legal framework, across global regions is needed. It would be foolhardy to rush into this technology without due care.

Progress with autonomous driving

Most automakers seem reconciled to an evolutionary trajectory starting with limited autonomy available for users under defined road conditions. In congested traffic with stop-and-go and low-speed conditions, risks are judged to be manageable. Similarly, on open highways with well-marked lanes, some degree of autonomy seems likely. The critical judgment that is called for is to recognize when acceptable conditions deteriorate and when the car's systems are no longer able to fully manage the situation.

For decades, automakers have operated test facilities and proving grounds to simulate all forms of road and environmental conditions. Thus far all these facilities have involved human drivers, often specially trained and skilled drivers. In June 2015 the University of Michigan's Transportation Research Center unveiled a purpose-built test track spread over 32 acres, dubbed M-City, that was designed specifically for autonomous vehicles. Imagine a Hollywood studio set, built at a cost of over $6.5 million, complete with downtown intersections, highways with on- and off-ramps, city street façades, and even a robotized pedestrian to simulate an absent-minded jaywalker. This facility will allow manufacturers to test their solutions and software in an environment free from humans or human drivers, and in that sense a safer environment. At M-City, autonomous vehicles will be driven by test and development software as the manufacturers work toward making their solutions saleable and roadworthy.

Already the ecosystem for autonomy has revealed very interesting contours as far as development is concerned. Prototype cars from such automakers as Daimler-Benz, Cadillac, BMW, and Hyundai are designed for limited context autonomy, such as when they are driven on a highway or in stop-and-go traffic on city streets. Super Cruise, the name of GM's semi-autonomous model, is intended to imply that the capability is an extension of cruise control functionality in which the car not only maintains speed and following distance but can also steer to stay in the lane and activate the brakes if the car ahead starts to slow. Delphi, Bosch, and Continental are examples of large global auto suppliers that have also made significant investments in this domain, sometimes by pairing with automakers.

Then there are specialists, such as Mobileye and Cruise Automation. These startups possess specific skills, typically in such domains as vision systems, radar and lidar sensing, sensor data fusion, and aspects of artificial intelligence and deep learning. They are able to make deep inroads into these specific domains but lack the full spectrum of vehicle integration skills and validation process knowledge that automakers possess. Most of the innovators in this space are looking for strong partnerships with automakers or even getting acquired by one. GM's acquisition of Cruise Automation in 2016 is an example of the probable outcome for many of these boutique tech innovators.

Google has been most visible among the nonauto players, and Uber has also ramped up its efforts in this domain. China's Baidu is another giant with immense resources that benefits from Chinese government policies likely to promote this technology, as deduced from the way it has invested in battery storage and solar cells. It is very probable that Google or even Baidu may choose to develop and possess the key "secret sauce" of autonomy even as both appear prepared to partner with traditional automakers to address the myriad other aspects of developing a car. Google's announcement of its intent to partner with Fiat-Chrysler and Honda in a preliminary stage of vehicle integration for autonomous cars is indicative of this trend. Each partner brings formidable competencies to the table, and no doubt the pairings will have the resources to pull off a major breakthrough. Yet when two giants dance, they can tire of each very quickly. It remains to be seen whether such partnerships will lead to enduring and game-changing business models.

Not all automakers have similar views on how to get to the end goal. For example, GM and Ford, cross-town rivals in Detroit, have chosen very different paths. GM had started up the incremental ladder from lower levels of autonomy to higher levels with Cadillac's level 2 system even as the company acquired Cruise Automation (with level 4 capability), which had demonstrated fully autonomous technology. Ford seemed to be wary of the incremental approach and had chosen to bet on a big bang and sought to target full autonomy (level 4+) directly. These two different approaches stem from very different views of risks on the road ahead and how the technology will mature. GM appeared to have realized that full-autonomy technology will take several years to master, and in the meantime it expected to address those customers who sought limited autonomous functions. Ford appeared skeptical that any system that needed to abruptly hand over control to a human driver when it was overwhelmed by a traffic or road situation would prove acceptable to drivers. Ford's head of research, Ken Washington, feared that there were "no reliable protocols" for such relinquishing of control to a human driver.[8] Toyota's Ken Laberteaux endorsed this concern by saying that developing such protocols is "fundamentally unsolvable."[9] Both sides had reasons to believe that theirs was the right approach for strategy that involves a complex medley of technological, business, and liability risks.

Figure 8.6 Automakers are accelerating their development of autonomous vehicles with carefully chosen acquisitions. GM's purchase of Cruise Automation is an example.
Source: General Motors Corporation.

Some of the challenges to technology were underscored by Jeff Owens, chief technology officer for Delphi, one of the largest global supplier groups. Delphi had one of its development prototypes driven in autonomous mode from Los Angeles to Las Vegas. The car generated three terabytes of data from the almost twenty sensors on-board, including cameras, radar and lidar. While the system could manage the drive because of the overlap of information provided by the different kind of sensors, these test drives provided a valuable learning experience to the development teams. To them, it was clear that dependence on camera-based sensors alone could be overwhelmed by a combination of visibility conditions, glare from the sun, inclement weather, and even the varying standards across states for marking lane boundaries. Yet, Jeff remains confident of the future for autonomous driving, although the challenges to be ironed out, he reckons, could take the better part of a decade.

These same technologies are equally relevant for other forms of urban transport. Similar systems with different software were applied to the Mercedes-Benz CityPilot bus, which has been tested in the Netherlands for urban transport. As the industry gains experience with this technology, migration of capability across the boundary between cars, vans, buses, and commercial vehicles will accelerate progress.

In the meantime, experiments continue, and with each passing year, more experience is amassed and more problems get solved. Most of the competing teams have been ramping up their on-road testing and validation. One measure of progress that is evident from these trials is that human intervention is being required less often as the systems gain maturity and sophistication. Google's former head of autonomous technologies, Chris Urmson, summed up an insider's perspective on this technology, saying, "I've gone from hoping this would happen, to thinking it might happen, to knowing it will happen."[10]

Business outlook for autonomy

Autonomy advocates foresee an enormous reduction in automotive fatalities. The basis of their argument is simple. The U.S. National Highway Traffic Safety Administration studies show that in 2015 there were just over 35,000 fatalities on U.S. roads, and human choice or error was tied to 94 percent of traffic accidents.[11] Adding to concerns about human drivers, that year traffic fatalities increased 8 percent over the prior year at a time when cars and safety systems were getting better.[12] Behavioral issues involving drunk drivers (involved in almost a third of fatalities) and, increasingly, driver distraction were identified as contributing to the increase in fatalities.

NHTSA's hope for a significant reduction, as autonomous driving technologies mature and get rolled out, is based on the fact that computers are not emotional, do not suffer from distraction or fatigue, cannot have their faculties dulled by alcohol or drugs, and have faster reaction times. A study by the Boston Consulting Group estimates that autonomous driving can lead to eliminating more than 30,000 fatalities annually on U.S. roads alone.[13]

Autonomous cars can have a major impact in the manner we use personal mobility. For current drivers, it can mean more productive travel. Freed of the responsibility of paying attention to the road, drivers can devote that time to other uses, such as sending emails, participating in conferences, having video chats, or watching a movie.

The critical decoupling of car from driver is the aspect that can also have very profound impact on shared mobility. As autonomous cars become part of car-sharing fleets, there may be further ramifications for housing. Autonomous shared cars mean fewer garages and parking lots, and cities will have the opportunity to convert many spaces to local parks and greenery. Global ride-sharing fleets like Uber, Lyft, and Didi Chuxing are aggressively investing in this technology. Uber has conducted pilot runs for Uber taxis to evaluate driverless operation. In the longer term they hope to trigger a revolution to catalyze a world where cars are no longer owned but are available on demand.

In terms of revenue, according to studies by the Boston Consulting Group, this industry could grow to over $40 billion by 2025, and a decade later such vehicles could account for one in every four cars sold.[14] The Boston Consulting Group also estimates the societal benefits at more than $1.3 trillion in the U.S. alone.

Such profound changes to transportation will likely give rise to a host of other outcomes, some favorable, some adverse.

Autonomous ride-sharing cars can be to cities what elevators are to skyscrapers. You step into one for the trip and step out at the destination. The journey will be devoid of any emotional attachment and will be evaluated on the metrics of speed, comfort, and cost. They promise efficient use of assets and investment. For large sections of industry related to autos, however, this revolution is expected to be a major challenge. This is especially true for automakers, which have jealously nourished their brands with elaborate communication and media expenditures and cultivated special relationships with their customers. Each car used and shared by many can dramatically lower annual vehicle demand.

The introduction of autonomous shared cars could potentially lead to some commuters switching from public transport to a personal autonomous car, attracted by the ease of use and the opportunities to improve personal productivity. This could have an adverse impact on carbon emissions.

Autonomous cars that need to be repositioned for the next use will require additional travel with zero occupancy. The movement of empty autonomous cars as they are repositioned for the next ride or shuttling to remote parking lots will increase their road presence and mileage. As office building and apartments reduce garage space, these cars may have to travel to a more distant location to be parked overnight, adding travel for zero revenue.

Box 8.1 A normal day—coming soon to your screen and your life

---

Not since the first automotive revolution have there been such stunning innovations in the industry. Autonomous vehicles will emerge to become an important part of the story.

KPMG's Gary Silberg has been passionate about the way mobility is changing. His work at KPMG has taken him into numerous customer clinics and automaker interactions to paint a credible scenario of what we might expect in the near future. The following scenes could play out every day for many commuters.

Consider this scenario of a new mobility ecosystem.

Mornings are non-negotiable. You have your cadence, your rituals. And your life is programmed accordingly.

5:49 a.m.: The sleep app on your phone senses your emergence from REM sleep and launches your wake-up soundtrack. You hit "OK," and your morning playlist fades in. Downstairs, on cue, a coffee maker starts. A connected health app checks your pulse and blood pressure. An alert blinks. You're not surprised. The end of the fiscal year is always a crunch time.

6:23 a.m.: You take a quick sip of espresso and head out to the garage. As you close the door behind you, you swipe the autostart app on your phone. Your car practically salutes: the motor boots on, the doors unlock, your apps light up the dashboard. It's all there: your email, your calendar, your call list. The seat glides back to your settings; your morning playlist pumps through the speakers.

6:28 a.m.: As you slide behind the wheel and buckle up, you see that your connected health app has already ratted you out. The dashboard displays your current vitals: 5.3 hours of sleep at less than 60 percent efficiency, blood pressure 139 over 90, resting pulse 72.

You're keen to drive; last night your operating system updated itself and you downloaded a new "travel docent" app that narrates the social and architectural history of the routes you take. But the connected health alert blinks yellow and flashes a message, "Medication alert: please take one Diruil and one multivitamin." You hit "OK," and Scarlett Johansson purrs, "Good morning, Steve. I see you haven't been sleeping so well. Why don't you let me drive?"

6:30 a.m.: As the car backs out of the driveway and heads toward your office, your calendar and to-do list appear on the dashboard screen. Two notices are flashing: "Primary care visit tomorrow at 8:00 a.m. Please complete pre-screening" and "Activate home security?" You answer yes to activate your home alarm system and set your smart grid on "energy-save," and then deal with your medical tests.

Does this sound far-fetched? On the surface, you may think so. However, the reality is that not since the first automotive revolution has there been such massive innovation and displacement of the status quo.

According to Silberg, "It's already here: the era of ubiquitous connectivity, the moment when you, your car, and your life are one. It will change your basic notions about mobility and revolutionize the way you think about and use your car. Because that car, like every other device you use, is part of an interconnected ecosystem that monitors and adapts to your schedule, your evolving priorities, your relationships, and even your health. Everything (including you) is networked, monitored. That car isn't just a mode of transportation: It's the control center for your mobile life."[15]

So will people still buy cars, even ones that drive themselves? Some will. Others won't. In some cases, the car one owns is a mobile locker for one's kids' myriad accessories and sporting goods, one's mobile office and gym locker, or a giant purse on wheels. And, especially in rural areas, the car provides the one thing most people still can't imagine living without: the freedom and flexibility to go where one wants when one wants. And there will be others who will unhitch one more needless possession when mobility truly becomes a service.

In closing

Without fear of overstatement, we believe that autonomous driving technology, when it reaches the mainstream, will change the contours of automotive sales and use, with reverberations all along the value chain and in the labor market. At scale autonomy will create the sort of disruptions seen once or twice in a century. In its fullest manifestation, this change in automobile technology could be as significant as when the earliest motorcars, then called horseless carriages, unhitched the horse for good. Autonomous driving has the potential to alter our expectations of mobility and fundamentally reshape the auto industry. The implications for technology are as large as the implications for business and indeed for how we live our lives.

9 Innovations and Variations in Traditional Mobility Modes

The best way to have a good idea is to have a lot of ideas.

—Dr. Linus Pauling[1]

Much of society, it seems, has been looking at mobility through a *bokeh* lens. Bokeh has been all the rage in the modern world of proliferating smartphone cameras. As Paul Mason of the BBC explained, "Bokeh is a Japanese term used by photographers to describe that pleasing effect where the background of a photo is defocused, often into blobs or hexagons, while the subject is razor sharp."[2] In the conventional perspective on mobility, the automobile as a dominant design has been viewed in exquisite detail while so many alternative options have been relegated to soft pastel hues in the background. Yet if one looks more closely, those alternate forms of mobility offer many compelling advantages. As technology is employed to amplify the utility of these modes, they reappear in diverse manifestations as attractive complements or alternatives to the use of personal cars.

Pedestrians and walking

Laozi, a contemporary of Confucius, is credited with the saying, "A journey of a thousand miles starts with a single step."[3] Many urban planners are rediscovering this truism. Walking may form a critical first-mile or last-mile connection to a journey to the other end of the world, whether the traveler lives in Paris, Tokyo, or New York.

A major attraction of city living is the proximity to work, family, and shopping. Thus in many cities a sizable fraction of the population walks to work or to local markets. In New York this figure is about 11 percent, in London about 26 percent. In Hong Kong it climbs to 45 percent, and in Mumbai it is 55 percent. Walking remains a simple yet important mode of travel across countries, both developed and developing. This pollution-free mode provides exercise and costs nothing. Further, cities that encourage walking also end up with cleaner and safer streets. Increasingly in such cities as London, Chicago, or Hong Kong, walking can be the quickest mode for short trips. Sadly, in many emerging economies, investment in sidewalks and pedestrian-access takes lower priority than investment in roadways and flyovers.

Walking is not only a mode of travel by itself but often an important connector for access to public transport. Urban planners have observed that when residential zones are well connected to proximate transit stations by walkways, the use of public transit increases. In many cities, planners will readily admit that all the investment in public transit and multimodal mobility will be for naught if the last-mile linkages to home or workplace are not provided for with clean, safe sidewalks.

Venues such as Hyde Park in London or Central Park in New York offer manifold benefits. To many commuters, they afford a pleasant route between home and work, while serving as a green lung in the midst of busy cities. They offer space for relaxation, recreation, and entertainment on weekends. No wonder cities as varied as Seoul in Korea and Boulder in the U.S. are constructing walking spaces that cut right across the city, allowing pedestrians to stroll from one end of the city to the other. Often, these projects use the edge of waterways or land reclaimed from disused railway lines. They can transform neglected areas into vibrant, activity-rich people spaces.

After decades of increases in use of automobiles for travel, the appeal of walking has grown in recent times. Traditionally, people walked for exercise or because walking is free transit. Many modern tools and gadgets increase the attraction of walking. Electronic wearables such as Fitbits and iWatches have made people more aware of the health benefits of movement and exercise. With the advent of mobile phones, a walking commuter can remain connected and entertained with music, videos or social interactions.

Many apps and tools have also emerged to increase the appeal of walking. Walc is a navigation app that demonstrates how technology can be incorporated into some rather mundane activities. Walc provides directions suited to the vantage of a pedestrian. Just as driving is now aided by navigation and search tools such as Waze, so too walking is becoming more efficient and attractive with similar aids. The app is designed to provide guidance through voice and can be used even when the smartphone is in a pocket, leaving the walker's hands free for holding a drink, eating, or just holding hands. Directions and cues are based on easily visible landmarks. Rather than instructions like "Turn right in 500 feet," the guidance one may

a.

b.

Figure 9.1 Many cities have taken advantage of unused urban spaces and converted them to attractive areas for exercise, recreation, and even pedestrian commuting. a. Seoul. b. Guangzhou. *Source:* ITDP and Karl Fjellstrom, New York.

hear could be "Do you see Starbucks? Then veer right." Like its peers in the world of apps, it is designed to learn the behavior and priorities of users and so enhance its own usefulness over time.

City planners have taken note of trends that draw more commuters to walking. Many new investments are directed toward mixed-use walkable neighborhoods. Further, some zoning regulations have encouraged new residential expansion along mass transit routes that are supported by walking spaces. In Berlin, for example, between 1998 and 2013 the modal share for walking increased from 25 percent to 31 percent.[4] During the same period, motorization dropped by 9 percent, and car ownership declined to almost half the national average. In 2013, approximately 27 percent of Berlin households did not own a car.

Biking and urban mobility

"Copenhagenize" has gained acceptance as a verb to denote transforming a community with a focus on bicycles for urban mobility. After experiencing significant traffic congestion and vehicular pollution in the 1990s, the city constructed more than 1,000 kilometers of bike paths within the Greater Copenhagen area. Safety was improved by imposing greater separation between cars and bikes. This infrastructure has drawn more than 45 percent of the working population into commuting to work by bicycle.[5] More than 63 percent of the population use a bike each day for some activity or other. These changes are contributing to the city's goal of carbon neutrality by 2025.

Strikingly, bicycle commuting works even through the snowy Scandinavian winters. There is an old Viking saying that keeps them motivated: "There's no such thing as bad weather, only bad clothing." In Copenhagen, when it snows, bike paths are cleared first, before the roads. As a result, three out of four Copenhagen residents continue to use their bikes in winter. In that city, the administrators estimate that the community saves 23 cents for every bike-kilometer traveled and loses 16 cents for every car-kilometer.[6]

The popularity of bikes is spreading fast in many neighboring areas of northern Europe. In the Netherlands, bicycle ownership runs at about 1.3 bikes per person. In London, where bike-share systems have been introduced only relatively recently, bike use has increased significantly, with the number of daily bike trips doubling since the turn of the twenty-first century. In Paris, where the established public transport system has been augmented by the Velib bike-sharing system, car ownership has dropped. In 2000, three

Figure 9.2 Some cities have elevated the importance of bicycles on their thoroughfares. The additional level of safety and ease of use draw more commuters away from their cars.
Source: Flickr CC0 1.0 Michael W Andersen.

out of every five Paris residents owned a car. By 2015, this figure had dropped to two out of every five Parisians. Studies in the EU have shown that more than 50 percent of urban trips covers less than 5 kilometers,[7] so that travel by bicycle is often as fast as travel by car, on a door-to-door basis, and involves less hassle and expense. As with walking, promoting bicycling in cities has required planning from the bottom up. Safe bike paths, designated bike parking spaces, the deployment of bike-sharing services, and facilitation of multimodal connectivity have all been included in the cities' master plans.

To attract more users to biking, some bikes have become high-tech gadgets. The use of advanced materials has lowered their weight and hence the required pedal effort. Many bikes sport battery and motor packs—a kind of a pedal-powered hybrid that increases the appeal of bikes to many among the elderly. And connectivity is as simple as snapping a smartphone to the handlebars.

Unfortunately, even as an increasing number of Europeans and Americans are abandoning their cars for bikes and walkways, large segments of the population in many emerging economies, including China and India, who might have used bicycles a few decades ago are quickly moving to motorized transport and leaving bicycles behind. As these governments invest in new infrastructure to support the growing use of cars, similar planning and investment for eco-friendly modes like bicycling are often absent. Since per capita automotive mobility is still relatively low in these countries, it is not too late for cities to revise their master plans to include the expansion of pedestrian and bicycling infrastructure.

Micromobility

Any visitor to Paris, London or Taipei will note the large number of motorized two-wheelers and three-wheelers that populate city center areas. No longer limited to students and young adults, motorcycles and motor scooters are the mobility tool of choice for many professionals who commute to or across the heart of a city. That these vehicles have come to enjoy the patronage of the well-heeled was underscored when no less a luminary than President Hollande of France was snapped by the paparazzi on his way to a rendezvous with his mistress aboard a scooter piloted by his security detail. His personal embarrassment had an unexpected positive—the scooter gained even more respectability.

Motorcycles and motor scooters enjoy several advantages in urban surroundings. They occupy less space than a traditional automobile, they can be parked closer to the intended destination, they navigate easily through highly congested areas and narrow streets, and they cost less and have a lower carbon footprint than cars. In Paris and Los Angeles, motorcycles and motor scooters are permitted to split lanes in clogged highways. In London they are permitted to use the relatively less congested bus lanes. Both concessions mean they often commute faster than cars.

Beyond motor scooters and motorcycles, a new breed of electric microcars is expected to straddle the gap between conventional cars and two-wheelers. Motivated by demand for very compact city vehicles that enjoy easier parking privileges as well as concessions for zero emissions, these are expected to embody the full complement of connectivity technologies making their way into conventional cars. Their compact size and limited range also moot many of the drawbacks associated with electric vehicles and the battery capacity handicap. Renault's Twizy, a two-person electric car, is one example of specific city vehicle brought by a large automaker to the market in many regions of the world.

Japan's interest in space-efficient cars has a long and successful legacy. In an effort to gauge interest in other markets, Toyota sent a few examples

a.

b.

Figure 9.3 a. The Renault Twizy. b. The Toyota i-Road. Slotting between scooters and small cars, these microcars are well suited to electrification and have a compact parking footprint. *Sources*: Renault and Toyota.

of its innovative i-Road microcar to Europe and the U.S. in 2015. The i-Road is a twin-occupant electric three-wheeler that is barely larger than a motorcycle. A fleet dubbed Cité Lib has also been deployed in the city of Grenoble, France, for longer-term evaluation. According to Jason Schulz, the project manager at Toyota responsible for this vehicle, "We were seeking an innovative mobility solution for highly dense environments, where people have to deal with congestion and parking difficulties."[8] These microcars would not only possess the full spectrum of connectivity and intelligence, they were also designed to be less harmful in case of collisions with pedestrians.

MIT's Hiriko folding two-person vehicle offers an interesting variation on space efficiency. On highways the car unfolds to offer better stability, but in cities or for parking, it folds to a compact length and takes up only one-third the space needed by a typical automobile. According to Kent Larsson, who led the development effort, a typical parking slot for conventional cars in a large urban apartment complex in a city like Boston could cost $70,000. That investment could be lowered, he said, to $10,000 if all residents drove around in Hirikos.

One idea that made a successful transition to market is the smart car. Mercedes-Benz does not often come to mind in a discussion of microsize city cars. Yet since 2000, the smallest Mercedes product, via smart, has been significantly smaller than the smallest Volkswagen. The offspring of a tryst between Swatch and Mercedes-Benz, smart attempted to offer modernity and chic in an affordable and compact city car. The partners were motivated by the same issues of fuel economy regulations, traffic congestion, parking constraints, and customers who found traditional cars increasingly inconvenient.

History often does repeat itself. The World War II years in Europe were marked by the imperative to conserve and ration the use of scarce resources. Scooters were popular in postwar Italy and Germany since they required very limited raw materials and were economical to use. Microcars also helped Europe and Japan gain mobility during those years. During the energy crisis of the mid-1970s, the British economist E. F. Schumacher's *Small Is Beautiful* successfully promoted the idea of conservation of materials and energy.[9] Yet gradually, affluence bred indulgence. Traditional mobility with a personal car wraps a 2,500 pound automobile around a person who may weigh less than a tenth of that. Viewed in those terms, it seems terribly wasteful. Reducing the weight of an urban vehicle to less than 1,000 pounds, as should be possible with microcars, would be significant progress.

Figure 9.4 Premium auto manufacturers are expanding their product portfolio to pay attention to urban commuter demands. Small city cars are valued for their ability to fit within crowded city streets with limited parking spaces.
Source: Car2Go, Daimler Mobility Services.

Historically, segment-busting solutions have not been easy to pull off. In 1985 the innovative millionaire Sir Clive Sinclair launched an electric micro-vehicle in London, the Sinclair C5, suited to carry one person through inner-city commutes. Even with a good pedigree and design, the project failed miserably, mainly because of primitive batteries, safety concerns, and a poorly managed marketing plan.[10] A decade later, BMW's C1 motor scooter was designed to appeal to converts from cars. Fitted with a windscreen, roof structure, and seat belts, the scooter offered these mobility enthusiasts a carlike experience on two wheels and the option of discarding the cumbersome helmet. It failed for being neither fish nor fowl, too heavy and insufficiently nimble compared to a motor scooter and not stable like a car. In the case of plans to develop Hiriko vehicles for initial implementation in the Basque region of Spain, a promising start with approximately $100 million in financial support from local and EU governments was derailed through poor planning, poor coordination, and possibly extreme self-dealing behaviors.[11]

But circumstances have changed since many of these misadventures. Urban densities have grown ever higher, emissions norms far stricter, and batteries and electric propulsion technologies several generations better. Cities facing the prospect of banning the use of cars in inner-city areas to protect their environment are more motivated to help incubate newer solutions. Furthermore, in many societies, the culture of conservation is coming back into fashion, and green mobility is in vogue. Microcars are likely to play a growing role in our future as well.

Such transformations need to be helped along. Many congested cities would do well to provide incentives and a suitable role for microcars because of their smaller size and lower carbon emissions, as many already do for two-wheelers. This is not a radical idea. In space-constrained Japan, the small *kei-jidosha* class of cars has enjoyed relaxed rules for over half a century compared to conventional cars. In Japan, sales of such cars account for almost 50 percent of the market, helping Japan achieve fuel economy leadership in the world.

Personal rapid transit

Adding *smart* to *small* should make mobility options even more attractive. Tracing the imagination of science fiction writers who dreamed of future travel, in which people would step into pods that would whisk them away to distant destinations, innovators have been experimenting with adding autonomous driving capability to microcars to further expand the envelope of personal travel.

Some cities have experimented with personal rapid transit systems with fixed guideways and podcars—small automated electric vehicles that run on special guides or tracks. Business commuters who shuttle between the car park and London's Heathrow terminals have been using such podcars since 2013. The operators claim that these mini-electric vehicles operate as quietly as a refrigerator and achieve significant per person carbon emission reduction—almost 50 percent lower than travel by bus and 70 percent lower than travel by car. The BBC has referred to their operation as "splendidly simple" and the experience as "delightful."[12]

Podcars like those used at Heathrow have a major limitation—they travel on dedicated tracks that are expensive to build and limited in flexibility. Ideally, one would prefer concepts that can share city roads and have greater flexibility of movement. In 2010 at the Shanghai Motor Show, GM unveiled its concept EN-V, the initials referring to electric networked vehicle. This was "a two-seat electric vehicle that was designed to alleviate concerns surrounding traffic congestion, parking availability, air quality and affordability for tomorrow's cities."[13] The Lutz Pathfinder project was a similar concept, which was partially funded by the government in the UK, to evaluate technologies related to autonomous microsize city cars. Such vehicles have very different requirements for parking. Most often they are intended for short distances, dropping off one passenger and picking up another, hence needing to stay parked for much less time. Cities have the opportunity to reduce parking spaces, which may then be converted to recreational areas, sidewalk cafés, and piazzas.

So far we have considered modes that offer a smaller footprint and lower carbon emissions to appeal to future urban communities. But the very high population density in many cities calls for modes that can be even more efficient in dealing with space and energy. At some point, the personal space we like to carve out for ourselves becomes a luxury and therefore needs to be shared. In the next sections we examine the many innovations addressing mobility for larger groups of people.

Bus and surface transit

Worldwide, 80 percent of all public transit commuters use a bus.[14] Yet contemporary debate on high-tech autos and future mobility hardly mentions buses. Let's face it, buses are not sexy. As a result, we have unwittingly failed to visualize modern renditions of intelligent and highly automated buses that can pack a lot more technology than the snazzy show cars that serve as the usual glamour toys of the auto industry. Buses badly need an image transformation. Maybe then their utility as a flexible, low-investment, urban mode will be appreciated and leveraged.

Mercedes-Benz, a large supplier of buses to cities around the world, decided to try to make buses more attractive to users. Its Future Bus, a semi-automated city bus with CityPilot technology, is capable of sensing pedestrians, synchronizing its movements with city traffic lights, and providing Wi-Fi connectivity to all its passengers. It is powered by advanced zero-emissions propulsion. Advanced buses of this sort are designed to appeal to residents because they are noiseless and emissions-free in crowded environments. The Future Bus is equipped with cashless and contactless payment modes that directly bill the accounts of passengers, who hop on and off at their convenience. With priority accorded to these buses at traffic lights, they can be faster for city travel. Powered by such technologies, the humble bus and public transit become formidable components of the urban mobility solution, greatly augmenting transport capacity, cutting down on congestion,

Figure 9.6 A modern city bus can employ a lot of the same technology that modern show cars boast—electric propulsion, zero emissions, semi-autonomous operation, and fully connected. *Source:* Daimler.

and contributing to cleaner air. Mercedes-Benz has demonstrated the use of Future Bus in Amsterdam over a 20-kilometer test loop.[15]

But it is one thing to add technology to the product. It is equally important to employ modern tools and technologies in the system they operate in.

Bogotá has been the poster city for demonstrating the effectiveness of bus rapid transit (BRT) systems. BRT systems can be thought of as low-investment metros suitable for medium-density routes where infrastructure funding is capped or route flexibility is necessary. Like a metro system, they have turnstiles that control access, and payment is made with smart cards or is contactless and is typically shared with other modes in the cities. Bus stops have platforms aligned with the bus floor, allowing faster ingress and egress of passengers and higher throughput. Dedicated lanes keep these buses flowing even on highly congested thoroughfares. This mode can be an important option for many cities where population densities are not high enough or where the city cannot afford the high capital costs of underground metros. Many cities, including Curitiba in Brazil and Ahmedabad in India, have deployed modern BRT systems to complement their portfolio of urban modes of travel. Since 1975 the population of Curitiba has doubled, yet its car traffic has declined by 30 percent.[16] For cities that have to deal with traffic congestion, these are important considerations.

The next wave of urbanization across the globe is expected to happen mainly in medium-sized cities with a population of 500,000 or less.[17] These cities will find BRT a more viable economic solution than metros. Slowly, U.S. cities are also finding merit in these solutions. BRT systems have been deployed in Boston, Los Angeles, and Cleveland, with numerous other cities assessing the options. As economic analyses adopt a more comprehensive perspective on costs and benefits, buses are being viewed with more interest.

Developers of future city master plans cannot afford to exclude an important role for buses. A host of developments and innovations can render investment in BRT systems very productive.

a. *Innovations in propulsion technology*. Across the world, buses are shifting to a range of cleaner propulsion options such as electric, hybrid electric, or biogas. They can make significant contributions to lowering carbon emissions.

b. *Innovations in pricing*. Most cities in the U.S. and Europe offer subsidized fares to promote ridership on public transport, justifying the move through demonstration of cost avoidance in other areas such as road maintenance, city pollution mitigation, and parking capacity increases. Pricing is increasingly employed to influence modal shifts.

c. *Innovations in electronics*. In parallel, many cities are also upgrading their mass transit fleets and investing in their physical and digital infrastructure. Buses and trams are being equipped with Wi-Fi to allow users to be productive or be entertained during travel. Timetables are dynamically updated, allowing online access for up-to-date information. User apps are rapidly gaining popularity, further increasing ease of use, adding flexibility, and lowering travel costs for commuters.

d. *Innovations in infrastructure*. Many cities are making their BRT corridors intelligent. These buses can communicate with traffic lights for priority and, in platooned convoys, travel faster through crowded thoroughfares. For example, data from Europe suggest that as the travel speed of buses from point to point is increased by 5 km/hour through intelligent links with traffic lights along these corridors, energy consumption can drop by a further 20 percent. An added advantage is that faster travel in cities attracts more riders.

Light rail, tramways, metros, and underground

Cities with very high population densities need to plan for higher-capacity solutions than buses. Typically, underground metros provide passenger throughput that can seldom be matched by other modes. Yet this requires very significant investment and an environment that encourages high ridership and use. While London's Tube and New York's metro are examples of early systems, and are almost a century old, newer systems such as those in Hong Kong, developed since the 1970s, offer many lessons in effective planning and operation.

The metro system in Hong Kong (MTR) may indicate the way these systems evolve. As an island with a very high population density and practically no suburbs, Hong Kong is well suited to metro transits despite the requirement for huge amounts of up-front investment. Private car ownership is maintained at low levels through a combination of fees, taxes, and parking

Figure 9.7 Modern bus rapid transit systems can offer high-capacity mobility for medium-density routes at much lower investment than underground metros.
Source: ITDP, New York.

constraints. Only six out of every 100 cars in Hong Kong are for private use compared to seventy in the U.S. It helps that over 40 percent of the population lives within half a kilometer of mass transit and over 75 percent lives within one kilometer of one.[18] The Hong Kong MTR is clean and efficient in a way that puts the tottering London and New York systems to shame. Most fares are collected through the use of contactless payment cards.

The Hong Kong system is also uniquely profitable. Across the world, in such major cities as New York, Washington, D.C., Paris, London, and Stockholm, fare-box recovery, which is defined as the ratio of fares collected to operating costs, ranges from 30 percent to about 70 percent.[19] For Hong Kong, this figure is almost 185 percent, achieved despite the relatively lower cost of travel per kilometer compared to many other cities. This profitability was achieved by planning the transit system as an integral part of the city's development. Without very high population density along corridors, metros cannot achieve the levels of ridership they need to be financially viable. Hong Kong has also realized that revenue collection must be efficient and be augmented by secondary income streams to justify the very large investment. In return the city gets an efficient, almost invisible high-capacity transit mode that has enviable economics and a very low carbon footprint.

Hong Kong's cityscape is dominated by people and their activities—not cars and parking. Other cities are taking notice and desire to replicate the benefits. India is a large country with many cities of exceptionally high population density. India's planning roadmap has earmarked twelve cities for implementation of modern metros.[20] As we gear up for more megacities around the world, each supporting more than 10 million inhabitants, more dependence on metros is inevitable and desirable.

Of course, not all cities can replicate what Hong Kong has done. Mobility has to be molded to local expectations and conditions. At a lower scale, many cities have deployed ground light rail or even aboveground monorail systems. Yet some of the same factors that support metros also apply to light rail systems, which require less investment and are sprouting in many cities. These cities are deliberately encouraging high-rise construction along these corridors. Cities such as Denver, Charlotte, and Portland in the U.S., not normally associated with congestion, are rapidly investing in mass transit, along with new housing projects located in the proximity of transit stations. These transit systems themselves can distort local development. Because of the proximity of these metro transits, rental values grow rapidly along these corridors. The high cost of land use then stimulates high-rise buildings to increase use of the land. These high-rise complexes generate increased travel demand, which is necessary to pay for the investment and the cost of operation of these metros and light-rail transits.

Light rail systems fill the gap between BRT corridors and metros. Where they are implemented effectively, many positive outcomes are visible. For example, Zurich, Switzerland, and Coventry, in the UK, are two cities of similar population (approximately 300,000). Zurich has a wealthier average population and a higher level of car ownership. Normally this would have meant a greater fraction of commuting undertaken by cars. Yet, owing to the utility and convenience of the light rail network linked to multiple alternative modes, only 29 percent of trips involve use of a personal car in Zurich, whereas in Coventry that figure is 75 percent.[21]

Across the globe, previously stagnant transit systems are adopting new technologies and reaching out to younger travelers through social media. To sustain the momentum, in 2015 the EU Commission approved a "cofunding" investment to deploy €28 billion toward improving transportation infrastructure and technology. This investment was expected to create an additional 10 million jobs while increasing the EU's GDP by an additional 1.8 percent by 2030.

Many cities in the U.S. have found the need to scale up their investments in public transit. Between 1980 and 2015, the number of commuter and hybrid rail systems in operation almost doubled, while the number of light rail and streetcar services grew fourfold. Since 1995, annual capital funding from the federal government to expand such systems increased from $3.5 billion to $7.5 billion. At the same time, the fleet for public transport, mainly buses and vans, increased by 50 percent to 178,000.

In the twentieth century, choice of mobility was often linked to the economic state of development of the city and the level of affluence of the individual. People moved up the mobility hierarchy to personal car ownership. In the current age, more and more crave the attractions of big cities. Concern for the environment has been a big leveler. Enrique Peñalosa has argued that "an advanced city is not one where even the poor use cars, but rather one where even the rich use public transport."[22] As many cities in emerging economies are witnessing a rapid increase in motorization, their leaders would do well to heed such counsel.

In closing

The course we have taken in this chapter has been deliberate. We started with simple individual modes, such as walking and biking. These nonmotorized modes are once again beneficiaries of a huge amount of interest and investment across the world. Micromobility with motor scooters and microcars also provides new opportunities for improving efficiency of motorized transport. Large-scale systems such as buses, light rail, and metros are employing technologies and systems that multiply their traditional productivity. To this we may add the variety we have seen in cars. Their future manifestations will be increasingly diverse. Combustion engines will compete with hybrids, pure-electrics, plug-ins, and perhaps even fuel-cell cars. This vast heterogeneous selection will provide customizable and personalized mobility to suit not just societies or customer segments but also individual customers.

Each of these modes is associated with unique signatures of cost, environmental impact, space required, invested infrastructure, and level of user convenience.

One strength of the CHIP mobility architecture is its encouragement of this heterogeneity of modes. The mobility options people need across the urban locations of this world will be as varied as the cultures and experiences they possess. To serve them to their satisfaction, a great variety of modes that conform to emerging societal norms will be needed. In this chapter we have seen how a variety of modes can be transformed and utilized for a wide range of future needs. Each leverages technology and innovation to render them more attractive, more efficient, and more productive.

Modern cities may utilize this spectrum of solutions as building blocks of a robust transportation system. These components can be configured to suit a specific context, though not every mode is suitable for every city. As city planners juggle many priorities, including peak demand, economics, and carbon emissions, they will have to assemble the combination that best fits their need.

The heterogeneity offered by these different modes, each with a unique attribute signature, underpins the flexibility and robustness of CHIP mobility. The objective is to ensure that as many locally appropriate solutions as possible are put in place to serve a broad cross section of commuters and travelers.

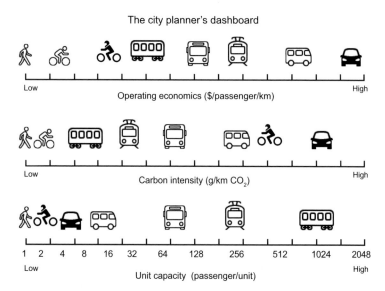

Figure 9.8 An urban planner's toolbox must contain many alternative modes and suit varied criteria. Each city, based on local conditions, demand, and affordability, has an option to configure a portfolio of solutions aligned with user expectations, environmental impact, and the city's budget.

10　Innovations in Marketplaces

Entrepreneurship is neither a science nor an art. It is a practice.

—*Peter Drucker,* Innovation and Entrepreneurship: Practice and Principles

Japanese culture retains a deep reverence for tradition even as it keeps pace with modern living. Yet many find some customs very expensive to sustain. A religious burial service, for example, can cost up to 2.3 million yen or about $25,000 and is affordable by fewer retirees these days.[1] While eager to perform the last rites for their loved ones in a traditional manner, many find it difficult and expensive to do so. Enter an innovative solution called *obosan-bin,* or "priest delivery."[2] That same worldwide Amazon website that can dispatch a box of perfumed candles can also arrange for a qualified Buddhist priest to perform the service at a fixed and affordable price. Although the practice is still controversial in conservative Japan, participating priests believe that this new medium at least allows people to remain in touch with Buddhism. An unlikely domain shows how inventive entrepreneurs, powered with modern technology, are creating innovative business opportunities.

The evolution apparent in the numbers and the power of online marketplaces across the globe is a natural outcome of long-term trends in society. Over decades, a combination of democracy and technology has empowered individuals and small businesses. Connectivity has enabled these distributed individuals and agents to link whenever necessary and to dynamically scale up their effectiveness and reach. Validation and authentication processes have permitted entrepreneurs to operate with a degree of transparency while dealing with distant entities, even those located across oceans. The propensity for contemporary society to rediscover the virtues of sharing and the growth of "crowd-based capitalism" have allowed the sharing economy to bloom.[3] Together they have shaped powerful new business opportunities. Following are some examples:

- *Products*: Amazon.com started as an online bookseller in the mid-1990s. Roughly two decades later that technology and retailing powerhouse reported 2016 revenues at over $135 billion.
- *Assets*: Airbnb experienced a meteoric rise in scale to build a network that offers more places to stay around the world than some of the largest hotel chains.
- *Services*: Launched in 2014, the UK's Just Eat serves customers with food delivered from more than 64,000 restaurants in fifteen countries. By 2016, the enterprise was already valued at over £3 billion.[4]

Whether in the realm of products, assets, or services, online platforms have unleashed a wave of business innovations that were unthinkable without the tools of modern society—the Internet and smartphones.

It is of little surprise, therefore, that the same types of platforms and a parallel wave of business innovations are reshaping mobility. A customer orientation and societal priorities have ensured that the benefits they deliver are aimed toward faster, smarter, and greener mobility.

Business innovations for mobility

Car ownership brings several benefits. First, access is predictable and full-time. Second, car ownership provides for some a statement of status. Third, a purchased car is personalized to the needs of the buyer: a person might buy an accessorized performance car, a red convertible, or a seven-seat minivan to meet a specific set of needs. But ownership has drawbacks as well. The average retail price of a car in the U.S. market in 2015 was about $33,000. Having that car sit idle for 96 percent of its life, as the average car does, suddenly seems improvident.[5] Yet this practice has been sustained over the decades for two reasons. Most often, cars have not been considered as merely a transportation utility; love affairs can explain many irrational choices. Second, as Carlos Ghosn, Chairman of the Renault-Nissan Alliance observed, "People buy the cars they do, not for their *actual* use but for their anticipated *potential* use."[6] Buying a car, however, also locked the purchase to a compromised set of criteria. Like a uniform, the car too was used for all occasions, even though a romantic drive along the coast might ideally call for a different kind of car from the one used for a Monday morning school run. In a fast-changing multi-option CHIP world, this one-size-fits-all philosophy of car ownership is out of date. Personal car ownership is an anachronism to many millennial digital natives living in a world where one can lease, rent, or share anything.

Modern economies are geared to emphasize the efficient use of time, money, space, and increasingly energy. These priorities are driven by a combination of customer priorities, competitive market forces, and regulations. Consequently, societal dynamics will look for ways to eliminate waste of any of these increasingly prized resources. An old adage maintains that a sculptor's skill is to remove all extraneous material that is not part of the final form. In our framework, the mobility that one needs should be similarly crafted, devoid of material or assets that are not needed. In this vision, we can access or synthesize the appropriate form of mobility for each journey or segments of a journey. In the future world, where virtually any item of desire can be obtained virtually instantaneously, it will be a matter of some astonishment if anyone lugs along extraneous assets, costs, or responsibility.

In other words, if the gap between actual use and potential use can be bridged by quickly configurable solutions, it is possible to operate closer to actual needs and significantly eliminate waste. In this chapter, we adopt that sculptor's perspective and attempt to eliminate such inefficiencies even while we recognize a consumer's perspective on convenience, experience, and economy.

To provide a framework for systematically exploring opportunities for improvement, we start with a few basic premises. If one car could be effectively used by two persons during different times of the day, it would see better utilization, and the allocation of fixed cost for each user would be halved. Further, if two people shared a ride to work, then both fixed cost and operating costs would be halved. If four persons are involved, the economics improves more. As each user claims a smaller fraction of the useful life of that car, and the attendant costs are allocated among a larger number of users, there is a significant improvement in economics. In the process, society would also reap benefits in the use of materials and environmental impact. The challenge is to execute this approach, while maintaining user preferences, priorities, and satisfaction.

Of course, there are many for whom car sharing is not an attractive or practical option. For some, especially those living in rural or poorly accessible suburban areas, there is a different relationship to and dependence on cars. For those with limited mobility options, the car will continue to represent a most versatile and flexible mobility tool. For others the car is not merely a utility tool but an object of emotional bonding. For this segment of users, mobility, recreation, and pride of ownership are intertwined in an inseparable package. Such customers will be prepared to pay a premium to be indulged. The CHIP mobility architecture is not inimical to these users. It accommodates the reality that these users expect more than just the quantifiable metrics of the functionality of travel such as speed, cost and carbon footprint—their travel "experience" is an important aspect of what they seek with their car and mobility. Our framework incorporates their right to exercise that freedom as long as they pay a fair share of the total cost to society for the use of space, resources and environmental impact.

That leaves a large and growing population, mostly urban, for whom the car is little more than a mobility asset. For this population, a multiplicity of mobility solutions may be attractive as long as these options meet their priorities, which may be constructed from the following factors:

a. Predictable access whenever needed;
b. Efficiency for duration of travel;
c. Affordable economics;
d. Ease of use and convenience;
e. Appropriate degree of privacy, and
f. Assured safety and reliability.

This is exactly the kind of problem entrepreneurs love to solve. Creative business models allow solutions to be configured to cater to modern customers by leveraging technology across a multitude of travel modes and options.

We start with some of the traditional solutions. According to data from IHS, a new car buyer in the U.S. holds on to the car for about 6.5 years.[7] In Germany, buyers retain a new car a little longer, for almost 8.5 years.[8] As leasing grew popular from the 1990s on, people typically held on to a car for shorter periods, about three or four years. That car would see several other owners over its life span. There are other situations when the desired period of retention is even shorter. Rental cars serve customers over very brief periods of time—typically, a few days to a few weeks, offering mobility without the need to purchase a car. Rental cars serve dozens of customers over a year.

Taxi rides last typically less than an hour. In a large city, the same taxi would serve dozens of customers per day with a significantly higher utilization than a personally owned car. The farther down the retention scale an asset is found, the more utility it has and the more people use it during its economic life. Riding a bus would cause the asset to be shared among dozens. A metro or subway ride would have an even larger population using the service at any given time.

Reducing the period of retention and sharing use of the service are two fundamental approaches to lowering cost and increasing efficiency. In the hands of entrepreneurs, they become tools for configuring solutions in innovative new ways.

Use, don't own

For someone accustomed to car ownership, the first and often the simplest step away from ownership is a lease. The bonds of ownership are severed, yet the lessee retains most other aspects of ownership, including assured round-the-clock access. Like a fledgling that takes its first flight, for many, this can be the first taste of life free of automotive asset ownership.

The capital-intensive airline industry discovered the operational benefits of leasing several decades ago. After airline deregulation in the U.S., Europe, and Asia happened in the 1990s, many new routes opened up, and many new airline companies were formed. Many airlines, especially the new ones, switched to a leasing model so that they could more easily reconfigure their fleets to suit volatile demand and serve a variety of routes and destinations. According to Boeing, between 1980 and 2012 the share of aircraft leased but not owned by airlines and charter flight operators grew from less than 2 percent to more than 38 percent. By 2020, leased aircraft are expected to account for 50 percent of global airline fleets. Going from owning to leasing shortens the period of retention of the asset and shifts an item of capital investment on the balance sheet to an operating cost on the profit and loss statement. This structure brings tax benefits while the business becomes more nimble to respond to changing dynamics. Travel sectors with declining load factors may call for smaller, narrow-body aircraft, while others may demand more business class seats. Airlines found that with leasing, they could align their fleets more easily to cope with such demand dynamics.

Most private car buyers may not care much about the implications of balance sheets and profit statements. But what can appeal to many car users is the flexibility that such arrangements can provide, especially if this flexibility is tailored to their changing needs.

In the U.S., where nominal vehicle sales hover around 16 million annually, one in every four new cars that are registered is now leased. Leasing used to be popular mainly for premium-segment vehicles. More recently, the proportions of middle- and lower-segment vehicles that are leased have also begun to grow as the practice finds wider appeal.

In Europe, the proportion of leased cars runs even higher than in the U.S. Many European customers favor leased vehicles because of tax advantages. In the EU it is common practice to provide company cars to many senior employees and executives, who use them for both business and personal travel. The UK market highlights this arrangement: more than 54 percent of new car deliveries are company cars. In Germany, 32 percent of new car deliveries fall in this category. Most of these cars are leased. The growing popularity of leasing means that more people are willing to relinquish the title of ownership to their cars if they can get their mobility needs served in other ways.

Leasing with variety

As entrepreneurship is unleashed, plain vanilla leases are morphing into a variety of solutions to serve a world that demands variety, continually sub-divides the unit of time, and seeks to carve out wasted effort or resources.

In the 1980s, when Japanese small car maker, Daihatsu, decided to expand in the European market, it chose the UK as a beachhead. The company's limited portfolio of products posed a problem. Daihatsu's managers were aware that their small cars would be suitable for city dwellers, but that the same customers could have very different needs during their annual summer vacation if they planned to take long trips with their families. Daihatsu's solution was to provide each customer with a voucher entitling the customer to two weeks of a rental car from one of the prominent rental car companies. Armed with this voucher, the customer could lease a small Daihatsu that was perfectly suited for most of the year and have hassle free access to a larger station wagon or minivan for the annual family vacation. Renting a car was always an option for this family, but the vouchers made that rental easier. Daihatsu's innovative solution was to bridge the gap between the customer's actual need and potential need with a voucher. This simple coupon allowed the customer to operate more efficiently. The waste of driving a cumbersome minivan around for the rest of the year was avoided.

Don Runkle is a technology-loving industry veteran who has had a long and successful career, first in GM and then as vice chairman at the automotive supplier Delphi. Chatting over a dinner in Detroit, he agreed that building more elaborately on the Daihatsu template was overdue. "We, in Buick, had made plans to offer a kind of membership to a Buick lease club that would allow members to vary the choice of the car they used during the year, selecting from various Buick models, within a lease agreement. So, rather than locking oneself into a responsible sedan for all seasons, imagine having use of a convertible for the summer, and a robust SUV to handle the harsh Michigan winters."[9] It was an idea that was close to launch in the 1990s but was scratched; it was probably too early for its time. A golfer would understand this concept easily. Imagine the absurdity of being asked to play an entire round of golf after being allowed to pick one good iron.

The Daihatsu example illustrates the simple linking of multiple solutions to satisfy the needs for every season of the year rather than choosing a single car for year-round use. Few automakers had the tools or the courage to go to market with the concept until recently. By 2015, groups such as BMW and Daimler had realized that for their new specialized products, such as electric vehicles, a similar solution was necessary. A buyer of a BMW i3 lease can also specify membership in BMW's car-sharing business DriveNow or even BMW's fleet leasing business, Alphabet GmbH (unrelated to Google's parent entity), to plan a longer-term range of mobility that is easily accessible with a single account and problem-free transactions.

The key to making any multisolution scenario work is to reduce the effort, inconvenience, and cost of switching from one mode to another. Sometimes this is enabled by technology like smartphones and apps, sometimes by establishing a membership account to be used with a smart card, and sometimes by supporting the physical transition from one mode to another. As we delve deeper into this analysis we will underscore the importance of reducing the cost and effort of switching as a way to increase user convenience and optimize the travel.

Shorter, more dynamic vehicle leases

Even leased cars often suffer from poor utilization and represent a lot of capital locked up. Particularly in Europe, where many companies offer cars to their employees, administering such programs is costly. Facing demands for continuous improvement in efficiency, employers may seek lower-cost solutions. Some leasing companies have begun to address the needs of such employers.

Large fleet owners, such as LeasePlan and BMW's Alphabet, offer to take over the ownership and management of the corporate fleet. For a fee, the leasing company maintains the fleets on-site at customer locations, and the cars can be easily accessed by employees with a smart card. Instead of having a dedicated vehicle for an employee, they make a car available on an as-needed basis. The same car may be assigned to multiple employees during a day, ensuring higher utilization. This solution offers cars to company fleets in a manner similar to how space rental specialist WeWork offers ready-to-use office space to startups. An individual user uses the resource temporarily and only when needed. Turnover is high. Access to the car or the workplace and exit after use are perfunctory and painless. Assets are shared, and each asset is used for a larger fraction of its life. The benefits are distributed between asset owner and user, leaving everyone better off.

The logical next step would be to do away with captive fleets and offer employees a mobility allowance and a "food court" of mobility solutions. Mobility Mixx in the Netherlands has moved forward this concept of managing the mobility needs of their customers' employees. Mobility Mixx offers member companies and their employees a smart card that entitles each employee to a range of transportation, both public and private, including the employer's own captive fleet. Employees may exercise their choice within their allocated budgets to select from the options for any given trip. Enabled by telematics, smart cards, and keyless access, the process allows users to assemble each journey from any combination of public transport, bikes, taxis, and car sharing, or to lease a car. These choices are priced according to their relative costs impact within a framework of entitlements and expense limits. Such plans accelerate the migration from company car entitlements to a mobility allowance. For employers, this leads to a significant reduction in overhead costs, as well as a means to motivate employees to use their transportation budgets efficiently. Few users of such a system will have a car parked twenty-three hours of the day as a leased car user might. They can more keenly sense their mobility budget evaporating if they do.

Car sharing and carpooling

A large majority of car users do not have the luxury of entitlement to a company car or a mobility allowance. Entrepreneurs have been innovating with new solutions to cater to this large population of users as well.

A few decades ago, investment in a family car was easier to justify. A U.S. suburban family, for example, that had a garage at home, local shopping malls with giant parking lots, and employers with generous parking policies, encountered rather few additional recurring expenses associated with car ownership. In a more urban setting, things are very different. For many city dwellers, there are several other costs associated with car ownership. Tenants usually pay additionally for access to a parking space at their apartment buildings. Parking in urban parking garages can be even more costly. In Tokyo, even the cost of registering a car in the city is very expensive. Before long, the freedom of mobility the car represented becomes overshadowed by a plethora of expenses. Understandably, residents of many large cities have turned away from car ownership, encouraged by improving public transit services. The Japanese, who live in a highly urbanized country, even have a special word coined for modern society's disaffection for cars, *kuruma banare,* which translates as "de-motorization."[10] Ideally, for many of these users, cars should be available on those few occasions when needed and disappear after use.

Continental Europe was better disposed to car sharing than the U.S. Cities and countries are more compact. Products and services cost more than in the U.S., and disposable incomes are often lower. The social fabric encourages a collective rather than an individual perspective. Hence it is not surprising that car sharing originated in Europe in the 1990s. Community groups received some startup subsidies from local governments to acquire a limited fleet of cars, which were shared among the members for short-term use for a fee. Germany and Switzerland saw these limited-scale efforts grow, and over the course of time they attracted a few corporate patrons, such as Lufthansa and Swissair.[11] Many of the airlines' crews and staff needed only temporary use of a car to serve their irregular schedules, which centered on an airport location. The focus on specific nodes, such as a town center or an airport, meant that managing the fleet and sharing were easy.

Millennials living in modern cities across multiple nations check many of the same boxes. Urban locations increase the cost of vehicle ownership and operation, even as affordability remains constrained for many of this younger population. For example, millennials who have grown up with cars in the family are not necessarily drawn to owning a car for status. According to Donna Miller, executive vice president–consulting for GfK Automotive US, "Urban millennials are seen to be much more open to car sharing than their older counterparts."[12] And with the power of online services, the domain for structuring such an operation can be much greater than the limited zones in which the European predecessors operated. They needed entrepreneurs to connect the dots. And some, like Zipcar, did.

Box 10.1 The Zipcar story

Robin Chase is an energetic entrepreneur and alumna of MIT's Sloan School of Management and a pioneer in scaling up car sharing. We met Chase at Café Andala, a unique Cambridge coffeehouse of her choice. It had taken us twenty minutes to find street parking in the crowded neighborhood of Central Square. The area is full of apartment buildings and detached houses, which are mostly occupied by students, university staff and hipster millennials who work in the hundreds of startup companies in the Boston/Cambridge metropolitan area. The café was alive with students working on their assignments amid the aroma of Turkish coffee. From this café in 1999, Chase founded Zipcar, inspired by the experience of a friend from Berlin. Her company was to provide students and local residents access to private cars for very short periods of time. "We started with just four cars," Chase explained, "and with such a low density of availability, the enterprise could have faltered." Yet with meticulous attention to detail, this small fleet expanded into a wider operation.

While the business might superficially resemble nothing more than a short-duration rental car service, the appeal lies in greater flexibility and ease of use. "We were inspired by the concept of data plans that were rapidly growing in popularity for cell phone service providers," Chase said. A major advantage over traditional rental car companies was the leverage afforded by connectivity and the ability to order a car using the rapidly grow-ing Internet. Smartphone apps would come later, but when they came, mobile phones became the perfect partner for car sharing. Apps can dispense with the bothersome paperwork and validation, as was typical at a rental car location. Contemporary tech-nological innovations were crucial enablers. A user could order a car by phone, using a smart card to lock and unlock it, and to link usage to billing on credit cards. As with a data plan shared among family members, the car could be shared among customers on an as-needed basis.

User demographics, typically indicating young adults, often drawn from college cam-puses, enabled Zipcar to connect with an attractive population likely to grow in economic clout. Asked to pinpoint what allowed Zipcar to succeed, Chase maintained that "our branding had a lot to do with it—cool, hip, smart, fun and innovative." She did not men-tion economics.

Zipcar's course resembles that of many other startups, with several rounds of funding and, sooner or later, the arrival of a new management team and CEO. By then Chase had decided to move on to other things. As Zipcar grew, special arrangements were made with manufacturers such as Mini and Honda that also saw this platform as a way to get potential future car buyers to experience their newest compact cars. When Avis finally saw the light and acquired Zipcar in 2013, it was already worth almost $500 million.[13] For Avis, this was a step to connect to a new range of customers and offer a new kind of service to augment its traditional business.

The Zipcar business model for car sharing involves breaking up a day's rental into several shorter rental periods of a few hours each, for users who have limited and specific use for a car. The smartphone app reduces hassles in transactions, allowing cars to be picked up from designated spaces on a self-serve basis. One might have expected that car rental companies such as Enterprise, Hertz, or Avis in the U.S. or Europcar in Europe would have been the first to embrace the new connectivity technologies that are now seen to disrupt this domain. However, this was not the first instance in which incum-bents were slower to react to new opportunities.

While Zipcar quickly established dominance among its peers in the U.S., in Europe the business evolved a little differently, where automakers such as

Mercedes-Benz and BMW got involved in the business. The former launched Car2Go while the latter's solution, called DriveNow, was founded in partnership with the Germany-based rental car specialist Sixt. As premium manufacturers that had been obliged to launch a range of fashionable city cars, they sought to latch on to the chic, young, and affluent city dwellers to whom they thought these services would appeal. Because of compact, denser cities and scarce parking lots, however, their model is significantly different from the U.S. model in one important respect. Unlike a Zipcar, which is rented from and returned to specific Zipcar parking spots distributed across the city, shared-use cars in the Car2Go or DriveNow program can be dropped off at any parking spot in the city. Mercedes-Benz and BMW counted on a higher fleet density and on the fact that locating and tracking cars would be enabled by GPS and smartphone apps. As a result, these "free-float" car-share services offer an even higher degree of flexibility and ease of use. Both Car2Go and DriveNow have also been busy signing up with various city administrations to buy bulk parking rights for street or city lot parking, so that their users face fewer hassles when dropping off their cars. By 2016, Car2Go had signed up more than 2 million members across the globe.

Figure 10.1 Zipcar boosted the popularity of shared vehicles by leveraging a network-connected customer, simplifying the transaction, offering local pickup spots, and allowing very short periods of use.
Source: Zipcar.

Car sharing with peers

Businesses like Zipcar, Car2Go, and DriveNow represent valuable complements to traditional rental car agency services. To other entrepreneurs, that the average car owner still saw his or her car languish unused in a parking spot for 96 percent of the day was a tantalizing problem in search of a solution. This was the opportunity Turo (originally named RelayRides) chose to address. Turo is like an Airbnb for cars. Both use a business model in which low-cost connectivity is leveraged to increase the utilization of high capital investment assets. Both, in their essence, are matchmakers in virtual space, connecting customers with asset owners.[14]

Earlier generations might have had reservations about either business model. With Airbnb, a stranger rents space in your apartment for a night. With Turo, a stranger rents your car when you are not using it. These ideas may seem uncomfortable to some. But to those "born on the Web," with social media sites as their constant companions, such sharing experiences come more naturally, especially with fellow members of a club or affinity group. Joel Stein of *Time* magazine described life in this new economy in a cover story titled "Strangers Crashed My Car, Ate My Food, and Wore My Jeans."[15]

Imagine a scenario in which a business traveler leaves her car in an airport's long-term parking lot during a three-day trip. Turo can put the car to alternative productive use, renting it out to a customer, over those three days. The car owner earns some money instead of paying for parking. The renter gets a lower-cost rental car, claimed by Turo to be about 35 percent lower than the cost of renting a car from traditional players such as Hertz or Avis.[16] To be sustainable, this business model must work for both renter and owner. Turo claims that its program allows an owner to afford a car that may otherwise not have been affordable. By 2016, Turo was operating in more than 4,500 cities.

A major challenge Turo faced was to set up the enterprise around the central concept of peer-to-peer business transactions. Average owners had to be quickly transformed into service providers. The easier part was to manage the technology platform to facilitate operations. Some owners proved to be outstanding at service while others needed a lot of help. As the business scaled up, self-governance evolved through a complex system for rating the renters and the owners.

The proliferation of such new business models, breaking traditional boundaries, does not happen without some trial and error. A typical challenge that these peer-to-peer businesses faced was managing insurance and liability. In 2012, a renter in Boston was involved in a fatal collision.[17] Unlike renting a car from a typical car rental agency, which has standard insurance coverage, renting a car in these new businesses involves a complex cast of characters, including the car owner, car renter, renting facilitator, and the third party, and assigning liability for such a collision may be difficult. Not all aspects of the business model are clearly sorted out. Yet, according to another Silicon Valley entrepreneur whose startup was also involved in peer-to-peer car rentals, it is not possible for innovative business startups of this genre to fix all issues before getting launched. Often it is a matter of moving forward and solving problems as they arise. Those advocating such innovation and entrepreneurship exhibit high risk tolerance and assert that the dynamism of the current environment will churn out solutions as fast as it does issues that need to be resolved. To them, the world is moving too fast for neatly packaged solutions. To many others, society and individuals need to be better protected from risks.

But the genie is out of the bottle, and entrepreneurs are busy hunting down other services and solutions that leverage valuable but underutilized assets. Another example of how entrepreneurs are leveraging the sharing economy and aiding cities in their quest to improve mobility is offered by Parkatmyhouse. The company brings to parking the same business model that worked for Airbnb. Private driveways and parking spots in congested cities are voluntarily converted to parking available for booking and use through an app that links the home-owner with the driver looking for parking. The home-owner gains some additional income, the driver finds a parking spot closer to a destination, and the city's parking capacity is expanded. In Sydney, Australia, Divvy Parking has concluded agreements with many large commercial property groups and offers their app users the option of parking in many vacant parking spots in large commercial office complexes.[18]

One of the key factors that make sharing work is the broad reach afforded by online platforms and digital connectivity.[19] These platforms create an efficient framework to set up public marketplaces and provide additional opportunities for efficiency of commerce. Platforms also enhance the ability of both the buyer and the seller of the service to review their counterpart's performance from engagements. This review and ratings feature allows better monitoring of performance and establishes a mechanism for reputation formation and quality assurance—on both sides of the market. Individuals with poor ratings, whether renters or owners, are weeded out, fostering self-governance of the system.

Analysis of car sharing

Does car sharing help address needs of our evolving society? There are many aspects to consider. Proponents believe that car sharing is ecologically a better solution. Fewer cars need to be built in a world in which a larger fraction of the fleet is shared, and this means less use of Earth's material resources and a gain in conservation.

Susan Shaheen of the University of California at Berkeley leads a team whose research shows that cities with better transport infrastructure are more conducive to shared-car services.[20] This outcome is enabled with a good multimodal transport infrastructure so that a large fraction of journeys may be completed without the use of a car. The existence and availability of such infrastructure encourage multicar families to reduce the number of cars in their household and encourage many single-car families to become car-free. They are reassured that when they need a car, one is easily at hand through a car-sharing service.

As car sharing expands, it has been shown to result in reduced sales of new vehicles. In Philadelphia the city administration was able to retire its captive fleet of 330 cars by offering its workers car sharing.[21] The University of California study posits that with every additional car entering shared fleets there could be elimination of sales of anywhere from nine to thirteen new cars. According to PricewaterhouseCoopers, between 2013 and 2025 the car rental business was expected to grow annually by 2 percent while the car-sharing business was expected to grow by 23 percent annually.[22] As a result, according to a study by the Boston Consulting Group, by 2021 global car-sharing fleets could impact as many as 550,000 new-car sales, leading to a potential revenue loss of $8 billion for automakers.[23] As autonomous vehicle technologies are employed on shared vehicles in the future, the impact could be even greater.

Walter Hook of the Institute for Transport Development and Policy adds, "If every additional trip had to be taken with a shared car, one is compelled to pay, for that trip, the incremental cost of that rental, which embodies not only the variable cost but also a fraction of the capital cost of the asset. In that sense, it motivates a user to combine chores to gain maximum value from that rental."[24] On the other hand, in a scenario in which the car is owned and available for use all the time (and the investment is viewed by the car owner as a sunk cost), the perceived cost of every incremental trip is limited to the incremental variable cost. In other words, one never thinks of the fixed cost element in an idling asset, and so every additional trip is judged to be relatively inexpensive. This leads to more trips being undertaken. Drivers dependent on car sharing actually drive less than drivers who own their own vehicles. This behavior helps lower carbon emissions.

There are other aspects of this business model as well. As was intended in the launch of Zipcar in the campus community of Cambridge, by dividing the customary unit of time into smaller durations, these business models provide access to cars to people who might have not had such access so easily. A student can more easily afford to rent a car for two hours than to rent it for a minimum of 24 hours, as was normal at a traditional rental car agency. Lower-income families too can have limited use of a car for specific chores. Zipcar and its rivals have certainly validated this aspect of enterprise, which has larger implications for emerging markets, where levels of vehicle ownership are relatively low.[25] Car sharing can make car use affordable to many who would not have been able to afford it otherwise.

A reciprocal benefit is that for many car owners who participate in peer-to-peer car sharing, such as through Turo or Getaround, the earnings from such rentals often are adequate to cover a good fraction of their monthly car payments. This makes car ownership affordable for many owners who do not need to use their car every day. For a Ford or GM or Nissan, offering buyers the opportunity to participate in managed peer-to-peer car sharing means an easier sale of the car.

As with so many new developments, automakers are not sure whether this trend is good for them. Yet many feel they cannot afford to look away or remain on the sidelines. GM had announced a partnership with Turo allowing GM owners with cars equipped with OnStar to place their cars in service through Turo. In 2015, GM also acquired Sidecar, a pioneer in the peer-to-peer car-sharing business and the owner of several patents in that business. Soon after this acquisition, GM also launched its own car-sharing brand, called Maven. Its Detroit rival Ford has also invested in the business of car sharing with GoDrive in the UK and the San Francisco–based peer-to-peer business Getaround. All these services are variations on the core concept of car sharing. As is typical of new business offerings, many avenues are explored as investors and operators seek to identify a winning business model.

Automakers have come to understand that their long-running business model, which mainly dealt with designing, building, and selling cars, is no longer sufficient. To be relevant to customers of the new millennium, they must attend to the wide diversity of choices customers are demanding.

Shared vehicles, taxis, and aggregators

Car sharing with Zipcar or using Car2Go typically involves trips that last a couple of hours. But a large number of urban trips may last no more than fifteen to thirty minutes. This is the domain traditionally served by taxis. A car is summoned when needed. It serves the purpose of the journey. The user is released of any obligation after the completion of the journey. No wonder it has served travelers' needs for temporary mobility from the days of hackney carriages. But taxis are often expensive, not available when needed, and, sometimes, offer an indifferent quality of service. If these issues could be solved, an enhanced appeal of taxis could persuade even more car owners to give up their cars.

Innovators have been having a crack at this problem as well.

The earliest taxi license was issued in 1654 in London.[26] Traditional taxis evolved alongside motorcars over much of the last century. From the days of pre-1800 hackney-carriages, these businesses evolved to be governed by several common principles. First, they operated on the basis of a license issued by local administrations. Second, the vehicles were hired for a fee that was typically regulated by an authority. The origins of the word "taxi" go back to the Latin *taxa*, meaning a tax or fee. Third, the drivers and operators of these services were commonly unionized, and their collective bargaining ability maintained equilibrium with the mandates stipulated by the owner and often also the regulator. Today taxicabs in New York are governed by the New York City Taxi and Limousine Commission, which regulates more than 40,000 vehicles in the region, including around 13,500 taxicabs with medallion licenses.[27] Similarly, London has more than 21,000 licensed cabs in operation.

Along the way, the trade accumulated regulations. Vehicle specification was sequentially enhanced for all sorts of legitimate causes—automatic door locks to protect passengers, barriers to protect drivers, and hybrid or compressed natural gas power to protect the environment. Some standards imposed by regulators were meant to make taxis accessible to people with disabilities. Drivers were tested for driving skills and familiarity with complex routes and byways. Most cities required screening of drivers for criminal records and medical tests for fitness. Customer interests were protected by fixing tariff rates, so that they could not be gouged for rush hour calls. Travelers were guaranteed access to a taxi even if this meant travel to remote or crime-prone areas of cities.

However, over time, some regulations worked against the interests of customers and society. The size of taxi fleets was often limited, to maintain profitability, and this led to the value of individual licenses or medallions, which were traded, creeping out of control. Acquiring a New York cab medallion could set the owner back by $1 million, and the medallion cost needed to be recovered through fares.[28] As with all well-established regulated systems, new technology induction was slow. Hailing taxis involved calling a dispatch center or trying to flag an unoccupied taxi on the street. Anyone who has attempted to hail a taxi in Los Angeles or Paris in rush hour has faced futility. Some regulations are well beyond their sell-by date. A six-month training process to memorize obscure streets and alleys makes little sense in a world where a $50 smartphone is powered with comprehensive maps and can support navigation guidance around temporary congestion.

The disruptors

Into this environment have rushed new-age service providers such as Uber, Lyft, Didi Chuxing, and Ola. Their business offering was deliberately different. In fact, they positioned themselves as little more than online technology platforms where user and service provider could transact. Of course, there is more to it than meets the eye.

These businesses, in their early years, tapped the large pool of informal, nonregulated car owners and drivers eager to make some extra cash, many of whom had other jobs. Drivers were encouraged to use their own vehicles as taxis, and this meant that the value of their car was seldom treated as a capitalized asset as it would be in a conventional business. Their vehicles were standard models any car buyer could acquire, and this meant that the capital costs were much lower than those of a taxi equipped to conform to regulations.

Most important, the business model leveraged the full power of modern connectivity technologies. Drivers were equipped with suitable smartphones that on a single affordable platform combined the functions of communication, tracking, navigation, and fare payment management. The driver's smartphone was tuned to be seamlessly operable with the customer's. Customers created accounts and used apps on their smartphone for hailing a ride and defining pickup location. They were provided a response time for pickup and an estimate of the cost of the trip. Payment was as simple as walking away after the trip and allowing one's account to be billed.

Interacting with the driver over the fare and decisions regarding the tip were done away with.

An information technology–enabled control room with little or no human involvement used algorithms to identify the closest available taxi while also getting proximate drivers to bid for the fare and tagging the designated driver for that journey. Real-time tracking of the vehicle while it was in operation allowed some degree of supervision. Quality control was expected to be further augmented by feedback from both customer and the driver after the journey was completed. Over time, this database began to accumulate information on the quality of service provided as well as on demand patterns and preferences. The growing application of modern analytic tools to this database is expected to deliver even more impressive improvements in meeting customer needs and system efficiency.

Is this efficiency or merely cutting corners?

In a sense, like many innovations, these new services have revamped standard operating practice by throwing out some good with the bad. A core issue concerns the ambiguity of the role of the platform provider. Service providers such as Lyft, Ola, and Uber have positioned themselves as online taxi aggregators, mediating between independent drivers and customers. Yet customers, using their apps and drawn to their service by the appeal of the brand and its advertising, implicitly place their trust in these service providers. The ambiguity was forced into focus when isolated cases of assault revealed loose accountability. In 2015, a customer was raped in an Uber taxi in India.[29] In 2016, a driver operating with Uber was charged with six murders in Michigan.[30] That year, Uber agreed to pay $28 million to settle federal litigation in the U.S. on behalf of customers who claimed misrepresentation by the company.[31] To be fair, deviant behavior by other classes of drivers or services also occurs. The issue in this case was the need to identify formal accountability for a service that purports to offer customers a better, more comfortable and hassle-free ride.

Several other issues of ambiguity have also given rise to conflict.

In April 2016, a U.S. federal judge rejected a proposed settlement between Uber and Uber drivers in two U.S. states. At issue was the status of drivers. Uber contended they were independent contractors who worked according to their schedule. The lawsuit charged that the drivers were employees and therefore entitled to a minimum set of benefits, including overtime and health insurance.[32] Disputes over similar subjects have flared up in many countries, especially in Europe.

Figure 10.2 Protests like the one shown in London have emerged out of a sense that there is an uneven playing field for operators like Uber and traditional taxis.
Source: (CC BY 2.0) David Holt.

These services initially started by allowing part-time drivers to give people rides in their own personal cars. Soon, as the businesses scaled up, they became full-time ride providers. In many cities, cars designated for contract hire must comply with expensive regulations governing safety, access for passengers with disability, and even low-emission engines. Traditional taxi fleets have protested the unfair exclusion from compliance for cars used by drivers of these ride-hailing apps.

Customers too faced disappointments in some situations. Raw economics, driven by relative balance of supply and demand, meant that during peak demand periods, fares were unexpectedly inflated, a practice called "surge pricing." Customers faced an unexpectedly higher and perhaps unaffordable cost of rides. In its defense, Uber has argued that the higher prices during peak demand times will pull more drivers into the marketplace, providing more supply just when it is needed. Efficiency in markets to some may be gouging to others.

After the dust settles

History is replete with instances in which disruptions of business models aided by technology have generated angst in society. Such perturbations of the status quo may ruffle many feathers, but they can catalyze a process leading to adjustments and shifts to a new improved level of service. Uber and similar services will likely be forced into compliance with a minimal set of norms that society views as non-negotiable. Other regulations that no longer serve a useful purpose will be retired. And traditional incumbents will raise their game and adjust to revised competitive landscapes.

In the half decade that the service has been operating, Uber's growth has been sensational. By 2015, it was operating in more than 330 cities in sixty countries and boasted a market cap in excess of $40 billion, which means that Uber as a company is valued more highly than Renault, Peugeot, and Fiat-Chrysler combined. By 2015, the number of Uber operators in New York City exceeded the number of Yellow Cabs, and the effect of the disruption was being felt by all. Between April and June 2015, in the core of Manhattan, Uber rides increased by 3.8 million while the number of pickups by Yellow Cabs declined by almost the same number.[33] As a result, the value of a New York City Yellow Cab medallion collapsed by 40 percent from a peak of $1 million. Certify is a leading U.S. travel and expense management service and hence processes expense reports for a large number of corporations. By 2016, according to a report derived from Certify's data, Uber use by business travelers had accounted for 43 percent of ground transportation transactions, higher even than rental car transactions, which were at 40 percent. Uber was not only affecting taxi use, the service was also causing rental car drivers to switch to being chauffeured on business trips.

Impact on mobility

The average resident of New York City would need to allocate around $9,000 annually for operating a private car. This same budget would allow a large number of Uber trips to be made, each including a free chauffeur. This is another mobility trend that threatens to adversely affect new car sales for automakers. Yet to many automakers, disengagement or fighting this change is not an option. In 2015, GM's acquisition of a stake in the ride-sharing business Lyft was a sign that automakers intended to stay closely connected in the evolution of this business.

There is already some consolidation under way in this space. To tackle Uber's preeminence, Didi Chuxing, a market leader in China, systematically acquired stakes in Uber's global rivals, including Lyft and Ola. Backed by a combination of Tencent, Baidu, and Alibaba in China, it too has the kind of deep pockets needed to take the fight to Uber; by 2016, its market capitalization had crossed the $16 billion mark.[34] China has proved to be a tough battleground for both services. Their aggressive campaigns to woo customers with lower fares and drivers with better incentives had left both rivals bloodied.

In response to the heavy losses it was suffering in this battle, Uber chose to sell its Chinese business to its main rival and become an important shareholder in Didi at the same time.[35] Uber also freed up its internal resources to grow elsewhere. This was expected to result in a situation in which Didi Chuxing would command more than 90 percent of the Chinese market. Formal approval from regulators was anticipated. Yet such deals should give rise to grave concerns. Many of these operators have been gaining market share with very aggressive pricing and in the process have eliminated a lot of the competition. Once they emerge in a dominant position in any market, they can have undue influence in urban mobility. Because such services divert trips from public transport in many cities, the interests of customers and drivers will need to be adequately safeguarded.

On the other hand, traditional taxi companies are rapidly integrating similar technologies into their services. Apps like MyTaxi, Way2Ride, and Flywheel empower the traditional taxi company to raise its competitiveness to match the new interlopers. They mimic the functionality of Uber's apps by locating, hailing, and using taxis. They have recognized the power of connectivity.

It seems likely that the traditional concept of taxis or vehicles for hire will change irreversibly. Whether Uber as an enterprise will survive and succeed depends on whether it can withstand challenges and emerge with the bugs fixed. Even if it does not, the company has changed society's expectations and the rules of the game.

Are you lonesome today?

Zipcar and Turo are motivated by providing personal mobility options at lower cost to owning a car or using traditional rental cars. Uber, Lyft, and traditional taxis have made it possible to use a car with considerable flexibility for getting from one place to another, yet most often they too serve individual travelers. Our CHIP framework is, however, relentless in demanding faster mobility, more flexible options, better environmental performance, and lower cost. Appropriately, market forces and entrepreneurship have delivered more variations and additional options.

To start with, even operators like Uber and Ola have started to offer carpooling in several countries. This entails expanding the capabilities of their operating software from selecting and planning the assignment of cars to individual customers based on location to planning around the demands of several travelers with similar journey profiles. Many users in a given locale may seek travel to common destinations, such as airports or railway stations, within a narrow time window. By combining their travel using one car, users who are willing to share the ride realize a lower cost of travel. In the process, they contribute to easing congestion and lowering carbon emissions. In 2016, Uber reported that within six months of its launch in London, over a million users had used this travel option. Further, UberPOOL already accounted for 20 percent of journeys with Uber.[36]

But consumers are moved by more than just economic motives. After all, Facebook is not just a tool for communication. There is a social angle as well. If a stranger can share companionship and cost with the owner on a trip, that solution might offer a combination of social, economic, and carbon emission benefits.

The concept of carpooling has been around for decades. The energy crisis of the 1970s triggered drastic measures in the U.S., including encouragement of carpooling. Many highway ramps were soon provided with parking lots for car pools. Any small group of two to five commuters could share the journey, typically to and from work, and in the process save fuel. These car pools were further incentivized and allowed use of high-occupancy vehicle (HOV) lanes where vehicles enjoyed use of a restricted lane and could hence make the commute faster.

That such a concept would be improved on by contemporary entrepreneurs, especially when augmented by connectivity technology, is not a surprise. BlaBlaCar is a new kind of service that now calls itself the world's largest long-distance ride-sharing membership. Founded in 2003, this service taps into the emotional value of social contact with like-minded peers by combining the element of camaraderie with the economics of shared travel costs: Commuting meets Facebook. Present in nineteen countries and counting 20 million members in 2016, this business has found resonance in many parts of the world. Riders in the car get a significantly lower cost of travel compared to travel by train or an equivalent public mode. The owner-driver has a large fraction of his or her cost subsidized by fellow riders. More important, unlike in an Uber taxi, riders are encouraged to play the role of peer, sitting in the front seat and providing both driver and rider a sense of companionship. Drivers and riders are rated by each other not only for the service but also friendliness, and this becomes an important element of self-governance. Profiles and stated interests can steer a rider to a group that he or she may enjoy traveling with. BlaBlaCar services not surprisingly show much higher levels of per vehicle occupancy. In Europe, the average car carries 1.7 persons. In the case of BlaBlaCar, this rises to 2.7.[37] Managers of large events such as music festivals and sporting events, where large crowds are expected, increasingly find this service favorable to their interests. They help reduce vehicle congestion and parking demands.

Blurring of the divide between public and private modes

Since 2000, the proliferation of smartphones and connectivity has spawned a range of technologies, apps, and business models that have further blurred the gap between private and public modes of transport. For well over three decades, across countries, transportation services have been on the road to privatization. In many cases, entire systems and services were transferred to private entities by their erstwhile government owners. In others, governments have transferred their management and operations to corporations that may still enjoy significant government ownership.

New private services such as BlaBlaCar find use for those infrequent travels, typically on longer journeys. But many commuters who still choose to live in suburbs and commute to the city are eager to lower their travel cost and reduce carbon emissions. For them, modern tools have created variations of the traditional van-pools where aggregations of four to eight commuters typically sign up to travel together, willing to synchronize their travel time to enjoy these benefits.

Rideshare is a vanpooling service owned by the car rental giant Enterprise that operates across the U.S. The company has been busy acquiring local vanpool operators and linking them with a common software and technology platform that takes advantage of better planning and coordination. Operating on a hybrid business model, many vans are owned by drivers who are compensated for giving rides to the pool members. In other cases, drivers are allowed use of a van that they agree to drive for the pool. That such services go beyond urban boundaries and often substitute for public transit means they are expanding the domain of applicability of the kinds of innovations that have been incubated in cities. It is not just urban professionals who enjoy the value of these new technologies. These services are being recognized for their impact on lowering highway congestion and carbon emissions and enjoy many incentives from governments. For example, U.S.

Figure 10.3 Smartphone-hailed, crowd-sourced van rides are helping to blur the divide between public transit and private cabs.
Source: Ford Smart Mobility LLC.

federal government employees are eligible for a tax-free benefit when they use vanpooling.

Increasingly, cities are obliged to rely on third-party service providers to help effect tight connectivity among the different modes.

San Francisco's Bay Area shares many problems with Los Angeles. The region is characterized by sprawl and an almost continuous distribution of cities—Milpitas, San Jose, Santa Clara, Sunnyvale, Mountain View, Palo Alto. They share another similarity—inadequate public transit. There is perhaps no better place than this to ask for technology and entrepreneurship to mask the poor public transit infrastructure in the suburbs. Many large employers contract with vanpool operators to offer subsidized rides to their employees. As with Uber or Lyft, riders use smartphone apps to schedule pickups.

In San Francisco itself, Chariot has been expanding its fleet of vans, which often work in tandem with the city's bus fleet. By 2016, Chariot was operating on twenty-eight city routes using fifteen-seater vans. Van frequency and stops along routes were based on crowd-sourced requests from Chariot's dedicated app. As cofounder and CEO Ali Vahabzahdeh explained, "Chariot's mission from day one has been to solve the commute by providing a mass transit solution that is fast, reliable and affordable for people living in today's cities."[38] Chariot, which was acquired in 2016 by Ford Smart Mobility, a part of Ford Motor Company, had outlined plans to add dynamic routing based on up-to-the-minute demand analysis and to expand their service to an additional five cities.

In some regions, demand on some routes can be very low and yet require transit options. Pinellas Park, Florida, in a bold and novel experiment announced in 2016 that the city would stop running two bus lines and instead offer an equivalent subsidy to offset the cost of an Uber ride for a city traveler.

While San Francisco and Pinellas Park roped in private operators to provide alternate services to public transit on lower-density routes, other cities have found it necessary to link public and private services in tandem. The city of Centennial, a suburb of Denver, was grappling with the issue of first-mile and last-mile linkages to its brand new light-rail public transit system. The city's solution was to pay commuters to use Lyft taxis to get to and from the light-rail stations.[39] The city managers viewed private services like Lyft as integral to the functioning of the public transit system.

Future mobility frameworks are likely to offer a very high degree of flexibility that will place a premium on seamlessness. Public and private transport used to view each other as competition. That distinction is no longer relevant or useful. Modern cities will be obliged to weave their own public services very tightly with private mobility solutions, keeping in mind the interests of travelers as well as their obligations to society.

A heterogeneous smorgasbord of options

In previous chapters we discussed a range of technologies and innovations to travel modes such as electric vehicles, microcars, and bus rapid transit systems, which have enriched our mobility options. In this chapter we looked at how the business models being adopted and altered by a host of entrepreneurs have similarly enhanced our choices. Our digitized world has propelled us into a new orbit that has dramatically collapsed space and time, fostering networked cooperation. In the process, a lot of power has shifted from established governments and businesses to dispersed innovators and entrepreneurs who are empowered by the technology of networking.

These entrepreneurs have used the tools of connectivity, analytics, and payment gateways to conjure solutions where none previously existed. In all cases, these new business models are seeking ways to improve the economics, efficiency, and enjoyment of travel. Where an asset could be used for more of its life, they have found ways to do so. Where more people could share a resource, they have created opportunities. Where two modes could combine to offer a better solution, they have created linkages. Like the sculptor chipping away material superfluous to the core form, they have taken mobility concepts such as cars, taxis and vanpools and sculpted them to become more targeted offerings.

Innovating on the Goldilocks principle, they have interpolated solutions to create new hybrids. Between any two solutions, there can be a hybrid that combines a little bit of the positives of the two bookends. We traditionally had personal cars and rental cars. Peer car-sharing is an additional hybrid solution. We have had friends offer a ride and we have had traditional taxis. Uber is an additional hybrid solution. We have had fixed-route vanpools and we have had public transit. Chariot-like services are crowd-sourced van transit routes that are an additional hybrid solution. And new business solutions, powered by a digitized economy, facilitate multimodal linkages. This heterogeneity is a fundamental building block to configure the mobility solutions of the future and is a crucial component of the CHIP architecture.

For many urban residents, especially in developed economies, car ownership is no longer necessary for expression of status. Ownership-free mobility on demand may actually fit a desired lifestyle better. Furthermore, collectively, the businesses discussed in this chapter help assure users of round-the-clock access to a car or suitable mobility. Assured of such easy access to desired forms of mobility whenever needed, customers may be able to purchase mobility to fit their actual needs and not necessarily their contingent needs. Two-car families may downsize to one car in this scenario. As options like those discussed in this chapter facilitate opportunities to vary one's vehicle and transport mode at will, can we really expect anything but the decline of long-term vehicular investments by individual buyers?

III   Implementation of the CHIP Mobility Architecture

In this final section of the book we discuss how the CHIP mobility framework can be implemented and the roles of some of the key stakeholders.

This framework is built on the foundation of the understanding we developed in part I, concerning societal changes and the trends in urbanization, sustainability, and culture.

In part II, we observed that technologists and entrepreneurs have been busy shaping innovative mobility solutions and services. Safety, sustainability, connectivity, and customization have all been enhanced. Cars are acquiring intelligent systems, and autonomous driving is around the corner. These developments will alter the boundaries and assumptions of human mobility. A legacy of lumpy discrete travel modes is being altered and augmented to form a more continuous mobility solution spectrum. With this heterogeneous portfolio of options, we are better equipped to serve modern consumers and modern societies.

In this final part of the book, we discuss how heterogeneous modes may be connected to deliver end-to-end solutions. In a world of dazzling variety, the options must be intelligently sorted, filtered, and connected to be of practical use.

Finally, we expect that future mobility systems will deliver personalized solutions for each and every traveler. In our view, effective deployment of this framework implies prominent roles for cities and their administrations, existing mobility providers, including automakers and transit operators, and the host of technologists and entrepreneurs who are reshaping the landscape with a combination of technology and innovative business models. Effective orchestration of all these stakeholders will be needed to deliver a unique mobility architecture that is faster, smarter, and greener.

11   CHIP Mobility: Framework and Architecture

Thirty years ago the average family in the industrialized world had a landline telephone connection, typically provided by a monopoly service provider for two-way voice communication. Today that family has numerous options to tailor its choices to the specific context, based on length or volume of communication, nature of transmission (voice-only or with video), and preferred device—phone, smartphone, tablet, or computer. Applications such as WhatsApp, Skype, Google Talk, Facetime, and WebEx expand the nature of services on offer. People are likely to use different tools to communicate with family members, friends, and colleagues. As a result, most users typically employ a heterogeneity of apps and communication channels on any given day. Devices intelligently switch across cellular networks or from cellular to Wi-Fi networks to maintain permanent connections based on signal strength and preferences. Similarly, connectivity services abound, ranging from traditional monthly plans to data packages for smartphones and shared access to free Wi-Fi hot spots. Family data plans are personalized, allowing pooling of data limits within the family, which helps lower bills and amplifies flexibility. As a modern user initiates any communication, he or she chooses from this portfolio of offerings the combination of device, application, service plan, and communication format best suited for the immediate purpose.

Today's communications systems thus function in a *c*onnected, *h*eterogeneous, *i*ntelligent, and *p*ersonalized (CHIP) environment. In this chapter we draw inspiration from these remarkable advances as we complete our articulation of the conceptual CHIP mobility architecture and discuss how it can be made operational. We also define the related CHIP mobility framework, which serves as a conceptual tool to visualize and analyze the prevailing mobility architecture and foster key stakeholder dialogue so that societies are able to transform how their future mobility needs might best be served.

Principles underlying the CHIP framework

Decompose, optimize, and synthesize

In the 1950s, during the Cold War, Paul Baran was employed as a researcher at the U.S.-based Rand Corporation on a Department of Defense contract.[1] At the time, Western nations were eager to ensure that their defense command-and-control infrastructure would withstand a nuclear first strike by the Soviet adversary. Baran's and his team's efforts and inventions resulted in a concept called *packet switching*, which led to a radically new, more efficient, and more robust way to effect communications. This breakthrough revolutionized modern telecommunications and serves as a critical foundation for the Internet and its wealth of options.

Packet switching involves breaking down a digital string of communication into fragments or packets, which are routed to their destination through multiple nodes in the communication network. The packets are then recomposed in proper sequence at the receiver to reconstruct the original message. Compared to a circuit-switched communication line, in which an attack at one location could disable critical end-to-end communication links, packet switching provides multiple pathways and adequate redundancies to create a robust network for the transmission of data.

This approach to moving data has delivered many impressive benefits. It has rendered communication more robust and less vulnerable to disruption. It has distributed elements of the total communication enterprise and attracted many service providers and entrepreneurs. It has hosted a vibrant environment for innovation, nurturing a multitude of communication formats and content. It has replaced the need to own software on individual computers and devices and has facilitated the use of software embedded within services. Communication costs have plummeted while customers' choices have multiplied.

In many ways, this transformation in communications offers lessons for transforming mobility. Society will likely demand an analogous combination of speed, flexibility, and economy from future mobility systems. The CHIP mobility architecture as postulated embodies these desired characteristics. In this chapter we review many instances in which the elements of such architecture are being successfully deployed and offer suggestions for increasing their use. We also discuss the potential for the CHIP mobility framework to help provide a roadmap for societies in their endeavor to achieve faster, smarter, and greener mobility.

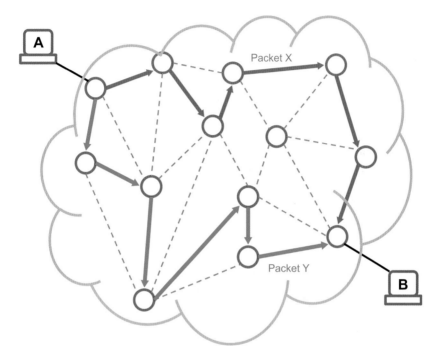

Figure 11.1 Paul Baran's concept of packet switching underpins the Internet. It is dependent on subdivision of the data string, the use of multiple alternative path segments, and system redundancies.

Steps toward decomposing, optimizing, and synthesizing mobility

To assemble and deploy the CHIP mobility architecture, it is necessary first to understand the way mobility is usually orchestrated.

Every trip we undertake, no matter how trivial, involves a few basic steps of planning and execution. In most cases we do this intuitively, with assumptions about modes we prefer, routes we are familiar with, and known priorities. Usually this is second nature and we do not formally undertake a rigorous articulation of the steps involved. If we did so, the process might be decomposed as follows.

Step 1

The full journey is broken into possible routes or multiple route segments. A modern city provides numerous routes and travel modes to get from one place to another. Some options may be chosen out of habit—just getting in the car and driving to a destination, for example even when such choices may be known to involve significant time spent in slow, dense traffic. Several other options might remain available, and travel using these options may involve making connections and choosing among multiple modes. Some combinations may actually require a brief segment of counter-direction travel (for example, to the closest bus stop or highway ramp) to reach a destination. When a journey is broken up into segments, each offering a choice of several modes, the traveler confronts a wide variety and combination of possibilities for making that trip.

Step 2

Of the multiple options available, some are likely to be more suitable than others. User preferences are usually based on multiple factors, including (1) the time consumed by the journey, (2) the cost of the trip, (3) convenience and comfort, (4) the level of privacy desired, and (5) the specific requirements of the trip, for example, the need to transport children or carry groceries. Each travel mode and journey routing, whether with car, bike, taxi, train, or bus, is characterized by its signature combination of (1) cost, (2) speed, (3) convenience and comfort, (4) carbon emissions, and (5) ambience. The multiple options offered on the basis of this signature of characteristics are matched to the traveler's preferences. The factors listed are not exhaustive and can vary depending on how deeply the traveler wishes to evaluate the options and the traveler's unique perspective.

Increasingly the sorting is not easy and defeats intuitive assessment. The variables are expanding, and many are unpredictable. Any multimodal trip warrants aggregating such information across many segments of travel. A football game may cause congestion delays near the stadium, increasing driving time. A forecast for rain may imply a drenching walk from the metro station. Many modern modes, including app-hailed taxis, may vary their pricing during periods of very high demand, changing cost assumptions. Each such circumstance may cause the traveler to alter routing or mode of travel.

In the face of these complex choices, mobility apps are constantly evolving to provide up-to-the-moment information, such as the current status of traffic or disruptions in specific services, weather, and pricing. Most people are familiar with online airline bookings that offer lower fares when seats remain unsold or when passengers accept flexible travel dates or are willing to endure additional stops en route. Similarly, travel through an airport hub may be cheaper and offer more options than flying direct. Flying from Denver to Detroit with a stop in Chicago or from Mallorca to Munich stopping in Frankfurt may be both quicker and cheaper than seeking to fly direct to the destination. Such options might be available for urban commuter travel as well. But aggregating and processing this growing quantum of information, which changes dynamically, is getting more complex. A host of modern tools help travelers sort such information quickly and effectively.

Step 3

Once multiple viable options, along with their cost and benefit profiles, are identified, the traveler can make an informed decision. Based on overall trip objectives, intelligent apps or advisers can be engaged to filter the many options. Powerful back-end computing ensures that numerous scenarios or options can be considered and assessed. A limited set of filtered solutions can then be presented to the traveler. Many modern tools learn user preferences and habits, apart from using traveler-specified parameters. A student and a business executive may have different priorities relating to the value of time and the affordability of travel. A trip for dinner or to attend the theater may call for different priorities than commuting to work. This personalization becomes a critical component of making mobility user-friendly.

Needless to say, in a fast-changing world, situations remain fluid, and hence any practical application must remain engaged, ready to recommend alternatives to routing or travel plans as circumstances change.

A social psychologist might argue that any individual constantly seeks to increase the value of his or her efforts. It stands to reason that we have innate motivations to seek the best value for mobility we undertake. The objective of the CHIP mobility architecture is to help users navigate the steps elaborated above in such a way that for the traveler, the expenditure of effort and resources is minimized while satisfaction and value of travel are maximized.

Connections, intelligent agents, and personalization

In part II, we reviewed how city administrators, entrepreneurs, and vehicle manufacturers are placing at travelers' service an ever expanding set of travel modes and solutions. The following discussion looks at the next crucial steps, which involve connecting modes and solutions and the use of intelligent filtering to deliver personalized offerings.

Connections: Linking modes and expanding utility

All the innovations in mobility modes will be for naught if they are not easily accessible to travelers or not well connected to other modes. Paul Baran's communication strategy would have ground to a halt if there were not parallel developments in high-speed switches and routers at each node. Well-connected physical infrastructure and well-connected digital communication are necessary to keep people mobile. These are the key elements that allow mobility users to swiftly and conveniently switch modes. If mobility is envisioned as a service, then connectivity becomes an important component of the platform.

With regard to physical infrastructure, effective solutions begin with getting the simple things right. Good sidewalks, for example, promote walking to the nearest public transit station. When residential zones have easy connections to a transit station, usually defined as location within a third of a mile or 500 meters of a transit stop, use of public transit increases. Bike rentals at metro stations and bike paths and linking them to nearby residential localities expand the reach of metros.

In many large Asian cities, shopping and commercial establishments form the basis of productive linking spaces. In Tokyo, rail stations and bus stops are connected through convenient walkways to shopping malls, office complexes, and residential blocks. As a result, almost 24 percent of total trips involve walking.[2] Singapore, another well-connected city, is investing in integrated transport hubs (ITHs), which are comfortable, air-conditioned interchanges for bus stops and subway stations, often complemented by retail and commercial spaces.

The Hong Kong metro, which is profitable and frequently cited as a benchmark, owns sizable chunks of real estate in and around their stations. Shopping malls adjacent to stations are persuaded to share investment and some operating costs. In return, the metro disgorges huge masses of people at the stations that help sustain the establishments in those malls.

The value of good connectivity is also evident for trips that bring travelers into cities. For example, it is possible to land at the airport in Frankfurt or Zurich and, within 500 meters, have access to long-distance trains to travel anywhere in Europe, to local trains and trams for travel to the city or the local region, and to buses, taxis, and rental cars for short-distance commutes.

Sometimes the best way to ensure connectivity is to carry it with you. Visitors to Europe or campus towns in the U.S. are familiar with the sight of buses carrying bicycles, which allow students and commuters to cycle to and from the closest bus stops. Without the bike carriers, the catchment area of the buses would be reduced and their utility to the community and to customers lowered. Buses with carriers promote access to low-cost and low-carbon transport solutions for many more commuters.

At the 2016 Consumer Electronics Show in Las Vegas, Ford Motor Company unveiled its MoDe:Me concept, which features a foldable city e-bike that packs neatly into the trunk of a Ford car. The bike's battery can be charged from a port provided in the car during the drive. As the commuter drives the car toward a city center, the parking app advises the driver of the

Figure 11.2 Bike racks fitted on buses are a common sight in many university towns. They help expand the catchment area for public transit.
Source: Flickr CC0 1.0 Martin Ljungqvist.

Figure 11.3 Ford's MoDe:Me concept. These e-bikes are folded and transported in a car and used to overcome a common hassle in cities: the lack of proximate parking.
Source: Ford Motor Company.

best location to park the car. At the parking garage, the driver gets the bike out and achieves her last mile of transport by pedaling or using the battery-assisted feature of the bike. Destination information and navigation seamlessly carry over from the car to the smartphone mounted on the bike. This combination overcomes a common hurdle in many cities—finding a parking space close to the destination.

Physical connectivity hence can be improved with a range of innovative approaches involving city planning, investments, infrastructure design, and product features. Such approaches facilitate easier transfers across modes of travel and enhance flexibility.

In the modern era, there is also a growing role for digital connectivity. Most nations and most cities are accelerating the roll-out of domain wide digital connectivity, recognizing that this constitutes an essential element of a modern economy. The ability of smartphones to keep travelers connected to information sources and travel solutions is vital to planning journeys and to choosing or combining travel modes. Online accounts and e-payment allow seamless transition from one segment to another and from one mode to another. The experience of cities such as London, Tokyo, and New York confirms that if good physical infrastructure is combined with modern digital connectivity, commuters will choose to mix their modes of travel for a more efficient total commute.

Apps can also access a wealth of information surrounding the user. Increasingly, successful apps depend on being connected to a large set of data sources. Many progressive service providers offer suitable hooks to third-party apps to improve user convenience. In London, for example, Transport for London's policy of sharing its data encourages entrepreneurs to develop peripheral products that enhance the utility and services Transport for London offers to customers. One such app is Citymapper, an independent third-party app widely used in many large cities, including London. It allows people to plan their mobility with a combination of walking, bicycling, and taking buses, taxi, metros, and surface rail, fully utilizing Transport for London's database.

On a global scale, data exchanges and protocols are being set up so that diverse sources of information can be piped to serve the needs of specific apps. These protocols allow various agents such as traffic police, meteorological departments, highway maintenance departments, event organizers, railways, public transit authorities, parking garages, and fuel stations to manage the flow of information related to traffic, transit schedules, weather, fares, and pricing.

Once the benefits of digital connectivity are added to those of physical connectivity, the positives multiply. Not only does public transit benefit from better connectivity but the success of modern car-sharing services such as DriveNow and Car2Go also depends on both physical and digital connectivity. What enhances their appeal and utility has to do with the way they are operationalized. The ability to find a car, use it, and drop it off at the end of a travel segment has simplified the transaction. Hence this business model encourages use of a car only for a specific trip, and not for an entire day. In other words, as the effort and cost to switch from one mode to another are reduced, multimodal mobility becomes easier. And with easier multimodal mobility, each segment can be uniquely optimized.

The Art Center College of Design in California is one of the preeminent institutes for industrial design. Its considerable focus on transportation has ensured that over the decades, some of the best-known automotive designers around the world have emerged from the program. A good designer is expected to marry aesthetic form and good industrial function. So it is not surprising to walk into the design halls and see student portfolios dominated by swoopy forms that they hope will adorn the next-generation Ferraris, Lamborghinis, or Teslas.

As frequent visitors, we have noted trends and evolutions in design form and language. The functional 1980s gave way to the lozenge-inspired aerodynamic themes of the 1990s and later to the bolder expressions of the 2000s. Yet on a recent visit to the Art Center, we found that many of the student projects had grown in scope. There was a greater emphasis on system performance rather than just on product design. Students were conceptualizing whole transportation systems, including their interfaces and connections, to make the full mobility experience more attractive. Many expressed the view that while creating stunning automotive shapes was exciting, conceiving integrated mobility systems was more challenging to an industrial designer.

In a sign of the times, one major automaker had commissioned a study to propose a complete future mass transit system, with design cues aligned with that automaker's brand. No wonder today's auto and industrial designers are speaking a very different language! They are egged on by fresh-thinking automakers that are beginning to look beyond the car as a product and at mobility as a system.

Faraday Future is a new kid on the block in California. Just as Tesla proceeded to rethink electric vehicles, Faraday Future claims to have positioned itself to rethink electric mobility. The company's focus is on fully connected, autonomy-enabled mobility. According to Nick Sampson, Faraday's Vice President of research and development, "We have a willingness to be more like a tech company than an automotive company. While the traditional auto industry is focused on making better cars, we are redefining the very nature of vehicles and mobility"[3]

It is not just automakers who are viewing the value of connected systems that work well for the user. Deutsche Bahn, Germany's prominent rail network operator, is also seeking to provide connected mobility components. More than 12 million people are moved each day in its network of 40,000 trains, 5,700 stations, and several feeder bus routes. Like many traditional rail operators, Deutsche Bahn fears being overtaken by the complex blend of mobility solutions that strive for seamless connections. It has responded with a new suite of services, including multimodal mobility planning and booking apps, car-sharing services (through a service named Flinkster, to prove that the staid Deutsche Bahn is trying to be young and funky), and bike-sharing services that operate out of railway stations, affording rail customers better options to begin or complete their travels.

From automakers to transit operators, they have all seen the writing on the wall. Modern societies are embracing well-planned physical and digital connectivity within an integrated transportation system to facilitate quick and efficient multimodal journeys.

Intelligent assembling of options to deliver personalized solutions

Once multiple modes and the connectivity to link them are available, the next step is to make them serve users effectively. This requires adding the elements of intelligent filtering and personalization of the many possible options.

The increasing number and possible combinations of routes, modes, and services, together with their attributes, give rise to a bewildering array of options for mobility. A user would be hopelessly lost in trying to sort through this mass of information and put it to practical use. Thankfully, technology is available to do just that. Apps get into computational crunching and sorting in diverse ways, depending on context and requirements. Just as Internet bots crawl through numerous sites to unearth best value, travel apps may query multiple modes to assess the best option according to the user's filter settings and preferences.

Furthermore, advances in artificial intelligence (AI) are expected to power some of the most significant information synthesizers in a generation. Modern AI-driven systems monitor and learn from observing user behavior. Progress with cognitive computing pushes the envelope of possibilities even further. They operate similar to the human mind. They can make use of unstructured data and detect patterns that defy being formally defined as rules. They can accommodate uncertainty and grey areas of both questions and observations.

Even the largest players will enter this space. Google's Assistant and Amazon's machine learning projects develop algorithms to understand people's preferences and to predict purchasing behavior. In 2016, Mark Zuckerberg resolved to have Facebook roll out an AI-powered personal assistant modeled after the Jarvis character in the movie *Iron Man*. As these technology giants with their comprehensive reach and perspectives on communication, transactions and opinions commit their involvement into mining and making sense of ever larger volumes of data, we may expect far more contemporary and granular understanding of society's habits and values.

These capabilities will receive a significant boost when they are able to access rapidly expanding data generated in a world in which devices and tools are increasingly embedded in the Internet of Things. Practically each device will be contributing data every day toward having its user's habits being better understood. With the benefit of such a vast training database, modern AI systems will increasingly compete with humans for effectiveness in a domain where they used to be deficient—in interpreting personal and social needs.

At this stage, a natural question for many travelers would be: can we actually trust technology to comprehend personal preferences in a complex environment and demonstrate their utility?

The domain of financial services is already seeing the fast deployment of similar intelligent robo-advisers. Here too there is an exhaustive variety of products whose value and characteristics may change rapidly with time. Recommendations must be aligned to the expectations and risk tolerance of a world of investors, no two of whom are identical. Now used by many large investment firms, robo-advisers use algorithms to design investment portfolios that suit the temperament and objectives of clients. This segment of the business is growing rapidly: it is expected that by 2020, more than $2 trillion will be managed by robo-advisers.[4]

Similarly, mobility tools that undertake the task of intelligently sorting through a huge volume of information and presenting only user-relevant options will be widely deployed, each seeking to carve out a slice of the mobility pie and potentially a share of the user's wallet. Like Paul Baran's packet-switching algorithms, such advanced mobility apps can break up a full journey into segments (if necessary) and fine-tune them, together with connections, then present them to users in the form of a limited, manageable set of options along with relevant information such as duration, cost, and carbon footprint of the travel. For specific journey segments, they can hail a taxi, guide the user to the nearest transit station, and book a train ticket. They can link multiple trip segments across different modes, ensuring effective and timely connections.

Such apps may recognize that the Saturday morning drive should take the scenic route compared to the weekday commute. They also sense context. For example, a user's calendar may allow the app to anticipate potential travel complexities such as those associated with an early morning departure to the airport, when fewer taxis are about and additional time may be needed to hail one. Intelligent apps can anticipate the need to stop at a florist on a personal anniversary and even identify a few the driver will pass on the usual drive home. Likewise, an app can tailor recommendations to adjust for a subway strike that has been called for at noon and suggest a change of mode.

Owned by Daimler Mobility Services, moovel is a mobility app or robo-adviser that is agnostic with respect to mobility modes and service providers, notwithstanding its ownership by the parent of Mercedes-Benz. Klaus Entenmann, chairman of Daimler Financial Services and head of the mobility services, explained, "Our current strategy is to ensure that our mobility customers find the right choice of mobility for them. We strive to deliver mobility at your fingertips."[5] In addition to analysis and recommendations, moovel can make travel bookings aligned to the user's preferences. The public transportation app Moovit is another popular app that provides multi-modal connectivity guidance in 800 cities across sixty countries, while the mostly North American Transit App is used in more than 100 cities. These apps seek to manage all segments of a journey from start to finish. Increasingly, they also partner with or sometimes integrate functions with specialist third-party apps. For example, as a traveler approaches her destination, apps like the GPS-enabled SpotCycle can help her cover the last mile by bicycle if necessary. For the driver, other apps, such as Roadify, provide traffic updates and alerts, while Waze provides route guidance and identifies where fuel prices are low on a given day.

A previous generation of enterprises had achieved considerable progress through more effective use of facts, data and logic to deal with their customers. The modern generation of enterprises will be challenged to deal with more complex aspects such as feelings and values of contemporary customers. The role for intelligent filtering and personalization of mobility solutions is critical to this society.

Figure 11.4 Smartphone apps pack a lot of power to aid mobility. They have become valuable robo-advisers to help travelers manage day-to-day movements.
Source: Daimler Mobility Services.

a.

Heterogeneity of modes

b.

Connectivity of modes

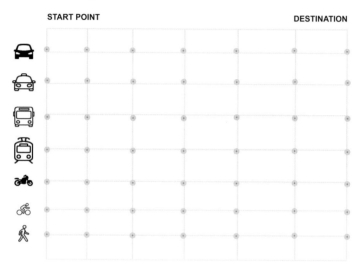

c.

Intelligent analysis

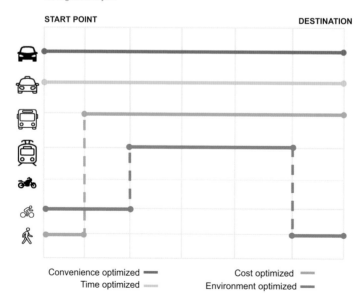

Convenience optimized ▬   Cost optimized ▬

Time optimized ▬   Environment optimized ▬

d.

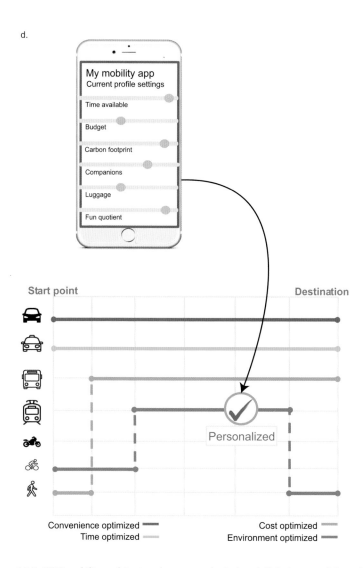

Figure 11.5 CHIP mobility architecture leverages physical and digital connectivity to intelligently synthesize a specific trip based on a menu of heterogeneous travel modes and their respective performance signatures in such a way that it is steered by each user's unique preferences while being influenced by societal priorities.

Box 11.1 TRusted Intelligent Personalized (TRIP) advisers

John Hagel is founder and cochairman of Deloitte's Center for the Edge, located in Silicon Valley. His work focuses on the intersection of business strategy and information technology. Hagel is currently concerned with a concept he calls "return on mobility." Hagel elaborates, "What we increasingly need and desire is to improve our return on mobility. What's that? It's a simple calculation starting with the notion that mobility is a means to an end."[6]

Most people, most of the time, have particular places to go and specific reasons for getting there. This leads to the use of personalized analytics to assess the satisfaction and benefit derived at the destination, as well as the enjoyment and pleasure experienced in getting there. This calculation is weighed against the cost, inconvenience, effort, and time it takes to get there. The decisions travelers make, powered by these motives, will depend on the data, information, and analytics that are packaged for them individually and personalized with respect to each one's value system. So getting to that serenely beautiful campground may count for a lot, just as taking the picturesque coastal road may add to the value. If the drive offers the prospect of great companionship and the car has brilliant driving dynamics and offers the right music and ambience for the drive, then the value is enhanced even more. Conversely, getting stuck in traffic while on the way to a critical meeting, dodging aggressive taxi drivers, and searching for parking may all detract from the mobility experience. And, of course, there are shades of experiences between these two extreme situations.

Now imagine a mobility adviser being available to help throughout the travel. Hagel explains, "There's an increasing need for a 'trusted mobility adviser,' someone who knows us as individuals better than anyone else (at least in the commercial world) and who could proactively recommend people and places that would provide us with the greatest value, given our specific context, needs and aspirations." This adviser's utility would depend on its knowing the user, the user's objectives, the user's preferences, and the user's values as much as it depended on the adviser's awareness of the context and circumstances related to the particular journey. Fortunately, the digital world we live in does not require one to afford a personal valet, a sort of sublimely competent Jeeves, to prevent us from bungling through our daily chores. The digital economy we engage in, powered by analytics, already knows a lot about each of us and what we like to do. As Hagel observes, "The economics of providing this kind of trusted adviser service are rapidly improving." As long as this source is authorized, validated, and trusted, its utility to our daily life can be immense.

According to Hagel, these trusted mobility advisers are likely to have the biggest impact in areas related to product purchases, entertainment, and social networks. Much of this is already experienced today. Online purchases are seldom executed without a web advertising suggestion for similar or complementary products. Choices of entertainment benefit from suggestions of activities in the neighborhood or something as simple as the music to suit the day streamed into the car. Social networks have made rapid strides not only in linking friends but also in connecting one to affinity groups and even strangers with compatible interests.

As the world is increasingly augmented with recorded transactions and events, and as the Internet of Things expands to touch more of the things mobility users deal with, these advisers will become both more useful and more affordable. And with trusted mobility advisers, mobility users can each get around to maximizing their own personal return on mobility.

CHIP mobility: The integrated view

The preceding chapters and sections have defined the building blocks of the CHIP mobility architecture. The functioning of this architecture is based on the four aspects of CHIP. The architecture depends upon and fosters proliferation of travel modes to enhance *heterogeneity*. It seeks to leverage the best of an expanding universe of physical and digital *connectivity* to take advantage of the combinatorics and hence synthesize multiple journey options for the traveler. It then uses *intelligent* machines and intelligent systems to assess costs and benefits among the various relevant options. As the final step, it seeks to recommend or select the most appropriate choice or choices that are *personalized* to the traveler.

The CHIP framework is a conceptual tool to visualize and analyze the operating architecture of a mobility system and foster a dialogue to improve its function. This framework is depicted conceptually in figure 11.6.

This framework is expected to play two kinds of roles. For cities across the world, no matter how mature their mobility architecture, the CHIP mobility framework may help conceptualize and orchestrate the interplay of mobility service providers, regulators, and city administrators with the users of mobility. In this role the CHIP mobility framework can guide the development and operation of existing mobility architectures. In its second role, the CHIP mobility framework serves as a conceptual foundation for modeling, evaluating, and road-mapping new scenarios, thereby fostering technical and business model innovations, as well as reform of policies. In this role it can aid societies that are preparing to improve and revamp their urban mobility architectures.

The CHIP mobility framework helps define and make visible the main stakeholders and the key functions of any mobility architecture. It can help people assess how well extant mobility architectures are assisting users stitch together end-to-end mobility, based on contextual priorities at that time. The framework recognizes four important factors:

- *Societal policies:* Mobility solutions operate in an environment in which societal imperatives are expected to be articulated through a combination

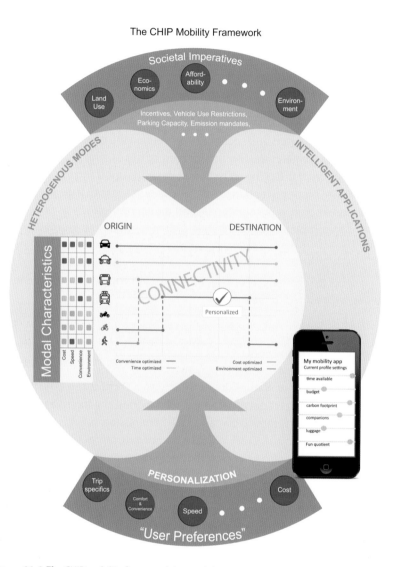

Figure 11.6 The CHIP mobility framework is a tool that promotes dialog and helps analyze the dynamics of interactions between the key stakeholders and the functioning of the architecture. It can help identify gaps and shortcomings and hence provide clues to improve the system.

of regulations, policies, investments in infrastructure, incentives, and fees. These policies will require frequent tuning to keep in alignment with overall goals.

- *Modal characteristics of mobility products and services:* An ever expanding universe of heterogeneous mobility modes and solutions is characterized by their respective signature for cost, efficiency, convenience, etc. Analysis of these signatures can identify gaps and provide clues for the opportunity to offer innovative new modes and solutions that may offer a competitive advantage.
- *Infrastructure and technology for connectivity:* Both physical and digital connectivity infrastructures are required for the CHIP architecture so that the variety of modes can be linked and connected in various combinations from the start of a journey to its termination. Information and data pertaining to these modes and solutions must be accessible to computing resources to intelligently sort through numerous options, taking into account the diverse modes and their characteristics, as well as updated information about traffic, weather, and emergencies.
- *User's preferences:* Users' priorities will need to be analyzed and tracked. Powered by such data and analytics, solutions should be able to present personalized options best suited for the traveler from start to finish.

The CHIP mobility framework is a tool with which to visualize and highlight interactions, identify gaps and opportunities for improvement, and promote a focused dialogue among all stakeholders, thereby leading to an ongoing ability to reenvisioning future mobility.

In the CHIP architecture, mobility is a service

Deploying the CHIP mobility architecture can open up a new paradigm for the way people move about. Mobility essentially is available on tap. When we access computing resources today, usually through an app, we seldom worry about who owns the computer server, where it is located, or what software needs to be purchased. Similarly, when communities deploy the CHIP architecture, mobility becomes a readily available service that each user may configure individually for each journey, on an as-needed basis. This service will be scalable across technology platforms and will eventually include autonomous modes. Erik Brynjolfsson, director of the MIT Initiative on the Digital Economy, agrees, saying, "Cars as a service is a likely outcome in this environment."[7]

Far from being commoditized, however, the CHIP architecture will enable personalization and will preserve the variety and differentiation that users and marketers require to make travel options responsive to individual needs.

There will be special occasions when "return on mobility" is maximized with a sporty convertible for a drive on a scenic mountain road; on other occasions it may be maximized with a rugged SUV for a backwoods camping weekend. The CHIP architecture will cater to all sorts of scenarios. The objective is to generate the maximum benefits with minimum of inconvenience, effort, or resources.

Enabled by technologies, future cities and communities will see private enterprise and corporations step into the middle ground between private and public services. For example, Mobility Mixx operates a fully flexible platform in the Netherlands that covers cars, buses, trains, metros, and bikes—all accessible to members with a single smart card. The company had announced their intention to expand their service to many large metropolises such as London. As Hein du Plessis, head of product development of Mobility Mixx's parent organization LeasePlan explained, "From LeasePlan's perspective, we really are moving away from the vehicle and more towards the journey."[8]

Box 11.2 Demographics and views on mobility as a service

Based on KPMG's extensive analysis of future mobility trends, KPMG partner Gary Silberg explained, "In every age group, participants showed significant attraction to 'mobility-on-demand' for specific conditions or circumstances, including safety, weather, premium experience, and leisure time."[9] KPMG's research showed that even young and elderly populations, not normally viewed as prime consumers of mobility, will add significantly to consumer demand for mobility as a service in the future.

The forty-five- to seventy-five-year-olds: Among the boomers-plus, people are living longer, delaying retirement, and moving to cities, often as empty nesters. Older boomers, however, have concerns about the safety of their driving as they age. So do their children. They are not going to stop being active, however, and won't be intimidated by mobility options. They want their freedom of mobility. With mobility services, adult children don't have to worry about taking the keys away from older parents, and don't have to worry about their driving.

The ten- to fifteen-year-olds: Children and the parents of young children share the boomers' interest in mobility-on-demand services but for different reasons. For the children, it's all about freedom without having to get their parents or someone else to drive. Relying on Uber? Via? Lyft? No problem. They've grown up not only tech-savvy but instinctively trusting in technology. In fact, the only limitation on their use of mobility-on-demand services will be their parents' view on when they are old enough to use an Uber or Lyft service on their own. Parents like the idea of not having to be taxi driver for their kids. Mobility on demand will be especially attractive for such parents in the future, and they will hesitate less to use these services.

For both populations, the benefits are even more attractive when we add autonomous cars to the heterogeneous mix. For example, the very elderly can retain an independent quality of life well into their sunset years assured that their freedom to be mobile will not be restricted. Now also imagine strapping kids into an autonomous car and sending them off to grandma's home 10 miles away. This would be liberating to moms and dads conscripted into the role of chauffeur. No more school runs or hauling a minivan full of kids to soccer practice.

As Silberg cautioned, "Think of it this way: ten years ago, how many of us would have predicted that most ten-year-olds would be walking around with smartphones? We grossly underestimated that trend. The automotive landscape will significantly change as a result of autonomous vehicles, and consumer behavior will dictate the rate of adoption. As with the smartphone, let's not underestimate the power of these changes and the vast potential for new business models to satisfy them."

Having defined the CHIP mobility architecture and its dealing with mobility as a service, we will now assess how it meets contemporary society's expectations.

CHIP mobility is pragmatic

CHIP mobility is defined as an architecture rather than a solution: we recognize there can be no single "winning solution" applicable to diverse environments. Differences in approaches and solutions are motivated by geography, economics, climate, culture, and the nature of local government. The CHIP architecture is conducive to pragmatic configurations to suit local needs reflecting local conditions and governance structures. A centrally controlled Beijing may effect changes quicker than a New York City that needs to first attract and consolidate community support. The sprawl of Los Angeles requires different solutions from high-density Hong Kong. Mumbai can ill-afford many of the options suitable for Tokyo.

We envisage the CHIP architecture as placing one in a celebrity chef's kitchen. Within reach is a fascinating array of ingredients—the heterogeneity of modes. Many recipes are available, suitable for many palates, along with dietary guidelines and information. Cities can assemble very different meals suited to their taste.

CHIP mobility is organic and dynamic

CHIP mobility is organic in evolution and dynamic to change with the times. In its ideal implementations, it will support an open innovation environment that allows new entrepreneurs and new ideas to constantly bring enhancements to the system. The architecture will benefit from a regulatory environment that allows open access as long as fundamental rules of the game are observed. The architecture makes room for logical redundancies and multiple parallel options, recognizing that no system can accommodate innovation without some experimentation and overcapacity.

CHIP's flexible architecture encourages continued differentiation, essentially varied genetic mutations, across travel modes, business models, and changing regulations. Zipcar, for example, is one mutation of a rental car business paradigm that recruits technological innovations (connectivity, analytics, access) and a new business model (mobility on demand, ultra-short duration of rental). A CHIP environment encourages a stream of new genres of mobility. Affordable new microcars may be slotted in between two-wheelers and cars, just as the group ride-share vehicle UberPOOL may be slotted in between buses and taxis.

Like biological systems that survive and evolve in complex environments, the CHIP architecture is highly adaptive and, where allowed to thrive, will morph to suit local needs.

CHIP mobility is democratic and equitable

Many modern technological developments have been regarded warily by society. A world that is racing to adopt the latest trends often leaves a large fraction of the population behind. Technology has often been elitist, benefiting the well-to-do, who can indulge in the latest gadgets and improve their own personal outcomes. This worry is compounded by society's concern over the increasing gap in global distribution of income and wealth.[10] The widening gulf between the upper economic classes and much of the rest of the world further discriminates in access to productivity tools. Similarly, a tech-fueled economy moves at a pace that often handicaps older populations. Those less familiar with or less adept at using basic tools that support everyday living in a digitized economy are greatly disadvantaged.

Mobility should be a basic right for every human being. Thus, any architecture for future mobility has an imperative to be inclusive. We believe that the construct of CHIP mobility passes this essential test.

Affordability is enshrined in the CHIP architecture in many ways and for many reasons. First, the CHIP architecture emphasizes the importance of heterogeneity of modes. Mobility starts with sidewalks and walkways, since walking is a chosen mode for a large fraction of the population, especially in emerging urban economies.

Further, the emphasis on a critical role for shared resources and public transit fosters lower-cost mobility. In many emerging economies, investment in public transit has badly lagged economic development, and these countries pay a high price for inefficiency in mobility. In such situations we foresee the CHIP architecture harnessing technology and business models to compensate, to some extent, for investment deficiencies in transport infrastructure. CHIP enables supply to emerge and meet unmet demands. CHIP mobility permits blurring of the public-private divide, which helps ensure that a city captures the energy that is unleashed when private enterprise, entrepreneurship, and private investment are encouraged to help solve problems. Chariot in San Francisco is a private mobility service that uses vans to complement public transit. Although San Francisco is far from a poor city, such services allow cash-strapped city administrations to deploy private capital and leverage technology-based efficiency to provide multiple transit options. Chapter 12 addresses the role of cities and societies in ensuring fair access to mobility for all sections of the population.

Similarly, with a rapidly aging population in many countries, there will be increasing demand from elderly travelers for low-cost, easily accessible, and not physically demanding transit options. The CHIP architecture incorporates solutions like UberPOOL or city versions of BlaBlaCar that offer personal door-to-door transport at fares that are considerably lower than the cost of traditional taxis. Since the CHIP architecture emphasizes a mobility-as-needed system, it avoids idling of assets and hence lowers the cost of mobility.

The CHIP architecture preserves use of cars and is not dogmatic in seeking a decline in their use. We do not believe that the combination of utility, value, and satisfaction provided by the car will quickly be expunged. But CHIP mobility places cars within a basket of alternatives, including car sharing, so that cars play their role in a full spectrum of solutions and suggests that they pay their fair share toward societal and environmental costs. In Denmark, for example, progressive policies have promoted environment-friendly bicycling and public transit. New cars are burdened with a tax in excess of 100 percent of the pretax price. Yet Denmark remains a vibrant car market and in 2015 registered more cars than ever before.[11]

CHIP mobility is green and sustainable
CHIP mobility promotes a greener future. Steering future mobility to a sustainable platform cannot be accomplished by technology alone. Sustainability will be attained through voluntary changes in behavior derived from improved awareness, but also through governments motivating behavioral changes in populations. Framing regulations, prescribing product and

service standards, and levying fees or imposing penalties are all levers available to governments to mold the mobility architecture. Many cities facing deteriorating air quality are advancing emission standards, and incentivizing zero-emission vehicle fleets to good effect. The CHIP architecture also preserves a role for road-use pricing, congestion fees, and even planning inner-city parking capacity and pricing as additional levers to motivate changes in user behavior. The architecture anticipates that societies and their administrations need to offer both inducements and disincentives. With a mix of offerings, government policies can motivate users to voluntarily pick from a palette of options and select solutions that are both greener and easier to use. London has transformed mobility, achieving its objective of a faster shift of commuters to public transit by offering sweeter carrots (increased travel mode options, integrated contactless payment, the Oyster card, intelligent Citymapper apps) and harsher sticks (congestion fees, limited-capacity high-priced parking, more bus lanes and fewer auto lanes).

CHIP in summary

The CHIP mobility architecture seeks to balance benefits against costs to deliver a sustainable and efficient future mobility architecture. For both benefits and costs, there is a user's perspective as well as a societal perspective. The CHIP architecture is motivated by individual preference, which is moderated by societal imperatives. The CHIP architecture relies on better tools and sensors to render hidden costs and constraints visible. Urban land use, environmental impact, and congestion, for example, are better tracked, and their implications for economic and social outcomes are better understood. This visibility allows cities and administrations to orchestrate a range of policies to encourage favorable choices. The CHIP architecture also relies on market forces to stimulate technological breakthroughs and business model innovations to deliver solutions that offer both customers and society faster, smarter, and greener mobility.

The next chapter examines how cities and stakeholders can play their respective transformative roles as societies start to deploy CHIP mobility.

12 Implementing CHIP Mobility: The Roles of Stakeholders

> Who you are is what you have been. Who you will be is what you do now.
>
> *—Buddha*

The CHIP mobility architecture and a framework to assess and improve mobility were presented in previous chapters. This chapter examines the roles of many of the key stakeholders who can effect desired change and transformation.

Cities and their administrations

Excavations of intricate ancient cities in Mesopotamia, in the Andes, and in the Indus Valley lead to wonder at the level of planning that went into these urban centers, with their roads, canals, drains, and public spaces. The Roman Empire was sustained by cities and settlements connected by well-planned paved roads, many of which remain in existence even today, two millennia later. Human aggregation has required a high degree of forethought and design beginning even in early times. Los Angeles, London, and other cities traversed their respective urban trajectories primarily in the twentieth century strongly influenced by city planning and policies. As modern society contemplates ever larger cities and greater population densities, the administrators of these urban regions must have the appropriate tools and frameworks to take on city planning challenges. The commitment to sound long-term planning and sustainable mobility can have a positive impact on very large populations in the future, especially for many of the fast-growing cities in the emerging economies.

Cities thrive when they prove attractive to residents and investment. A 2013 survey of fifty cities from around the world revealed that the top three criteria for attracting new investment to a city were environment, economic development, and mobility.[1] Specifically, in their quest to configure sustainable and user-friendly future mobility architectures, large-city administrations will need to undertake many of the following steps as they employ the CHIP mobility framework.

Focus urban master plans on desired future urban form

As the planet prepares to go from 55 percent urban population to 66 percent, and many urban areas hurtle toward their destinies as megacities, the world's priciest real estate continues to spiral upward, especially in Asia. Hong Kong is twice as expensive as New York City, an erstwhile benchmark for expensive property. Singapore, another vibrant metropolis is one-third pricier than New York. Even in developing countries such as India, Mumbai can be a more expensive city in which to buy real estate than Tokyo, another benchmark for expensive real estate.[2] This trend of population densification imposes huge pressures for effective use of urban land. Planning the trajectory of the urban form, keeping in mind social capital, economic efficiency, and environmental responsibility is a crucial obligation for planners and is a task that is often poorly accomplished.

Noting the inter-dependence between urban forms and mobility architecture, planners need to ensure congruent approaches. In their efforts to accommodate larger populations while respecting these social goals, many cities would benefit from more compact urban forms, with local neighborhoods designed around people, not cars. Accomplishing such changes would require addressing issues such as densification, zoning principles, the size of city blocks, the utilization of public spaces and incorporation of transit oriented development principles.

Many cities confront the need to reform archaic zoning laws. Many obsolete regulations curb housing density and were a consequence of earlier experiences when poor planning and inadequate infrastructure proved incapable of supporting high-rise construction. In many rapidly expanding cities in emerging economies, retaining such flawed zoning policies has skewed development adversely in the direction of sprawl. This consigns residents in these cities to dependence on personal transport with a high likelihood of consequent traffic congestion and environmental degradation. In such cities as Jakarta, Manila, and São Paulo, the pace of growth has been so rapid that planners have struggled to keep up. The National Capital Territory region around New Delhi in India has been growing at 50 percent per decade and almost thrice as fast as forecast in the Regional Plan of 2001.[3] However, residents in such cities are often in no mood to wait patiently for public mobility solutions to be put in place. If citizens perceive that invest-ment in public transit is delayed or inadequate, they fulfill their demand for mobility with personal vehicles whenever possible. Over 80 percent of New Delhi's fast spreading population is dependent on private transportation to serve their mobility needs. This solution is both economically inefficient and environmentally damaging.

As a result, a number of cities are now convinced that they need to encour-age expansion vertically. The economic and environmental advantages of cities like New York, Hong Kong, and Tokyo with their many skyscrapers and efficient mobility architecture are being recognized. Sky-high real estate val-ues also demand that the cost of expensive land be shared among more people, thereby improving access to wider income demographics. Higher population densities automatically make related investment in efficient transport infrastructure, modern utilities, and amenities more viable.

Policies to support CHIP mobility architecture

Many futurists fear that as megacities develop, governance challenges can lead to large expanses of lawless slums or favelas. Democracies depend on enfranchising and empowering all sections of their population. In many cit-ies, the poor and the very elderly lack access to safe and affordable mobility. A mobility architecture that provides access to all segments of the population facilitates engaging the full population in positive economic development.

Encouraging a shift away from priority for personal modes   As multiple modes jostle for space in crowded cities, many find the need to prioritize allocation of space and public assets in favor of public and shared mobility. For many cities, the development of more mass transit options is necessary.

Growing and populous economies have recognized the need to be pre-pared to move large populations at affordable cost in their major cities. This is very evident in fast-growing economies like those of China or India. Met-ros or sub-ways offer unbeatable efficiency for mobility in high density cor-ridors even though this solution requires significant investment. According to a global survey, in 2015 China had more than 2,700 kilometers of metros in place and was building another 2,800 kilometers of new lines in twenty-three cities.[4] Similarly, India is moving forward with deployment of metro rail transits in more than twelve cities.

For their moderate capacity corridors, Bogotá, in Colombia, and Curitiba, in southern Brazil, road space which was traditionally allocated for personal cars was reduced and the lanes thus freed up were turned over for use by their fast-expanding bus rapid transit systems. As supporters of bus transit have argued, based on the relative footprint in urban traffic, a bus can be ten to twenty times more efficient than a car for moving people in crowded thoroughfares.

Seattle represents a major U.S. city that is rapidly transforming its urban mobility pattern with emphasis on public transit. According to Scott Kubly, Director of Seattle's Department of Transportation, "We can't handle any more cars than we currently have."[5] The city's residents have voted to increase funding toward investment in a combination of new bus lines (the largest such expansion in the U.S.) and light rail along with an expansion of bike lanes. The public transit system, under the brand of RapidRide, is supported by a host of parallel initiatives including restriction of cars from some bus-only downtown streets during rush hour, electronic fare payments, and better traffic management with priority for buses. The network expansion will bring buses in closer proximity to 72 percent of residents from the current level of 25 percent. With this, they expect single-occupancy vehicles to drop from 30 percent to 25 percent over ten years. Since 2002, Seattle has witnessed bus ridership increase at twice the rate of population growth.[6]

The Estonian capital city of Tallinn has taken a bolder step. In 2013, the city made travel on public transit free for city residents. At the same time, cars were restricted from some roads, and parking fees in the city center were hiked. Almost immediately, traffic on city streets fell by 10 percent. While overall ridership increases were lower than expected, the policies generated enough benefits to sustain the subsidy for this change. In a very different part of the world, in Omaha, Nebraska, city planners, after evaluating many options, reduced the number of parking spots and increased the capacity of the urban transit system for the same reason. In democratic societies, these policies must pass the test of being seen to be fair and to serve public good.

The C40 Cities Climate Leadership Group, comprising city administrators from around the world, has created an urban action scenario showcasing declining trends in the use of personal vehicles in cities across the OECD economies, where similar policies have been successfully rolled out. By getting cities to adhere to compact urban redesign and invest in modern mobility infrastructure, the C40 Group anticipates that the share of mobility provided by private vehicles will decline from a level of about 64 percent in 2015 to 53 percent by 2050. The group's analysis reveals that greenhouse gas emissions from OECD cities had already peaked by 2015. Taking into account a combination of vehicular technologies, modal shifts, changes in use patterns, and urban design, it estimates that between 2015 and 2030, greenhouse gas emissions resulting from transporting people in urban environments could decline by half.[7]

Inducing private players to augment capacity and competition   Many cities across the world face acute financial constraints. Moreover, the demand for transit investment has grown so rapidly, particularly in emerging economies, that few states have exchequers big enough to fund all their needs. Over several decades, many nations have slowly distanced themselves from the principle that transport infrastructure should fall exclusively under state or public ownership. Private capital has become necessary in a variety of ways for making an investment in building or improving tunnels, bridges, and highways. Sometimes private investment is viewed as a temporary measure, and business models such as build-operate-transfer allow for gradual transfer of the asset back to public ownership.

In keeping with modern trends, the CHIP framework encourages blurring of the boundaries among public, shared, and personal mobility, essentially increasing the degrees of freedom for administrators to act. The engagement of private enterprise and innovative new solutions marshals a broader set of resources to address the mobility challenge. For example, many cities in Southeast Asia allow motorcycle taxis to ply where public transport is inadequate. Such mobility components can be fast, efficient, and affordable. Motorcycles can navigate through crowded thoroughfares better than most other kinds of vehicles and are therefore highly popular.

The Kutsuplus service in Helsinki and the Chariot transit service in Silicon Valley had come to serve as alternatives to public transit, moving five to ten people at a time, using platforms similar to Uber to expand their reach and efficiency. The orchestration of the hundreds of privately owned tuk-tuks in Indonesia or share-autos in India can be significantly enhanced with regulations that encourage their wider use and their adoption of low cost apps for hailing and route optimization.

These shared modes of transit can be a significant addition to affordable transit capacity in many cities. These services are typically funded by private capital and so can be put into use even when public funds are highly constrained. Yet the approach requires considerable care to ensure proper governance and transparency in operation.

Aligning to environmental goals   Increasingly, cities are also obliged to adjust their development trajectories to align with national and global commitments to the environment. Such commitments require mobility architectures to meet quantified sustainability goals. Many modern cities have rediscovered the value of nonmotorized modes of mobility. Walking and bicycling are enjoying a resurgence of interest in a large number of urban environments.

Motorized modes have been obliged to clean up their act and produce much lower per capita carbon emissions through increased fuel efficiency, and the use of innovative technology (such as electric vehicles), while new and improved business models (such as carpooling and vanpooling) contribute by more effective passenger aggregation. A growing number of cities are depending on these advances and are enacting laws limiting entry to central areas to only those vehicles that are deemed "zero-emission" or "ultra-low-emission" to ensure the city meets its sustainability target. The proposed Urban Mobility Plan for Barcelona in Spain will call for reducing circulation of private cars by one fifth by 2018 in order that the city may comply with the European Union regulations for air quality. "This is not a war against the car, but we need to make a radical change, mainly due to a health issue," said the Councilor for Mobility, Mercedes Vidal.[8]

The CHIP framework may be used to assess whether cities are employing a full spectrum of heterogeneous solutions that offer the best prospects for improving the environmental performance of mobility. At the same time, the framework can help evaluate how effective various innovative business models and mobility connections are. Analysis of gaps and shortcomings can motivate encouragement of new solutions so that citizens have a wide array of more sustainable mobility choices.

Some cities have sought to ban cars from entering specific areas. The Innere Stadt area of Vienna and the city of Brussels observe a ban on cars in certain city center areas. Oslo is another European city that is considering a proposal to severely limit the use of cars in the city center beginning in 2019.

In many emerging economies, even where car ownership rates are much lower than in industrialized economies, rapid development and a very rapid increase in motorization are causing similar pressures, leading to curbs on personal vehicle use. Two Sunday mornings a month, the city government of Kuala Lumpur, in Malaysia, hosts the KL Car Free Morning, when the downtown city streets are taken over by joggers, bicyclists, walkers, strollers, wheelchairs, skateboards, roller-bladers, and even marching bands. Mexico City, Beijing, Shanghai, and New Delhi have been pushed into taking action on two parallel strategies. On one track, public transit infrastructure is receiving significant investment to provide people with alternatives to the use of personal vehicles. At the same time, on the other track, curbs on licensing new vehicles and restrictions on the use of personal cars are being imposed.

As these cities are discovering, curbs on cars can be successful only if the city has prepared itself with a host of alternative public and shared modes to compensate for capacity. The CHIP framework can be used to guide capacity expansion with a combination of shared and private modes.

Align fiscal policies: The principle of "user pays"

Allocation of public spaces, investment in roads, city parking and connectivity infrastructure, and setting up new mass transit systems are all expensive initiatives and usually involve commitment to sustaining some form of subsidy. The important role played by urban mobility in the trajectory of cities demands that the investments made, as well as the incentives offered and levies imposed are all carefully aligned to deliver desired outcomes. The CHIP mobility architecture relies on a dynamic set of fiscal tools to fund infrastructure and influence patterns of consumption and the demand for mobility.

Paying for public assets and infrastructure   Traditionally, taxes were blunt instruments that primarily served the purpose of revenue generation for the nation or the city. The U.S. interstates and the German autobahns were initially funded by national taxes and made freely available for all users. Taxpayers paid their dues, whether they used these highways or not. Similarly, across the world, drivers of cars have often not been required to pay the full cost of their use of public assets. A World Bank study points out that most surface streets and main roads in urban areas are underpriced, even after the taxes imposed on fuel sales are taken into account.[9]

The same has historically been also true of parking costs in many cities. Parking spaces have often been treated as legacy assets that local authorities have failed to value in a contemporary urban setting. An EU report noted that parking capacity and pricing are important complementary tools for controlling vehicular traffic in inner cities. Parking fees not only pay for costs of infrastructure but also induce people to use public modes, reduce congestion, and lower air pollution.[10]

Future societies will find they can ill afford such oversight or disparity. The growing demand for use of urban land will need to be addressed through zoning policies and regulations and fees governing use of valuable assets. As a result, cities are increasingly adopting the principle that users must pay their full and fair costs for the use of public assets and resources. Toll roads and tunnels have long been used to allocate costs directly to users. Many other assets and resources, however, have not been appropriately priced, usually because tools to accurately measure their use were unavailable or limited in utility.

Modern tools, methods, and technologies allow a sharper and deeper analysis to be undertaken and hence promote more accurate allocation of costs. With technologies such as video cameras and transponders for vehicle identification and numerous electronic payment modes (as is deployed in London's system), cities can more easily price the use of roadways and parking in proportion to the amount of use and in real time.

The CHIP framework anticipates the use of modern technologies to allow far greater precision in implementing such pricing and fee collection. Inevitably, many heretofore "invisible" subsidies for personal transport will disappear as cities balance ever tighter budgets and acquire better tools to implement a "fair" approach to pricing public resources. The challenge for city administrators is to articulate societal priorities, estimate the full cost and impact of various transit modes, and integrate a staircase of modal offerings across the price spectrum within the CHIP framework.

Paying for related economic costs   Policy makers have also found the need to allocate other costs that cities incur but that were typically less visible. Lowering the environmental impact of transportation is worth a lot to a modern city. Many cities face penalties for failing to meet minimum air quality norms. Efforts to remedy environmental degradation are costly and increasingly consume considerable city investments. Moreover, in some cities, residents, particularly children and the elderly, court serious long-term ailments from breathing polluted urban air.

The costs of congestion were similarly diffuse, and used to be hard to quantify. Traffic paralysis can be debilitating to an economy. During the 1980s and 1990s, governments in the U.S. and Europe struggled to build roadways to keep pace with growing vehicle populations. As they invested billions to build roadways to ease congestion, the expanded capacity only encouraged more travelers to buy and use cars. The newly added road capacity was quickly saturated, and the long-term problem remained.

With the additional data now more easily available, the impacts on environment and congestion, hitherto invisible, can be estimated in financial terms. Electronic sensors can measure traffic density and the dynamics of congestion in bottlenecks, and can even identify individual vehicles using the road. Using such tools, and computer modeling, cities today have much better estimates of the financial costs of air pollution and congestion. In chapter 2 we had dealt with estimations of the economic consequence of a combination of these two factors. This expenditure can be more effectively assessed against cost of new investments and economic outcomes from a different mobility architecture.

After attempts to curb congestion by adding capacity failed, congestion pricing came to the fore, imposing additional fees on users of roads in an effort to allocate such costs better or to modify user behavior. In explaining its basis, the World Bank has noted that "the concept of congestion pricing is that road users should pay a price that reflects the short-run marginal social cost of road use."[11] This pricing is designed to be dynamic, and hence variable, based on actual levels of congestion.

After London imposed a congestion fee for vehicles entering the city center areas, data showed that vehicular traffic dropped by 16 percent, traffic delays fell by 26 percent in the first three years after the charge was instituted, and particulate emissions dropped by 12 percent.[12] The last factor was estimated to contribute to marginally increased life expectancy for residents in the congestion zone. These figures lend themselves for use to estimate economic consequences and guide use of fees or incentives. From 2020, personal vehicles that enter London and do not conform to the ultra-low-emission vehicle (ULEV) category will also be levied an additional fee of £12.50, beyond the congestion fee, to help offset costs of complying with clean air standards.

Cities are no longer able to ignore the social and economic impacts of car use, notably environmental degradation and congestion. They are obliged to reform their mobility architecture and steer user behavior toward achieving societal goals. Many cities have concluded that they have been chasing the wrong problem. Instead of investing in more efficient public transit to ease congestion as Tokyo, London and New York had done, they were going down a path that was essentially an endless and adverse spiral.

The CHIP framework can help administrators with a rational basis of evaluation of existing or proposed deployment of incentives or fees through modeling of the possible outcomes, valuing resulting benefits or cost to society, and factoring fair pricing of public assets and services.

Managing subsidies in an era of privately funded infrastructure   In an era when for-profit enterprises engage in infrastructure creation and operation, a more complex basis of pricing is required. Policies need to blend the for-profit motivation of the investor with the obligations of the city to provide access to mobility across all economic classes.

Public transit services in most cities enjoy subsidies. As private operators engage in the provision of public services, a more complex approach to estimating their contributions to public good is warranted. A case in point is that of Centennial, Colorado, as we had noted in chapter 10. The city allows commuters to be partially compensated by the city for use of Lyft taxis to access and ride the light-rail network. By expanding the use of public transit, the city identified a host of other benefits. This program implies that taxpayers are not only paying the cost for these users, they are also paying a share of the profits of the private operator. When such funding is provided after due care and transparent articulation of the net benefits to the whole community, it can allow those cities to more effectively leverage private capital and private operators' services to the public.

When cities put in place robust governance, their options to engage private enterprise to aid city operations are significantly enhanced.

Keeping policies and the mobility architecture nimble.   Cities need to be prepared to deal with the dynamic nature of the mobility environment. Technologies change, habits and landscapes evolve, and new business solutions appear, ever faster. Both the mobility framework and administrations responsible for supporting it must be nimble to keep pace with and accommodate these changes. The CHIP architecture, like Baran's packet-switching philosophy, expects a continuous induction of new mobility modes, and incorporation of novel ways to link modes (both physically and digitally). The system thrives when the universe of options and combinations is ever expanding. The CHIP framework is a useful tool to simulate "what-if" scenarios and encourage the induction of new modes and mobility services even as some, that have failed to deliver expected outcomes, are replaced.

Oversee and monitor mobility operations

In the future, cities will also bear new responsibilities as they play a more central role in orchestrating urban mobility. The tragic deaths that occurred in the three-day-long traffic jam described in chapter 2 in Indonesia were an unfortunate outcome of poor planning and coordination. That many other cities have come close to confronting a similar tragedy as a result of congestion places a big onus on cities to be prepared to respond dynamically to evolving situations. Cities are typically equipped to deal with disaster management for floods and earthquakes. Mobility management, not only at times of calamities and evacuations, will be a growing responsibility for cities.

A dynamic mobility landscape with many more modes and many new regulations and policies leaves cities with a complex task of licensing, monitoring, and oversight. The number of interfaces has grown enormously, and the task of ensuring compliant operations is challenging. As one example, the induction of app-hailed taxis like Uber in many cities around the world has led to numerous legal issues. Such a system is affected by labor laws, vehicle compliance regulations, pricing policies, operator liability, and competition law. Singapore has modified regulations to allow a trial of driverless taxis in a restricted-access industrial park as it evaluates the possibilities of wider deployment of that technology. Cities often find themselves having to invent and oversee new rules as technological solutions and business models evolve rapidly.

The success of cities such as Singapore and London in aligning policies and driving towards desired outcomes is striking. After a combination of such policies, involving investments, curbs on vehicle use, incentives and fees, and induction of private enterprises, was implemented by Singapore since 2000, traffic volumes dropped by almost a fifth, while traffic speeds increased by a third without any new roads being required. Singapore had prepared itself with a host of alternative travel modes, including mass transit, so that the inconvenience caused was minimal. These policies have lessened congestion in the inner city, improved air quality, and reduced traffic accidents and injuries.

Smart cities

This book has chronicled the fascinating evolution of technology in cars and mobility. At the scale of an automobile, we find these products are embedded with more software than early spacecraft. Cars are expected to "talk" to other cars and infrastructure, and cars even drive themselves. How much more technology could be embedded at the scale of entire cities, as every aspect of city operations is visualized and made interactive!

Cities are indeed on that journey. Within a few years "smart" cities are anticipated to make residents' daily lives safer, more productive, and more satisfying. Across the world, nations are rolling out sizable investments as they endow cities with information and communication technologies (ICT) to render them "smart," or at least smarter than they were. From South Korea (in Songdo), to Japan (in Fujisawa) to the U.S. (in Peña Station, a suburb of Denver), pilot programs are embedding technologies across a variety of functions and urban infrastructure.

Now they are joined by fast-developing economies in Asia. By 2013, China alone had kicked off more than 193 pilot projects for smart cities. In 2016, the government of India announced a national plan to roll out deployment of funds to promote ninety-eight smart cities over a five-year period. Smart-city technologies leverage the power of information and connectivity to boost economics, services, governance, mobility, and sustainability.

Contrary to some misconceptions, smart cities need not be impersonal and sterile environments. New Urbanism as a philosophy deals with cities as living and dynamic organisms. Organisms survive and evolve by sensing and monitoring external stimuli and creating appropriate reactions. We expect smart cities to resemble living organisms that wake up every morning. As any time-lapse video of city life shows, the stirring of life as people start their daily commutes on thoroughfares can be visualized as blood coursing through arteries. Sensors, like nerves, will communicate pain points that will be locally acted upon, just as in a living organism with local instinctive reactions. In addition, a master control room will keep track of overall conditions, much like a brain, and orchestrate actions across domains.

Cities have complex evolutionary trajectories that defy simple correlation between plans, investments, and outcomes. People and the way they live shape cities. Cities can serve residents better when they can sense people's interactions with the city, starting from their local neighborhoods, for such services as utilities, health care, and mobility. In the town of Enfield, in the U.K., an intelligent virtual personal assistant named Amelia is available on call on behalf of the town council ready to respond to queries across a range of topics from residents, using natural language much like a human, round-the-clock, seven days a week.

Technological progress is now placing some very powerful tools in planner's and city managers' hands to help with the task of sensing and listening to the pulse of the city. In a recent survey of more than fifty diverse cities from around the world, respondents identified the need for cities to be "self-aware" as an important aspect of governance.[13] Smart city technologies help nudge what used to be concrete jungles towards becoming more self-aware entities. Smart cities rely on sensors and data to measure everything from traffic flow, rainfall, and water and sewer functions to health care intervention needs and even crime. Smart streetlights turn themselves on based on ambient lighting and even get their bulbs changed when necessary. Sensors in water pipes and sewage lines optimally manage supply and flow. Garbage bins broadcast a signal when they need to be emptied. In Songdo, a more advanced pilot renders garbage bins and trucks obsolete, with a pneumatic waste-disposal system that conveys all waste to a central underground processing center. With more data and more analytics, city administrators have a better sense of the pulse of their domains.

Smart cities and CHIP mobility

The CHIP architecture thrives in data-rich environments. When rich external data sources, derived from the data network of the smart and connected city, augment their own internal generation of data, the effectiveness of the CHIP architecture is greatly boosted. Mobility essentially becomes one of many services orchestrated by the city; mobility serves as a module within the entire system.

Improving information and data flows   In the CHIP framework, smart cities will deploy an expanded set of tools to influence mobility.

- Smart data-driven traffic management is now in place in many cities. Modern traffic control rooms with real-time data can anticipate problems before they escalate. Smart systems can be used to manage traffic lights based on actual traffic load and not on the basis of predefined intervals, saving time, energy, and environmental impact. City administrators can use technology to predict bottlenecks and sources of congestion and dynamically reroute traffic to avoid backups.
- Monitoring and disseminating information about air quality will become easier. Ambient air quality in cities like Los Angeles and New Delhi is strongly dependent on prevailing weather. City managers in a city that sees a warm day with temperature inversion can advise more commuters to swap their cars for alternative modes, hence avoiding a day that breaches permissible air quality thresholds.
- The improved synchronization of multimodal transit, linking buses, underground metros, and light rail, will create better connectivity for commuters. The capacity and frequency of transits on specific routes can be dynamically adjusted according to demand. Many of the smart city experiments are already using driverless shuttles in certain routes.
- Sensors can steer drivers instantly to parking spots based on the dynamic monitoring of empty spaces, saving time and fuel. The sensors will not only alert the driver when the parking duration is coming to an end, they can also pass on the same information to the parking inspector!
- Smart-city infrastructure can alert commuters to where bicycles are available and where they can be dropped off.
- In colder climates, smart cities can even monitor icy sidewalks, summon sidewalk cleaners and alert pedestrians.

Overall, by proactively intervening with the expanded set of levers smart cities now possess, they can allow commuters to experience more satisfying travel.

Improving vehicle-to-infrastructure communication and autonomy   The CHIP framework anticipates even more use of technology to integrate mobility in future smart cities. As the era of connected cars dawns, and vehicle-to-infrastructure technology becomes more widespread, the overlap of smart city infrastructure, connected cars and the Internet of Things will significantly magnify possibilities. Cars will be able to communicate to smart-city traffic lights and facilitate smoother flows and fewer stops. Idling time for cars at traffic lights will be reduced, saving fuel and lowering emissions. Cars will practically guide themselves dynamically altering routes to save time and energy.

Data from these multiple city sources will also be seamlessly employed in myriad smart device apps that guide users across multiple modes of travel. Travelers will be able to optimize segments of their travel more precisely, and the trip will be better tailored to their unique preferences and circumstances. Smart cities can help better accommodate the priorities of each individual, strengthening the bond between residents and the city.

In the near future, planners will also have to prepare for autonomous modes of mobility mixed in with conventional modes. The advent of autonomous modes will open up a whole new set of transformational possibilities for cities.

Enforcing compliance   Cities big and small, in industrialized and emerging regions, struggle to achieve effective governance in a manner that is fair and equitable. ICT can contribute to efficiency and transparency. For example, one seldom argues a speeding ticket with a police officer equipped with a smart radar that displays a picture of the car with its speed recorded in the image. ICT can eliminate much ambiguity to ensure impartiality and fairness.

Singapore has invested in ICT to improve surveillance and security. New York uses ICT and citizen involvement to identify illegally parked cars. In India, driver licenses with embedded chips help law enforcement access driving records and deal with habitual offenders.

A range of sensors, including cameras, is being deployed by smart cities to aid in security, traffic law enforcement, problem anticipation, and so on. These sensors continuously transmit data that may be employed for a wide range of analytical purposes beyond ensuring compliance.

Implementing pricing and fees   Information and communication technologies have revolutionized the domains of sensing and tracking. They are aided by "always-on" sensors carried by people and by vehicles. Electronic tachographs communicating to city infrastructure are used for everything from monitoring driver time on-duty, tracking vehicle use within specific "fences" such as highways, and dynamically levying tolls, which can be fine-tuned to the length of highway use, the time of use, the axle load, and other parameters.

The potential for such transformation of a city has drawn the attention of such global technology giants as Cisco, IBM, Siemens, Panasonic, and Google, which perceive a large new business frontier opening up. With the engagement of these and other similar solution providers, cities and mobility will be boosted by a new source of skills and competence to complement legacy mobility players. According to Phil Gott of IHS Automotive, "Smart cities are evolving simultaneously with connected vehicles: Mobility and transport solutions are a key focus for many current smart-city projects around the world and this trend is set to continue. IHS sees mobility and transport as a major growth area for the smart-city market."[14]

Deploying the CHIP mobility architecture in an environment that is boosted by adoption of many of the smart city technologies will offer those communities a significant multiplication of benefits.

Outcomes with CHIP mobility

As Einstein observed, "In theory, theory and practice are the same. In practice, they are not." In the following section we examine three cities that have embarked on bold plans to upgrade their mobility architecture. Mexico City and Helsinki, faced with dissimilar challenges and constraints, have deployed two very different orchestrations of the CHIP architecture elements. They represent work-in-progress and early results are encouraging. Masdar City in the United Arab Emirates is yet another distinct environment and is studied as a case in which the flexibility and heterogeneity demanded by the CHIP architecture are absent, which has led to the problematic deployment of an ambitious plan.

Mexico City   Mexico City fits the template of a large, rapidly growing city, with a population exceeding 20 million. In 1990, the UN labeled Mexico City the most polluted city on the planet. Even in 2013, air pollution was expected to cause 1,700 deaths per year. A Climate Action Program launched in 2008 has started to meet intermediate milestones toward an overall goal of cutting pollution by 30 percent by 2020. Former Mexican president Felipe Calderón outlined a vision for a "connected, compact, coordinated" city as a part of the roadmap.

Transport was identified as the largest source of pollution, contributing about 45 percent. Consequently, a large part of the total effort to tackle pollution has been aimed at mobility. In 2014, Mexico passed legislation guaranteeing citizens a "right to mobility." The plan reserved an important role for city administration to work with private enterprises toward achieving this goal. The plan relied on a multitude of mobility solutions, both public and private, to achieve improvements. The plan was rich in technology, employing smart sensing and traffic management even as it paid attention to social outcomes such as the human values of parks and inexpensive recreation for the whole family. While it is too soon to proclaim success, and Mexico City has a long way to go to rid itself of its polluted air, we can usefully review some of the main initiatives.

Among the measures, a bus rapid transit (BRT) system increased the use of public transit and lowered personal vehicle use. By 2016, it was the world's sixth largest BRT system, serving more than a million passengers daily. When city administrators observed that more than half of trips were less than 8 kilometers, bike lanes were expanded and a bike-sharing system, EcoBici, was launched. The largest urban park in Mexico was revitalized and provided walking paths and weekend recreation. Weekly car-free days and a pedestrian-only zone in the city's historical center were additional measures to improve air quality. Cars not complying with modern emission standards were restricted from entering parts of the city. Taxi services were encouraged to switch to electric vehicles, and this was also expected to extend to private vehicles. Gradually, the number of days on which the city was under high pollution alert declined. Nitrogen oxide concentrations in ambient air in 2016 had been reduced to a quarter of their value in the 1980s. That this was being done in a country where the economy was still growing and budgets were relatively constrained serves as compelling motivator to many similar cities in emerging economies.

Helsinki   Helsinki in Finland is very different from any of the previously mentioned megacities. Yet, urban quality of life, air quality and user-friendly mobility are global challenges. Helsinki had also embarked on a journey to fundamentally transform urban travel. The city's priorities and initiatives underscore the broad applicability of the CHIP mobility architecture. The city administrator's goals were specific: they had targeted deployment of a citywide mobility as a service (MaaS) solution. The objective was a system so convenient, flexible, and cost-effective that "no one would have reason to buy a car for travel within the city by 2025."[15]

City administrators in Helsinki hoped to provide their residents with a personalized, point-to-point mobility-on-demand system involving seamless and integrated public and private transport. The plan did not ban the use of cars. As the CHIP framework proposes, the city administrators expected cars, city-bikes, taxis, and vans that provide Uber-like service to coexist with traditional public transit and even ferries.

Helsinki's plans for achieving this goal depended heavily on the use of technology and participation by a populace in a city where smartphones and connectivity were ubiquitous. The transport network comprised different modes that were all technology-enabled. Cashless payment, facilitated through the Helsinki Travel Card, was a key enabler to achieve connections across private and public modes. The Journey Planner app serves as travel planner to synthesize individual journeys. Apps were also rolled out to bundle the planning and payment gateway functions across the multiple modes. Trial runs of a self-driving twelve-seat electric minibus were started in 2016. In Finland, laws do not require a driver to be at the wheel of a vehicle.

The CHIP framework is intended to be flexible and dynamic. It accommodates experimentation and anticipates that some technologies or business solutions may not prove viable. In these circumstances, the ecosystem is intended to adapt and evolve and to allow newer and better solutions to replace those that fail.

Not all of the elements in Helsinki have been successful. The Kutsuplus app-hailed vans, which worked on a principle similar to UberPOOL's, failed after three years and were terminated at the end of 2015. Failure was attributed to subscale operations and the need for greater-than-planned subsidies. However, Helsinki's other mobility-on-demand systems adapted to make up for the loss of Kutsuplus. The combination of heterogeneity and a dynamic and entrepreneurial environment will ensure workarounds when some solutions fail. To provide further encouragement, the similar Chariot service in San Francisco is an adaptation of the same idea and has been faring significantly better under a different operating environment.

Figure 12.1 Helsinki's course to deploy mobility as a service is heavily dependent on technology. An autonomous electric twelve-seat minibus is being evaluated to complement the city's transit system.
Source: EasyMile.

Masdar City   The CHIP framework emphasizes variety, flexibility, and the engagement of a dynamic population of entrepreneurs and technologists. When some of these characteristics are missing, even bold ideas to transform mobility can stumble, despite adequate commitment and funding. Few cities in the world have the luxury of starting with a clean sheet of paper in redefining mobility. Yet in Masdar City, a car-free community in Abu Dhabi, the United Arab Emirates, city planners did indeed find such an opportunity.

The UAE proposed that ambitious project to create a city with zero net carbon emissions. City blocks with streets shaded from the harsh sun by buildings, power generation from renewable sources, and numerous promising concepts were all part of the master plan. Blessed with a large budget, the planners' mobility architecture called for a citywide system of autonomous zero-emission electric podcars that could zip travelers from one location to the next, traveling on dedicated pathways. The Masdar City Master Plan was to enable mobility as a service by using podcars available on demand.

This case, however, provides an example of a promising concept that proved too difficult in implementation. In Masdar City the design required a complex interdependence between podcar tracks and the buildings they would serve. Thus, to get the desired system-wide performance, the streets, buildings, walkways, and podcar tracks all had to be designed simultaneously and integrally. The required architecture proved quite inflexible to the natural evolution patterns of cities. The numerous constraints proved daunting. The developers of many of the city's planned buildings were unprepared, both in regard to design constraints and in regard to financial willingness, to bear the cost of integration. Expansion of the Masdar City podcar project has been shelved.[16]

The technical feasibility and social desirability of many of these interesting concepts must be reconciled with system complexities and financial realities. Too often they fail because planners have not understood the full set of operational requirements. Urban environments require highly adaptable and heterogeneous solutions with a certain degree of capacity redundancy. To believe that a city's mobility architecture and operations can be optimally planned and run will lead to failure.

Box 12.1 Washington D.C.: Mobility on Demand

The waitress looked bored as she filled our coffee for the third time. No doubt she was waiting to close the breakfast room. It was the Marriott in Greenbelt, a leafy campus suburb of Washington, D.C. I had awoken on a lovely spring morning almost three hours earlier to a fairly full schedule of meetings in and around the city. With fellow board members who had flown in from Germany, we were taking stock of the previous day's meeting over breakfast. Wrapping up and exchanging good-byes, I was eager to get going. I noted with some anxiety that it was already ten minutes past ten.

My first meeting was in McLean, Virginia, another verdant suburb of Washington favored by many members of Congress, diplomats, and businessmen. I was going to meet an old friend who ran an institute for robotics. By my reckoning it should have been an easy ride, using the Beltway at a time when most commuters should have already reached their destination. My rental car's navigation system agreed with the assessment of Google Maps on my smartphone—the trip would take me about fifty-five minutes with prevailing traffic. The efficient voice commands from Google made sure there was little risk of losing my way.

A sumptuous Mexican lunch followed that meeting, and I was running further behind schedule for my next meeting, at the Library of Congress, close to the White House. Checking traffic, I was aware that I would barely make it in time. Further, I would have trouble linking this stop to my fourth stop of the day—an upscale Mediterranean eatery in northwestern D.C., where parking was scarce and valet service was notoriously slow. This called for a change of plans. After consulting my smartphone apps, I decided that the best option would be to drop off my car at the McLean Park and Ride station and take the Washington Metro. The ride cost me about $4 and got me to within 100 yards of my destination in twenty-three minutes, compared to the estimated forty-eight minutes had I traveled by car. I also managed to send a few email replies during the Metro ride, saving me precious time in staying on top of my correspondence.

After the Library of Congress meeting concluded, I had thirty minutes to reach my next appointment—dinner with a retired official of the EPA to discuss fuel economy regulations announced by the Obama administration. The best option was simply to call an Uber taxi, and I was at my next destination in twenty minutes, without the stress of parking or dealing with the maze of one-way streets, which were already filling up with commuters returning home. My host had graciously offered to drop me off at the Park and Ride at McLean. Being chauffeured meant I could enjoy an extra glass of Chardonnay over an enjoyable meal. It was past ten in the evening when I reached the Park and Ride to retrieve my car and drive back to my Greenbelt hotel.

In hindsight, I realized that I was indeed living in the new world of mobility. In normal circumstances, it would have been difficult to persuade me to abandon the cocoon of my car for the day's movements. Yet there I was, balancing time, cost, and convenience, effortlessly switching travel modes, supported by nothing more than apps on my smartphone. Dynamic rerouting and replanning were hassle-free. I could be pleased that I had managed my movements efficiently, traversing suburbs and city centers without being late to any of my appointments, and with minimum stress.

The day's movements, as they spontaneously unfolded, involved a heterogeneous combination of personal, shared, and public modes of travel. Each segment was intelligently optimized to suit my preference across constraints of parking, travel time, and hassle. As a bonus, I could feel virtuous that I had reduced my carbon emissions for those sectors when I used the Metro. It was supported by omnipresent connectivity to guide me through everything, including traffic status and the Metro timetable, as well as hailing and paying for the Uber taxi. I could only imagine that had I been a local resident, I might have had even better tools at my disposal to mix and match my mobility solutions with even greater economy and convenience.

We are just on the threshold of a new paradigm of mobility that is characterized by many options and is smartly customizable for specific individuals for every context.

Venkat Sumantran

The mobility industry and its role in the CHIP framework

One might expect traditional automakers to be unenthusiastic about the CHIP architecture. After all, it carves out more space for public and shared modes, and in high-density environments suggests increasing the price of access to cars. It promotes the idea that mobility may be treated as a service. It seems to intrude into that special relationship between auto brands and their customers, something automakers have painstakingly cultivated for more than a century. Having positioned autos as a dominant design for mobility over the past hundred years, automakers have much to lose as that comfortable equilibrium is upset. Automakers have traditionally resisted efforts by external entities to intrude into that coveted and intimate relationship they share with their customers.

Yet recent years have seen a noticeable change in the industry's outlook. "We're expanding our business to be both an auto and a mobility company, and partnering with cities on current and future transportation needs is the next major step," said Mark Fields, Ford's former CEO. "For more than 100 years, Ford has been part of the community and the trusted source for automotive transportation. Now, we want to work with communities to offer even more transportation choices and solutions for people—for decades to come."[17] He is not alone. In recent years, a chorus of auto industry CEOs has voiced a similar outlook as the leaders prepare their companies to face a very different future.

Automakers bring a lot of experience in dealing with people and their mobility. They can be valuable agents as nations and cities seek to transform this domain. Almost all automakers have well-established long-term planning functions charting roadmaps for R&D and investment aimed at future transportation. But a notable few have ventured further, with specific plans and investments outside their traditional core areas. They seem willing to step outside their comfort zone and address an altered view of future mobility. We examine how they can make an impact on the anticipated transformation.

Germany's Daimler Group may have started with one advantage as it embraced such change. As an automaker with a broad portfolio of products, extending beyond cars to trucks, buses, vans, and a strong presence in the taxi and limousine trades, it already catered to a wider spectrum of mobility than most of its competitors. Under the umbrella of Daimler Mobility Services it has acquired and nurtured a basket of companies engaged in a new portfolio of offerings, including short-term car rental (Car2Go), tech-enabled taxi services (MyTaxi) to rival Uber, personal limousines (Blacklane), BRT, low-cost intercity bus services (Flixbus), and a personal mobility adviser app platform (moovel). Taken together, these mobility offerings can serve the role of transport manager for an individual, prospecting solutions, optimizing journeys based on cost and time, and mixing public and private modes. Based on the configured travel, they can assist with hailing a taxi, booking a Car2Go rental car, or even booking tickets on local trains. This suite of solutions and offerings comes from an automaker that a decade ago would have been happy just trying to sell you a new car. Voicing the outlook of this breed of progressive automakers, Klaus Entenmann states, "It's clear that any viable car company in the future has to be more than just a producer of assets. The transition, for us, from a vehicle manufacturer to a mobility provider began nearly a decade ago."[18]

Bavarian rival BMW has also embarked on a similar suite of enterprises and solutions that includes Alphabet GmbH, a mobility management and leasing company. Alphabet too has a large portfolio of offerings for personal mobility. DriveNow is a free-float car-share service—users can pick up a car at a nearby location and drop it off at their destination. ReachNow offers a ride-sharing taxi service. Alphabet also offers corporations the option of a subscription, which then allows the corporation's employees to avail themselves of flexible modes, including the temporary use of cars from a fleet that usually consists of BMW and Mini models, in addition to their other services. BMW too is aimed at serving customers with mobility on demand. Anticipating another major constraint faced by most urban drivers, BMW's extended business services include dedicated apps that help drivers find parking. BMW owns stakes in JustPark, a service that aggregates information on private and public parking in many cities. For a brand that was narrowly focused on producing the "ultimate driving machines," BMW now finds it needs to be adept at negotiating parking access with city administrations and local residents.

Expanding into such very different domains calls for automakers to deal with many small startups and to manage nimble entrepreneurial businesses—something large automakers typically find difficult to do. Making and selling cars is very different from delivering mobility services. Providing multimodal connectivity across many global cities with minute-by-minute updating is a daunting challenge. As Entenmann explains, "We especially see the comprehensive intermodal experience challenging, when integrating a mobility platform like moovel into a city's existing infrastructure. Each bus, rail and bike company needs to sign on with us, and that usually takes time, which prevents a quick and efficient city expansion. Another challenge is the ability to harness big data in a meaningful way."[19] To endow these businesses with the speed and agility to be effective in such a dynamic environment, automakers usually carve these businesses into separate subsidiaries. Daimler has created Daimler Mobility Services, while BMW has formed a dedicated organization, BMW iVentures, to manage its expansion.

A few industry leaders, such as Bill Ford (Ford), Dieter Zetsche (Daimler), Harald Krueger (BMW), and Carlos Ghosn (Renault-Nissan), have acknowledged that in the coming decades, mobility will be influenced increasingly by technologies developed outside the auto industry. These industry leaders have chosen to aggressively engage with the tech giants and grapple with unfamiliar technologies and businesses rather than be passive in the face of transformation. As Peter Schwarzenbauer, a BMW board member, summarizes his own company's outlook, "We don't want to be shaped, we want to shape mobility ourselves."[20] Their responses incorporate many elements, including partnering for developing technologies, tapping innovative talent and startups in places like Silicon Valley and Israel, and creating organizational structures that can deal with the scale of the auto industry, on the one hand, while also engaging with small, fast-moving innovators and startups on the other. They are also clear that the onset of self-driving cars will further change mobility. The change is not just a matter of removing the cost or effort of the driver. Rather, self-driving cars will add a further degree of freedom to mobility to alter conventional business boundaries.

Box 12.2 Ford: "Finding New Ways to Move You"

Ford's new slogan clearly telegraphs the company's intent. Specifically, Ford seem to have boldly broken ranks with most traditional automakers in imagining a different future architecture for mobility. Under the stewardship of Bill Ford, chairman of Ford Motor Company, they seem willing to place bets that align with the CHIP mobility architecture. Speaking at a TED session, Bill Ford stated, "When you factor in population growth, it's clear that the mobility model that we have today simply will not work tomorrow."[21]

Bill Ford articulated the need for such moves, stating, "Ensuring the freedom of mobility requires us to continually look beyond the needs of today and interpret what mobility will mean to future generations. My great-grandfather helped put the world on wheels so everyone could enjoy the benefits of mobility. Our vision today is to expand that same thinking using advanced technology and new business models, and addressing the mobility challenges people face around the world."

Among the company's many initiatives, Ford has invested in car sharing through partnering with Getaround in the U.S. and easyCar Club in London. Through these new partnerships, Ford hopes to engage the peer-to-peer car-sharing service, with two objectives. First is to lower costs for owners of Ford products who choose to rent out their car some of the time. Second is to allow non-Ford owners who use the service to experience new products from Ford's lineup.

Related services as car-lease financing, vehicle insurance, and enrollment in Ford's SYNC subscription services have the potential to deepen the bonds between automakers and customers. In an age when the core business of automakers is increasingly challenged for viability, these wrapper services can increase revenue and profit streams over a longer period of time.

In 2016, Ford, like Daimler and BMW in Europe, created a separate subsidiary, Ford Smart Mobility, to deal with the complex landscape of new technologies, startups, and novel customer interfaces. Bill Ford says, "This new subsidiary will enable us to develop mobility solutions to address the rapidly changing transportation challenges of an increasingly crowded world."[22] This enterprise deals in all forms of solutions ranging from e-bikes to Chariot mini-vans that complement transit services in the San Francisco area.

Recognizing that this means a shift from a pure product focus to a wider view of products and services, Ford's former CEO, Mark Fields, said, "Our plan is to quickly become part of the growing transportation services market, which already accounts for $5.4 trillion in annual revenue."[23]

In addition to the broad range of advanced technologies that the core Ford Motor Company is working on, Bill Ford founded Fontinalis Partners to invest in and nurture the kind of new ventures that are emerging with all forms of mobility tools and solutions.[24] Fontinalis Partners has evolved into a sector-focused investor that already has made investments in many upcoming new brands and services.

Mark Schulz, founder of Fontinalis Partners, had long served as a senior Ford Motor official. He remains a trusted adviser to Bill Ford. The dignified oak-paneled boardroom of Fontinalis Partners' downtown Detroit office, overlooking the Detroit River, seemed an unlikely place to be discussing the next moves by innovative mobility startups in Silicon Valley. With the enthusiasm of an angel investor, Mark explained that their focus spanned connected vehicles, data and analytics, smart logistics, and mobility transactions. "We try to stay away from brick-and-mortar investments. Further, we remain stage agnostic and will gladly support ventures enabling bicycle use or parking infrastructure."[25] Noting, for example, that future city mobility will be constrained by availability, pricing, and ease of use of parking, Fontinalis has invested in parking adviser apps such as Parking-in-Motion and ParkMe, and the parking payment service ParkMobile.

Yet, even these bold steps may not be sufficient to calm anxious investors in the face of the oncoming disruption. Auto CEOs are expected to deliver on two very different objectives: (a) keep the organization's core business delivering above par results quarter after quarter; and (b) commit sizable investments in future technologies and enterprises, some admittedly speculative, to get prepared for the future. Bill Ford candidly admits, "We're going to have to make great cars and trucks for the rest of my life. But we're also going to have to invent the future. Most companies have a hard time doing one thing well, much less two things well, but that's exactly what we have to do."[26] In 2017, Ford's board was obliged to let their CEO, Mark Fields, go for failing to meet expectations of the board and investors in managing this dual challenge. He will certainly not be the last CEO to fall victim to this approaching storm.

The role for technology disruptors and business model innovators

Apple, Google, and Microsoft have all fired warning shots across the bows of the auto industry's behemoths, indicating their interest in joining the fray in mobility services. They have been the force behind much of society's recent transformation with respect to connectivity and data platforms. In most cases they have come to enjoy considerable customer intimacy, often greater even than that of automakers' with their customers. They are unwilling to cede the pole position in the competition to emerge foremost in the minds of customers. Their close intimacy with a large user population endows them with detailed knowledge of customer habits. To many customers, they already are an irreplaceable connection in daily life.

Mobility and the auto industry is a game of high stakes and very large capital demands. However, the technology giants have gained so much market prominence over the past two decades that, unlike aspirants from many other industry sectors, the scale of the required investment does not deter them. In 2015, Apple, Google, Cisco, and Oracle together possessed cash reserves in excess of $ 500 billion, or almost 30 percent of all cash held by nonfinancial U.S. companies. Projects like autonomous cars consume a lot of investment, but for a company like Google, this is not a roadblock for entry. The Chinese counterparts of these organizations such as Baidu and Tencent are similarly well funded and have been equally active in many mobility domains.

These tech companies have seen the entire auto sector and mobility industry rapidly move toward their strengths. Future auto technology is likely to be paced by four domains: electrification, sharing, autonomy, and connectivity. These players can strongly influence the last three of these four. As we have seen, cars are soon expected to have more than 50 percent of their value contributed by software. The strategy of built-in, brought-in, and beamed-in functions in a car is heavily influenced by these players.

Soon the human interface with cars will migrate to voice commands. Here too, these technology players hold a considerable advantage. Recognizing the value of these advances, automakers have sought to partner with the technology specialists to deliver customers the functions they will soon come to expect in their cars. By 2017, automakers were rushing to integrate the functions of AI-based virtual assistants to their cars. This has triggered a race among not only automakers but also among the tech giants as they prepared to dominate a very large potential market. Microsoft's Cortana had signed on both BMW and the Renault-Nissan alliance as their partners. Rival Amazon had executed a deal with Ford while Google's Assistant was chosen by both Hyundai and Daimler.[27] The objective in all these partnerships is to integrate the "smart" functions in the car with use patterns learned by these assistants in the home environment. Further, they are accelerating the use of voice as a prominent user interface so that user interactions can be natural and easy. A command from the breakfast table, "OK Google, get Blue Link to start my Sonata and set the temperature to 70 degrees" will ensure that one steps out of the house into a nicely cooled car for the drive to work.

The role of the technology specialists is growing for other reasons. Innovations in mobility have been highlighted by new business models and marketplace innovations. Mobility as a service and mobility on demand are concepts operationalized through software and connectivity platforms. Google, Microsoft, and Apple have a lot of experience in dealing with these businesses. That many of these services depend not only on connectivity but also on maps and layers of data related to commercial establishments and infrastructure means that owners of data hold a significant advantage. It is no surprise that Google, Apple, and Baidu have made heavy investments in ride-hailing apps such as Uber and Didi Chuxing.

Many of the innovations we have discussed for autos (vision-based tracking, autonomy, connectivity) have been the products of fast-moving startups; they have not come from large R&D centers. Similarly, the mobility services Turo, Uber, and Zipcar emerged from startups. Google, Apple, and their peers have amassed a great deal of experience living with start-ups and working at their clock speeds; not so long ago they were startups themselves. This helps them more easily nurture and groom many of the newer innovators. They are also more comfortable with the higher risk tolerance that characterizes such enterprises. Generations of dealing with serious product liability issues have made the traditional auto industry more cautious. Bosch, a major auto industry technology supplier, has noted the rapid pace of development led by many small startups, such as Mobileye and Cruise Automation, in places like Israel and California. Bosch chairman, Volkmar Denner asserted "What we're lacking in Germany is the willingness to start up companies, a lack of audacity. If Silicon Valley is a role model, then we must learn to be daring." [28] In fact, he is actually voicing an apprehension shared by many of his colleagues in the auto industry around the world.

Autos: A different game

Even as many among automakers and suppliers anticipate a fresh influx of robust competition from a very different field of business, many of the technology specialists, including Apple, have comprehended that the auto sector and mobility will be a very different and perhaps difficult game to play.

Unlike software, the auto industry has been shaped by more than half a century of regulations governing safety, emissions, fuel efficiency, and even sales channels. Regulated businesses such as pharmaceuticals and auto manufacturing are characterized by due care, elaborate validation and certification, and longer product cycles. The environment rewards patience and thoroughness as much as it rewards speed and innovation. The culture of "deploy and improve," often characteristic of software development, is not always effective in the auto industry. Safety, risks to customers, and product liability are major concerns in the automotive industry. As we have seen in the case of autonomous cars, premature beta software downloads can give rise to grave safety risks and vulnerability to very expensive legal liability obligations. Any single issue of product liability can have devastating consequences on even large organizations—Firestone tires and Takata airbags are two recent examples from the auto industry.

Automotive manufacturers are also obliged to support customers over a long period, even long after production of the product has ceased. Aftermarket supplies of spare parts may be called for even fifteen years after production has ended.

The nature of the auto business, involving very large investments and prolonged payback periods for capital, is yet another disincentive for many. As Dan Ackerson, former chairman of GM, responded when asked about his reaction to the speculation that Apple might have interest in making cars, "I think somebody is kind of trying to cough up a hairball here. If I were an Apple shareholder, I wouldn't be very happy. I would be highly suspect of the long-term prospect of getting into a low-margin, heavy-manufacturing business."[29]

Yet, as the saying goes, nothing ventured, nothing gained. The tech giants are anything but shy. Many of the issues noted above can be managed and many successful organizations have proven adept at migrating to new business sectors, learning the rules of the game and succeeding, even as they brought with them their own blend of fresh thinking and dynamism.

In closing

As society prepares a transition from the century of the automobile and begins drafting a new script for this century, the mobility landscape will be more complex and engage many more stakeholders. In this chapter we have identified pivotal roles for cities and their administrators, for automakers, and for technology innovators and business entrepreneurs. A traditional outlook that was characterized by heightened sensitivity to interference will need to be set aside in a new era when cooperative planning and orchestration becomes necessary. Carlos Ghosn announced Nissan's plan to cooperate with the 100 Resilient Cities initiative promoted by the Rockefeller Foundation. In his words, "The biggest transformations will not take place inside our vehicles, or even inside our companies. Rather, they will take place on the stage of the world's cities. From population growth, to the increase in elderly populations, to the stresses on transportation infrastructure, cities are facing challenges that could be solved, in part, by mobility solutions. To align technology, policy, and planning, automakers and cities must work as partners."[30]

Many of the changes that are expected to underpin future mobility also favor a prominent role for technology players and mobility solution providers. The addition of this culture, oriented toward faster clockspeeds, the rapid churn of ideas, and distributed sources of innovation, will greatly boost the dynamism of a CHIP architecture and introduce additional and much-needed venture capital.

Yet it would be simplistic to assume that this will lead the technology companies to a direct collision with existing automakers. What is certain is that the canvas of mobility will expand significantly. On this wider canvas, there will be room for a broader cast of characters, each of whom will bring a portfolio of mobility offerings. We expect that the powerful forces behind the auto industry and the technology industry will converge, cooperating in some areas and colliding in others. The CHIP framework depends on such continuous replenishment of the stock of engineers, technologists, and entrepreneurs to keep the pot stirred. This expanded landscape and the collective cast of characters will reward users and society with faster, smarter, and greener mobility.

Conclusion

Nothing changes until something moves.

—*Einstein*

In human evolution, every age has faced its challenges. So it is understandable that each generation has felt entitled to the view that it lives in times of great change. Yet the long lens of history does reveal periods of exceptionally vigorous transformation. The Industrial Revolution of the nineteenth century, for example, sparked major societal changes, replacing agricultural work with factory work for a significant fraction of the population across a swath of industrializing countries. The post–World War II years triggered a rebalancing of global power, the dismantling of colonial structures, and leaps in prosperity and democratization in many nations. In our age we see the digital revolution transforming society in a manner that is also as profound.

Mobility is the lifeblood of society, critical to economic and human development. Any vibrant, growing and developing society needs a robust, efficient, and dynamic mobility architecture so that its evolution remains healthy. The twentieth century vastly broadened human mobility options—on land, on the seas, and in the air—and supported unprecedented spurts in economic well-being. The automobile has been an important agent in transforming ground mobility and catalyzing a motorized century. The industrialized nations poured investments into interstates, highways, motorways and autobahns, knowing that increased personal mobility had the power to change the way people live. Expanding road networks and the huge popularity of automobiles enabled previously unimagined personal and commercial mobility. True to its promise, the automotive industry has played a strategic role in the economic development of many nations by creating jobs, advancing improvements in logistical efficiency, and stimulating technological innovations, which have spilled over into many other industries. This strategic value also explains the repeated interventions by governments across the world to nurture their automotive champions, foster industry growth, and, in calamitous circumstances, come to the financial rescue of automotive factories and jobs.

The reaction to predominantly car-based mobility took a long time to appear, but it is here. The beloved automobile gradually became a victim of its own success. Urban densification has shifted the emphasis of mobility investments from intercity connections to improved mobility within cities, where cars increasingly find themselves crowded out. Cities compelled to battle congestion and deteriorating air quality have steadily grown more averse to cars.

A contemporary society that is more frequently reminded of the specter of climate change and the imperative for environmental responsibility will encourage business models that relentlessly pursue efficiency and are oriented toward eschewing waste. Choosing the right tool or solution for the task at hand is important in this environment. Assets that are allowed to idle or mobility modes that have high carbon footprints will be displaced by other modes and solutions. Intelligent application of a combination of regulations and fees will speed the process.

These changes in attitudes have coincided temporally with a revolution in connectivity technologies, which is expanding the world of mobility possibilities and changing the way we live and do business. Concepts and assumptions of what constitutes user-friendly and efficient mobility are being remolded by the pace of digitization and the power of connectivity.

Less than three decades ago, companies such as AT&T, Siemens, and Fujitsu dominated global telephony. Consumers now look to Apple, Samsung, htc, and literally hundreds of generic smartphone manufacturers and rely on a smorgasbord of communication applications, including traditional telephony, Whatsapp, Facetime, WeChat, Skype, and Instagram, and others to communicate. Similarly, where companies such as Sony, National, and Philips once dominated recorded music, issuing products for analogue devices such as record players, tape players, and cassette players, today's smartphones, tablets, and laptops provide the gateway to the music services of XM, Spotify, Pandora, and others. Whether in communications or in music, people have come to expect solutions tailored to their personal needs and preferences.

In parallel to the experiences in digital world media, mobility solutions will also depend upon seamless connections, provided by both physical infrastructure and digital tools, across heterogeneous modes. Thus connected, these solutions will amplify the utility and flexibility of the mobility architecture.

The influence of cultural change is also accelerating changes in mobility. The seemingly contradictory philosophies implicit in a sharing economy and seeking personalized solutions and services will co-exist. One can seek to be a car user and not necessarily a car owner. A world where mobility is shared with others and can be approached as a service is liberating to many. At the same time, discrete, lumpy solutions are being interpolated with new products and services configured to more closely align with the personalized needs of individual consumers.

In this fast changing world, is there any reason to believe we will continue to rely exclusively on mobility provided by the cars we purchase or procure on a 3-year lease from a traditional auto brand? These purveyors of mobility products from the twentieth century face the challenge of transforming themselves or facing obsolescence.

Disruptive changes triggered by new innovations can occur over very short periods of time. In 1901, the typical street in New York City was a chaotic jumble of horse-drawn carriages and pedestrians picking their way through mounds of horse manure. Yet, a brief decade later, by 1911, the same streets were populated with motorcars, and horse-drawn carriages were rapidly disappearing.

The gathering "perfect storm," arising out of the confluence of societal imperatives, lifestyle changes, climate concerns, possibilities with new technologies, and innovative enterprises has automotive industry leaders hurrying to recast their strategic plans. Just as the telephone did not disappear but changed dramatically, the car is not likely to disappear but will be used differently, and will have new roles. As with communications, this new age in mobility will transform how people live, travel, and socialize.

A diverse set of actors will instigate this disruption. Technology innovators and new business model entrepreneurs will replicate the kinds of changes seen in telecommunications. New and reformed automakers, redefining their organizational mission and raison d'être, will join them. Cities and their administrations are stepping up to their role to steer public investment and guide the trajectory of this change, keeping in mind their obligations to society. Together, they are concocting diverse new mobility options from a mix of transit modes, infrastructure assets and digital tools.

In our view, the future of mobility will be connected, heterogeneous, intelligent, and personalized. We believe that the CHIP framework can provide a useful template for future mobility architectures in this new world. Its claim to validity and applicability is underscored by the following:

1. Innovation and globalization continue to drive new technologies, new business model innovations and new attitudes. To serve this environment, any mobility architecture must be flexible and adaptable. The CHIP architecture is designed for dynamic add-ons and substitutions. It is robust enough to ride the turbulent waves of change.

2. In a world that resolutely forges ahead by empowering people and democratizing opportunities, any mobility architecture must be inclusive. The CHIP architecture anticipates a heterogeneity of modes and allows pricing mechanisms to intelligently allocate scarce resources. Across income levels and age demographics, the architecture is suitable to an inclusive society.

3. Acute pressures for sustainability have, and will, come to bear on mobility and transportation. The world's current transportation trajectory is dangerously nonsustainable. The CHIP architecture addresses sustainability using many levers—technologies, business models, regulations, and fiscal measures. A diverse and growing set of modes and sharable solutions offer numerous options applicable to a wide range of context and local conditions. Even as regulations refine the trajectories of solutions, incentives and fees can nudge user behavior toward more responsible choices.

4. The CHIP architecture retains the noneconomic benefits—fun, enjoyment, utility, ease—of travel. The popularity of motoring over the past hundred years has been supported by the perception that it was convenient, flexible, and fun. The CHIP framework seeks to ensure that future mobility architectures are configured to suit personal tastes, enhance user convenience and maximize "return on mobility."[1]

The CHIP mobility architecture urges action by a variety of stakeholders. The auto industry dominated much of our mobility architecture in the previous century. Future mobility, especially in the urban domain, will likely have strong roles for elected officials, city administrators, citizen groups, automakers, technologists, and entrepreneurs. Designers and providers will be challenged by a society hungry for ubiquitous and responsible mobility, configured uniquely for each individual.

The CHIP mobility architecture is a practical, efficient, flexible, and contemporary system with which to meet such demands. Fueled by the collective actions of cities, innovators, technologists, and entrepreneurs, this architecture will deliver faster, smarter, and greener mobility.

Notes

Preface

1. T. S. Eliot, "Little Gidding," in *Four Quartets* (New York: Harcourt, 1943).

2. D.E. Davis, tagline at *Automobile Magazine.*

3. P. F. Drucker, *Concept of the Corporation* (New York: John Day, 1946).

4. H. D. Thoreau, *Walden; or, Life in the Woods* (Boston: Ticknor and Fields, 1854).

5. N. Gibbs, "Automakers outline how they will thrive in a digitally driven future," *Automotive News Europe,* June 5, 2016.

6. Gibbs, "Automakers outline how they will thrive."

7. C. Hetzner, "BMW's Robertson warns industry to brace for change," *Automotive News,* June 8, 2016.

8. G. B. Shaw, "Speech at the Einstein Dinner," London, October 28, 1930.

9. C. Darwin, *On the Origin of Species* (London: John Murray, 1859).

Chapter 1: A Tale of Two Cities

1. L. Nelson, "Los Angeles area can claim the worst traffic in America. Again," *Los Angeles Times,* March 16, 2016.

2. CBS, "By the numbers: The American vacation," *CBS News,* August 3, 2014.

3. M. Novak, "Nobody walks in L.A.: The rise of cars and the monorails that never were," *Smithsonian Magazine,* April 26, 2013.

4. R. Longstreth, *The Drive-In, the Supermarket, and the Transformation of Commercial Space in Los Angeles, 1914–1941* (Cambridge, MA: MIT Press, 1999).

5. E. Eidlin, "What density does not tell us about sprawl," *Access* 37 (Fall 2010).

6. P. Sorensen, "Moving Los Angeles," *Access* 35 (Fall 2009).

7. K. Anderton, "Private motorized transport, Los Angeles, USA," Global Report on Human Settlements 2013, UNHabitat.org, http://unhabitat.org/wp-content/uploads/2013/06/GRHS.2013.Case_.Study_.Los_.Angeles.US_.pdf.

8. Sorensen, "Moving Los Angeles."

9. Ibid.

10. C. Hawthorne, "Mobility Plan 2035 may be the cornerstone of a new L.A.," *Los Angeles Times,* September 18, 2015.

11. Eidlin, "What density does not tell us about sprawl."

12. INRIX, "Los Angeles tops INRIX global congestion ranking," INRIX.com, http://inrix. com/press-releases/los-angeles-tops-inrix-global-congestion-ranking.

13. D. Venugopal, email exchange with Venkat Sumantran, June 6, 2016.

14. GLA (Greater London Authority), "Population Growth in London, 1939–2015" (London: GLA, January 2015).

15. London TravelWatch, "TfL 2015–16 Quarter 1 performance report" (London: London TravelWatch, October 2015).

16. J. Leape, "The London congestion charge," *Journal of Economic Perspectives* 20, no. 4 (2006): 157–176.

17. M. Briggs, Frost and Sullivan, email exchange with Venkat Sumantran, November 13, 2015.

18. Ibid.

19. London TravelWatch, "TfL 2015–16 Quarter 1 performance report."

20. M. Briggs, Frost and Sullivan, email exchange with Venkat Sumantran, November 13, 2015.

21. UN Habitat, "Planning and design for sustainable urban mobility: Global report on human settlements 2013," UN Habitat, 2013.

Chapter 2: An Urban Century

1. P. Geddes, *Cities in Evolution* (London: Willams and Norgate, 1915).

2. M. Gottdiener, *The New Urban Sociology* (New York: McGraw-Hill, 1994).

3. T. Friedman, *The World Is Flat* (New York: Farrar, Straus and Giroux, 2005).

4. R. Florida, *Cities and the Creative Class* (New York: Routledge, 2004).

5. E. Glaeser, *The Triumph of the City: How Our Greatest Invention Makes Us Richer, Smarter, Greener, Healthier, and Happier* (New York: Penguin, 2011).

6. C. Watson, "Trends in world urbanization," in *Proceedings of the First International Conference on Urban Pests,* ed. K. B. Wildey and W. H. Robinson (Exeter: BPCC Wheatons, 1993).

7. UN, "World urbanization prospects: The 2014 revision" (UN, Department of Economic and Social Affairs, Population Division, 2014.

8. TNS and the European Commission, "Attitudes of Europeans towards Urban Mobility," 2013.

9. A. Kundu, "Trends and patterns of Urbanization and their economic implications," Indian Institute of Technology, Kanpur, 2006.

10. UN, "World urbanization prospects: The 2014 revision."

11. M. Spence, P. C. Annez, and R. M. Buckley, eds., *Urbanization and Growth* (Washington, DC: World Bank for the Commission on Growth and Development, 2009).

12. Spence et al., *Urbanization and Growth*.

13. Glaeser, *The Triumph of the City*.

14. UN, "World urbanization prospects: The 2014 revision" (UN, Department of Economic and Social Affairs, Population Division, 2014.

15. R. A. M. Stern, D. Tilove, and J. Fishman, *Paradise Planned: The Garden Suburb and the Modern City* (New York: Monacelli Press, 2013).

16. F. Cairncross, *The Death of Distance: How the Communications Revolution Is Changing Our Lives* (Boston: Harvard Business School Press, 2001).

17. E. Kneebone and N. Holmes, *The Growing Distance between People and Jobs in Metropolitan America* (Washington, DC: Brookings Institution Press, 2015).

18. S. Calvert, "For more US cities, downtown is a center of economic strength," *Wall Street Journal,* August 5, 2016.

19. Nielsen, "Millennials: Breaking the myths" (New York: Nielsen Co., 2014).

20. S. Humphries, "Detroit's revival template for struggling U.S. cities," *USA Today,* July 6, 2015.

21. S. Calvert, "For more US cities, downtown is a center of economic strength." *Wall Street Journal,* August 5, 2016.

22. J. Karp, "Suburbs: A mile too far for some," *Wall Street Journal,* June 17, 2008.

23. A. Nelson, *Toward a New Metropolis: The Opportunity to Rebuild America* (Washington, DC: Brookings Institution Press, 2004).

24. V. Chakrabarthi, *A Country of Cities: A Manifesto for an Urban America* (New York: Metropolis Books, 2013).

25. L. Gallagher, *The End of the Suburbs: Where the American Dream Is Moving* (New York: Penguin, 2014).

26. UITP (Union Internationale des Transports Publics), Mobility in Cities Database (UITP, 2015), http://www.uitp.org/MCD.

27. "Urban land: Space and the city," *Economist*, April 4, 2015.

28. Glaeser, *The Triumph of the City*.

29. H. Mallya, "With 3rd largest smartphone market in the world, India to reach 314 million mobile Internet users by 2017," YourStory.com, July 21, 2015.

30. A. Sarin and R. Jain, *Effect of Mobiles on Socioeconomic Life of Urban Poor* (Ahmedabad: Indian Institute of Management, 2009).

31. R. Dobbs, S. Smit, J. Remes, J. Manyika, C. Roxburgh, and A. Restrepo, *Urban World: Mapping the Economic Power of Cities* (New York: McKinsey Global Institute, 2011).

32. A. Gouldson, S. Colenbrander, A. Sudmant, N. Godfrey, J. Millward-Hopkins, W. Fang, and X. Zhao, "Accelerating low-carbon development in the world's cities," New Climate Economy Working Paper (London: New Climate Economy, September 2015).

33. World Bank, *Planning, Connecting, and Financing Cities—Now: Priorities for City Leaders* (New York: World Bank, 2013).

34. *Proceedings of City Transformations Conference, Rio de Janeiro, October 2013* (London: SE Cities, 2013).

35. J. Miller, "Davos 2017: Is the urban-rural divide increasing?," *BBC News*, January 17, 2017.

36. Michael Bloomberg, speech at the UN Economic and Social Council 2014 Integration Summit (New York: United Nations, May 2014).

37. Nelson, *Toward a New Metropolis.*

38. World Bank, *Planning, Connecting, and Financing Cities.*

39. Economic Development Board, Singapore, 2015.

40. C. Weller, "China is building a megacity that will be larger than all of Japan," *Business Insider,* July 23, 2015.

41. R. Moses, *Public Works: A Dangerous Trade* (New York: McGraw-Hill, 1970).

42. J. Jacobs, *The Death and Life of Great American Cities* (New York: Vintage Books, 1992).

43. M. Grynbaum, "For city's transportation chief, kudos and criticism," *New York Times,* March 4, 2011.

44. E. Durkin, "Bloomberg predicts Times Square pedestrian plaza will stay under de Blasio," *Daily News,* December 23, 2013.

45. E. Thomas, I. Serwicka, and P. Swinney, "Urban demographics: Why people live where they do" (London: Centre for Cities, November 2015).

46. A. Gouldson, S. Colenbrander, A. Sudmant, N. Godfrey, J. Millward-Hopkins, W. Fang, and X. Zhao, "Accelerating low-carbon development in the world's cities," in *Seizing the Global Opportunity: Partnerships for Better Growth and a Better Climate* (London: New Climate Economy, 2015).

47. D. Moore, "Ecological Footprint Analysis: San Francisco Oakland Fremont CA" (San Francisco: Global Footprint Network, 2011).

48. H. Metge and A. Jehanno, "A panorama of urban mobility strategies in developing countries" (New York: World Bank for Systra, September 5, 2006).

49. J. R. Kenworthy and F. B. Laube, "Patterns of automobile dependence in cities: An international overview of key physical and economic dimensions with some implications for urban policy," *Transportation Research Part A: Policy and Practice* 33 (1999): 691–723.

50. T. Litman, "Analysis of public policies that unintentionally encourage and subsidize urban sprawl" (Victoria, Australia: Victoria Transport Policy Institute; London: LSE Cities, March 2015).

51. G. Zhang, L. Li, M. Fan, W. Li, and Y. Chen, *More Efficient Urban Investment and Financing: Government Debt Security and Reform of Investment and Financing in Urbanisation* (Beijing: Urban China Initiative, 2013).

52. UITP, Mobility in Cities Database.

53. Glaeser, *Triumph of the City.*

54. "The future of urban mobility 2.0" (New York: Arthur D. Little, December 2013).

55. EU, "Final consumption of households for transportation," *EU Data Book,* 2015.

56. "The mobility opportunity: Improving public transport to drive economic growth" (Credo Business Consulting for Siemens AG, 2016).

57. "The cost of traffic jams," *Economist,* November 3, 2014.

58. D. Dash, "Delhi traffic chaos costs Rs 60,000 crore annually," *The Times of India,* February 5, 2017.

59. F. Creutzig and D. He, "Climate change mitigation and co-benefits of feasible transport demand policies in Beijing," *Transportation Research Part D: Transport and Environment* 14, no. 2 (2009): 120–131.

60. "Indonesia traffic jam: 12 die in Java gridlock during Ramadan," *BBC News,* July 8, 2016.

61. UN Human Settlement Program, *Planning and Design for Sustainable Urban Mobility: Global Report on Human Settlements 2013* (Nairobi, Kenya: United Nations Human Settlement Programme; New York: Routledge, 2013).

62. Enrique Peñalosa, "Politics, power, cities," lecture, LSE Cities Programme (London: London School of Economics, January 11, 2015), https://www.youtube.com/watch?v=8hWRXdUJPPA.

63. EU Commission, "Together toward competitive and resource-efficient urban mobility" (Brussels: EU Commission, December 17, 2013).

64. U.S. Department of Transportation, "Complete streets policies" (Washington, DC: Department of Transportation, updated February 2, 2016).

65. M. Bausells, "Superblocks to the rescue: Barcelona's plan to give streets back to residents," *The Guardian,* May 17, 2016.

66. R. Petersen, "Land use and planning urban transport" (Berlin: German Ministry for Economic Cooperation and Development, 2004).

67. J. R. Kenworthy and F. B. Laube, "Patterns of automobile dependence in cities: An international overview of key physical and economic dimensions with some implications for urban policy," *Transportation Research Part A: Policy and Practice* 33, nos. 7–8 (1999): 691–723.

68. Bausells, "Superblocks to the rescue."

69. "Superblocks: Barcelona's war on cars," *BBC News,* February 8, 2017.

70. M. L. Moss and H. O'Neill, "Urban mobility in the 21st century" (New York: NYU Rudin Center for Transportation Policy, November 2012).

71. R. Weinberger, J. Kaehny, and M. Rufo, "U.S. parking policies: An overview of management strategies" (New York: Institute for Transportation and Development Policy, February 23, 2010).

72. M. Friedman, *There's No Such Thing as a Free Lunch* (New York: Open Court, 1975).

73. V. Haché-Aguilar, "Syndicat Autolib' Métropole," http://www.avere-france.org/Site/Adherent/?adherent_id=4624.

Chapter 3: A Softer, Greener Footprint

1. O. Paz, "Vuelta," *Vuelta,* 1976.

2. D. Chazan, "How Paris is stepping up its drive against the car," *BBC Magazine,* May 2, 2016.

3. M. Phenix, "On 27 September, Paris goes car-free," BBC, September 2015.

4. S. Feng and Q. Li, "Car ownership control in Chinese mega cities: Shanghai, Beijing and Guangzhou," *Journeys* (Sustainable Urban Transport), September 2013).

5. R. Carson, *Silent Spring* (New York: Houghton Mifflin Harcourt, 1962).

6. Club of Rome, *The Limits to Growth: A Report for the Club of Rome's Project on the Predicament of Mankind* (New York: Universe Books, 1974).

7. M. McGrath, "CO_2 levels mark 'new era' in the world's changing climate," *BBC Science and Environment,* October 24, 2016.

8. UN, "Paris Climate Agreement to enter into force on 4 November, 2016," press release, October 5, 2016.

9. T. E. Romano, C. Pardo, and C. O. Medina, for the UN, "Creating universal access to safe, clean, and affordable transport: A status report on the contribution of sustainable transport to the implementation of Rio+ 20" (Rio de Janeiro: UN and Partnership on Sustainable Low-Carbon Transport, June 20, 2013).

10. A. Sieminski, "International energy outlook 2016" (Washington, DC: Center for Strategic and International Studies, May 11, 2016).

11. U.S. IEA (International Energy Agency), "Transport energy efficiency: Implementation of IEA recommendations since 2009 and next steps" (Washington, DC: IEA, 2010).

12. U.S. IEA, "Key world energy statistics" (Washington, DC: IEA, November 30, 2015).

13. Sieminski, "International energy outlook 2016."

14. Eurostat, "Sustainable development—Transportation," EC.Europa.eu, September 10, 2015, http://ec.europa.eu/eurostat/statistics-explained/index.php/Sustainable_development_-_ transport.

15. U.S. EPA, Air Quality Trends, 2016.

16. American Lung Association, "State of the Air® 2016" (Chicago: American Lung Association, 2016).

17. WHO (Word Health Organization), Global Urban Ambient Air Pollution Database (Geneva: WHO, 2016).

18. U.S. EIA, "Fuel economy standards have affected vehicle efficiency" (Washington, DC: U.S. Department of Energy, 2012).

19. National Highway Traffic Safety Administration, "Fleet fuel economy" (Washington, DC: Department of Transportation, 2015).

20. M. Oge, Driving the Future (New York: Arcade, 2015).

21. White House, "Obama administration finalizes historic 54.5 MPG fuel efficiency standards," press release, August 28, 2012.

22. D. Shapardson, "Fiat Chrysler buys emission credits from Tesla, Toyota and Honda," Automotive News, December 16, 2015.

23. EEA (European Environment Agency), "Evaluating 15 years of transport and environmental policy integration" (Luxembourg: EEA, December 14, 2015).

24. ITDP (Institute for Transportation and Development Policy), "Climate change ahead of UN climate summit" (New York: ITDP, September 17, 2014).

25. U.S. IEA, "Key world energy statistics."

26. L. Mearian, "Renewable energy represented more than half of all new power capacity in '15," CIO Magazine, October 26, 2016.

27. U.S. EIA, "Germany's renewables electricity generation grows in 2015, but coal still dominant" (Washington, DC: U.S. EIA, May 2016).

28. H. Suzuki, "Transforming cities with transit: Transit and land-use integration for sustainable urban development" (New York: World Bank, 2013).

29. R. Petersen, "Land use planning and urban transport" (Berlin: GIZ for the Federal Ministry for Economic Cooperation and Development, 2004).

30. UITP (Union Internationale des Transports Publics), "Latest figures on the urban bus fleet in the European Union," Public Transport Statistics Report, Issue No 1 (Brussels: UITP, 2010.)

31. U.S. IEA, "Key world energy statistics."

32. B. Bohr, personal interview with Venkat Sumantran, Stuttgart, November 6, 2014.

33. J. Dohmen, personal interview by Venkat Sumantran, Aachen, Germany, September 5, 2014.

34. A. Lovins, telephone interview by Venkat Sumantran. August 21, 2014.

35. S. Pacala, "Stabilization wedges: Solving the climate problem for the next 50 years with current technologies," *Science*, August 13, 2004.

36. Eurostat, "Sustainable development—Transportation."

37. S. DuBois, "The auto industry's best kept secret," *Fortune,* February 22, 2013.

38. R. Lucas, "End-of-life vehicle regulation in Germany and Europe: Problems and perspectives" (Wuppertal: Wuppertal Institute for Climate, Environment and Energy, 2001).

Chapter 4: New Attitudes

1. U.S. Census Bureau, "American Community Survey" (Washington, DC: U.S. Department of Commerce, U.S. Census Bureau, 2014).

2. U.S. Department of Transportation, "Licensed drivers by age and sex," Federal Highway Administration data.

3. U.S. Census Bureau, "American Community Survey."

4. IFMO, "Mobility 'Y': The emerging travel patterns of gen 'Y,'" IFMO, Munich, 2013.

5. U.S. Census Bureau, "American Community Survey."

6. DRI, "World car industry forecast" (DRI, 2011).

7. R. Nader, *Unsafe at Any Speed* (New York: Richard Grossman, 1965).

8. C. E. Wilson, Confirmation hearings before the Senate Armed Services Committee, 1952.

9. Federal Highway Administration, "FHWA forecasts of Vehicle Miles Traveled (VMT): Spring 2016" (Washington, DC: U.S. Department of Transportation, Office of Highway Policy Information, 2016).

10. T Dutzik and P. Baxandall, "A new direction: Our changing relationship with driving and the implications for America's future" (Boston: Frontier Group; Washington, DC: U.S. PIRG Education Fund, 2013).

11. Dutzik and Baxandall, "A new direction."

12. "The future of driving: Seeing the back of the car," *Economist*, September 22, 2012.

13. "Another bummer summer: Teen unemployment still at 24.1 percent going into summer 2013," Employment Policy Institute, EPIOnline, May 2013.

14. M. Sivak, "Has motorization in the U.S. peaked? Part 2. Use of light-duty vehicles," UMTRI-2013–20 (Ann Arbor: University of Michigan, Transportation Research Institute, July 2013).

15. "Millennials: Breaking the myths," Nielsen.com, January 27, 2015, http://www.nielsen.com/us/en/insights/reports/2014/millennials-breaking-the-myths.html.

16. P. Brasor and M. Tsubuku, "Japan is losing its drive to get behind the wheel," *Japan Times,* September 28, 2016.

17. R. Petersen, *Land use planning and urban transport*. German Ministry for Economic Cooperation and Development, GTZ. 2004.

18. UITP (Union Internationale des Transports Publics), "Public transportation in the European Union" (Brussels: UITP, 2015).

19. APTA (American Public Transportation Association), "Public transportation investment" (Washington D.C.: APTA, 2015.

20. B. Davis, T. Dutzik, and P. Baxandall, "Transportation and the new generation: Why young people are driving less and what it means for transportation policy" (Boston: Frontier Group; Washington, DC: U.S. PIRG Education Fund, April 2012).

21. R. Buehler and R. Pucher, "Demand for public transport in Germany and the USA: An analysis of rider characteristics," *Transport Reviews* 32, no. 5 (2012).

22. White House, "An economic analysis of transportation infrastructure investment: Report of the U.S. National Economic Council and the President's Council of Economic Advisors (Washington, D.C., July 2014).

23. K. Shaver, "One way to ease traffic: Let it get so bad that motorists give up," *Washington Post*, November 4, 2016.

24. U.S. Census Bureau, "U.S. labor force 2015" (Washington, DC: Economics and Statistics Administration, U.S. Census Bureau, 2015).

25. U.S. Population Census since 1940 (U.S. Census Bureau, 2012).

26. D. Goldman, "Walmart will close 269 stores this year affecting 16,000 workers," CNN, January 15, 2016.

27. "On-line retailing: Britain, Europe, U.S. and Canada 2016," Centre for Retail Research, UK.

28. CNNIC, "Share of online transactions in total retail sales," Statistical Survey Report on Internet Development in China, 2016.

29. "China's e-commerce market: Untapped potential for global companies," Nielsen. com, January 14, 2016, http://sites.nielsen.com/newscenter/chinas-e-commerce-market-untapped-potential-for-global-companies.

30. L. Fedor, "Tech investors taste success in food delivery," *Financial Times,* July 6, 2016.

31. T. Spangler, "Movie attendance among younger 'digital' audiences drops 15% in 2014: Nielsen," *Variety*, December 11, 2014.

32. Emails to Venkat Sumantran, January 19, 2016.

Chapter 5: Innovations for Sustainability

1. B. Blondel, C. Mispelon, and J. Ferguson, "Cycle more often 2 cool down the planet: Quantifying CO_2 savings of cycling" (Brussels: European Cyclists' Federation, 2011).

2. Volkswagen, "The new Volkswagen XL1 Super Efficient Vehicle (SEV)" (Wolfsburg, Germany: Volkswagen AG, 2011).

3. George Bernard Shaw. Personal quotes.

4. U.S. EPA (Environmental Protection Agency), "Milestones in mobile source air pollution control and regulations" (Washington, DC: U.S. EPA, 2012).

5. B. Halvorson, "Sacramento strong-arm: California now mandating EVs from Volkswagen," *Car and Driver*, December 22, 2016.

6. D. Hancock, interview with Venkat Sumantran, Detroit, September 10, 2014.

7. W. Bernhart, interview with Venkat Sumantran, Stuttgart, September 24, 2014.

8. A. Vance, *Elon Musk: Tesla, SpaceX, and the Quest for a Fantastic Future* (New York: HarperCollins, 2015).

9. M. Chafkin, "A broken place: The spectacular failure of the startup that was going to change the world," *Fast Company,* April 7, 2014.

10. J. Cobb, "Hybrid sales rising globally, says Toyota," *Hybrid Cars*, August 22, 2016.

11. Volkswagen, "Matthias Müller: We have launched the biggest change process in Volkswagen's history," press briefing, June 22, 2016.

12. Volkswagen, press release, September 29, 2016.

13. Mercedes-Benz, "Electric mobility: Mercedes-Benz flips the switch," press release, September 29, 2016.

14. China Association of Automobile Manufacturers, "Vehicle sales in 2016," Beijing.

15. M. Reuss, telephone interview with Venkat Sumantran. July 24, 2015.

16. "VW HR chief says expects five-digit number of job cuts," *Hindu,* October 31, 2016.

17. C. Ghosn, personal interview with Venkat Sumantran, Paris, January 15, 2015.

18. WHO (World Health Organization), "Global Status Report on Road Safety 2013.

19. FERSI, "The sustainable safety approach to road transport and mobility" (Brussels: Forum of European Road Safety Institutes, 2009).

20. T. E. Romano, C. Pardo, and C. O. Medina, "Creating universal access to safe, clean, and affordable transport: A status report on the contribution of sustainable transport to the implementation of Rio+20" (Rio de Janeiro: UN and Partnership on Sustainable Low-Carbon Transport, June 20, 2013).

21. R. Nader, *Unsafe at Any Speed* (New York: Grossman, 1965).

22. C. Jensen, "50 years ago, 'Unsafe at Any Speed' shook the auto world," *New York Times,* November 26, 2015.

23. J. Dang, "Preliminary results analyzing the effectiveness of electronic stability control (ESC) systems," DOT HS 809 790 (U.S. Department of Transportation, National Highway Traffic Safety Administration, 2004).

24. FERSI/ECTRI, "The sustainable safety approach to road transport and mobility" (Brussels: Forum of European Road Safety Institutes / European Conference of Transport Research Institutes, January 23, 2009.

25. M. Flegenheimer, "A safety plan with Swedish logic and city smarts," *New York Times,* May 13, 2014.

26. CARE: EU Road Accidents Database (Brussels: European Commission, 2009).

27. NHTSA, "Federal highly automated vehicle policy: Accelerating the next revolution in roadway safety" (Washington, DC: U.S. Department of Transportation, NHTSA, 2016).

28. NHTSA, "Traffic fatalities 2015" (Washington, DC: U.S. Department of Transportation, NHTSA, 2016).

29. WHO, "Road safety."

30. WHO, "Road Safety."

31. C. M. Farmer, A. K. Lund, R. E. Trempel, and E. R. Braver, "Fatal crashes of passenger vehicles before and after adding antilock braking systems," *Accident Analysis and Prevention* 29, no. 6 (1997): 745–757.

32. D. Burton, A. Delaney, S. Newstead, D. Logan, and B. Fildes, "Evaluation of anti-lock braking systems effectiveness," Report 04/01 (Noble Park North, Victoria, Australia: Royal Automobile Club of Victoria, April 2004).

Chapter 6: Innovations to Support Mass Customization

1. C. C. Tossel, P. Kortum, C. Shepard, A. Rahmati, and L. Zhong, "An empirical analysis of smartphone personalization: Measurement and user variability," *Behaviour & Information Technology* 31, no. 10 (2012): 995–1010.

2. B. Borzykowski, "What's so wrong about dressing up your desk?," *BBC Capital,* February 3, 2017.

3. E. Devaney, "The psychology of personalization: Why we crave customized experiences," blog post, November 10, 2014, http://blog.hubspot.com/marketing/psychology-personalization.

4. A. Issa, "Personalized medicine and the practice of medicine in the 21st century," *McGill Journal of Medicine* (January 2007): 53–57.

5. K. Murphy, "A personalized diet, better suited to you," *New York Times,* January 11, 2016.

6. H. Ford, *My Life and Work,* with Samuel Crowther (New York: Doubleday, Page, 1922).

7. C. K. M. Prahalad and M. S. Krishnan, *The New Age of Innovation: Driving Co-created Value through Global Networks* (New York: McGraw-Hill. 2008).

8. I. Kirby, "A smart move: Justin Bieber takes his new customised 'swag car' for a spin," *Daily Mail,* April 19, 2012.

9. C. Weller, "The identity crisis under the ink," *Atlantic,* November 25, 2014.

10. V. G. F. Ramaswamy, *The Power of Co-Creation* (New York: Free Press. 2010).

Chapter 7: Innovations to Stay "Always Connected"

1. W. Bernhart and Th. Schlick, "Connected vehicles" (Munich: Roland Berger, 2012.

2. OnStar, "OnStar Tops 1 Billion Customer Interactions," press release, July 29, 2015.

3. European Commission, "eCall in all new cars from April 2018," EC.Europa.eu, April 28, 2015.

4. Cisco, "Cisco Visual Networking Index: Global mobile data traffic forecast update; 2014–2019 white paper," Cisco Systems. March 7, 2015.

5. McKinsey, "Advanced industries report: Connected car, automotive value chain unbound" (New York: McKinsey, September 2014).

6. C. Grote, interview with Venkat Sumantran, Munich, September 24, 2014.

7. D. Hoheisel, telephone interview with Venkat Sumantran, November 13, 2015.

8. V. Prasad, interview with Venkat Sumantran, Ann Arbor, MI, May 5, 2016.

9. L. Yuantao, "OSGi-based service gateway architecture for intelligent automobiles," *Intelligent Vehicles Symposium Proceedings IEEE,* June 2005.

10. J. Owens, interview with Venkat Sumantran, Troy, MI, September, 12, 2014.

11. Ibid.

12. Bernhart and Schlick, "Connected vehicles."

13. CTIA (Cellular Telephone Industry Association), "Americans' data usage more than doubled in 2015," press release, CTIA, May 23, 2016.

14. Cisco, "Visual Networking Index: Global mobile data traffic forecast, 2015–2020," Cisco Systems, February 3, 2016,

15. F. Bi, "How Formula-1 teams are using big data to get the inside edge," *Forbes*, November 13, 2014.

16. A. Greenberg, "Hackers remotely kill a Jeep on the highway—with me in it," *Wired,* July 21, 2015.

17. NHTSA, "Federal Automated Vehicle Policy: Accelerating the next revolution in vehicle safety" (Washington, DC: U.S. Department of Transportation, 2016).

18. P. Rotella, "Is data the new oil?," *Forbes*, April 2, 2012.

19. D. Newcomb, "Inside Audi, BMW and Daimler's $3 billion bet on HERE's mapping business," *Forbes*, June 27, 2016.

20. M. Colias, "Can GM build on OnStar advantage?," *Automotive News*, November 23, 2015.

21. L. Mearian, "Once your car's connected to the Internet, who guards your privacy?," *ComputerWorld*, September 18, 2014.

22. Alliance of Automobile Manufacturers, "Automotive privacy" (Washington D.C.: Alliance of Automobile Manufacturers, 2016).

23. "Industry report: Platooning systems such as from Peloton offer significant fuel efficiency & safety gains," BusinessWire.com, October 4, 2016.

24. M. Martinez, "'Smart' freeway rises on I-96, I-696," *Detroit News*, August 24, 2015.

25. P. Gott, telephone interview with Venkat Sumantran, October 26, 2015.

26. McKinsey, "Advanced industries report."

Chapter 8: Innovations for Intelligent Cars and Autonomy

1. K. Korosec, "The most hyped emerging technology of 2015," *Fortune*, August 20, 2015.

2. M. Ruf, telephone interview with Venkat Sumantran, November 11, 2015.

3. ATR, "Growth of automotive electronics," *Auto Tech Review,* 2015.

4. D. Dvorak, "NASA study on flight software complexity," JPL and California Institute of Technology, 2009.

5. D. T. H. D. M. Gelles, "Complex car software becomes the weak spot under the hood," *New York Times,* September 26, 2015.

6. D. Newcomb, "For automakers and suppliers, Silicon Valley is as much a shift in mindset as a location," *Forbes*, November 24, 2015.

7. Reuters, "Germany says Tesla should not use 'autopilot' in advertising," *Fortune,* October 16, 2016.

8. K. Burke, "Big Three will skip a step in autonomy," *Automotive News,* September 26, 2016.

9. R. Wright, "Ford and GM split on the right road to self-driving cars," *Financial Times*, April 14, 2016.

10. Reuters, "Google's self-driving car guru announces he's leaving," August 8, 2016.

11. NHTSA, "Federal Highly Automated Vehicle Policy: Accelerating the next revolution in roadway safety" (Washington, DC: U.S. Department of Transportation, NHTSA, 2016).

12. D. Shepardson, "US traffic deaths jump 7.7% in 2015 to 32,500," Reuters, July 1, 2016.

13. Boston Consulting Group, "Revolution in the driver's seat: The road to autonomous vehicles" (Boston: Boston Consulting Group, April 21, 2015).

14. Boston Consulting Group, "Revolution in the driver's seat."

15. G. Silberg, interview with Venkat Sumantran, Chicago, September 16, 2015.

Chapter 9: Innovations and Variations in Traditional Mobility Modes

1. Quoted by F. Crick, "The impact of Linus Pauling on molecular biology," Salk Institute lecture, 1995.

2. P. Mason, "In praise of bokeh: The dilemmas of TV filming," *BBC Technology Report,* April 30, 2012.

3. Laozi, *Tao Te Ching,* chapter 64, https://en.wikipedia.org/wiki/A_journey_of_a_thousand_miles_begins_with_a_single_step.

4. P. Rode, C. Hoffman, J. Kandt, and A. Graff, "Toward new urban mobility: The case of London and Berlin" (London: LSE Cities, 2015).

5. "The 20 most bike-friendly cities on the planet," *Wired,* March 22, 2016.

6. "The 20 most bike-friendly cities on the planet."

7. J. Dekoster and U. Schollaert, "Cycling: The way ahead for towns and cities" (Brussels: European Community, 1999).

8. A. Del-Colle, "The Toyota i-Road is unlike anything you've ever driven before," *Road and Track*, December 18, 2015.

9. E. F. Schumacher, *Small Is Beautiful: A Study of Economics As If People Mattered* (New York: Blond & Briggs, 1973).

10. J. Stewart, "Was the Sinclair C5 thirty years too early?," *BBC Future,* December 9, 2014.

11. "How a folding electric vehicle went from car of the future to 'obsolete,'" *Morning Edition*, NPR.org, November 5, 2015; http://www.npr.org/sections/alltechconsidered/2015/11/05/454693583/how-a-folding-electric-vehicle-went-from-car-of-the-future-to-obsolete.

12. M. Phenix, "Hands-off with Heathrow's autonomous pod-cars," *BBC Technology Report,* November 13, 2014.

13. General Motors, "GM unveils EN-V concept: A vision for future urban mobility," press release, March 25, 2010.

14. U. Guida, "Increasing bus attractiveness through efficiency" (Brest: UITP, 2013).

15. Daimler AG, "The Mercedes-Benz Future Bus: The future of mobility," press release, September 2016.

16. Allianz, "How to design cities around people, not cars," Allianz.com, June 10, 2011, http://knowledge.allianz.com/mobility/infrastructure/?1532/new-urbanism-cities-for-p...22-11-2014.

17. H. Suzuki, "Transforming cities with transit: Transit and land-use integration for sustainable urban development" (Washington, DC: World Bank, 2013).

18. N. Padukone, "The unique genius of Hong Kong's public transportation system," *Atlantic*, September 2014.

19. A. Davies, "The 20 most expensive public transportation systems in the world," *Business Insider,* September, 2012.

20. M. K. Singh, "12 cities to get metro rail soon," *Times of India,* November 18, 2011.

21. FICCI, "Modern trams (light rail transit) for cities in India" (New Delhi: Institute of Urban Transport, September 2013).

22. Enrique Peñalosa, "Why buses represent democracy in action," TED Talk, Ted.com, September 2013, https://www.ted.com/talks/enrique_penalosa_why_buses_represent_democracy_in_action?language=en.

Chapter 10: Innovations in Marketplaces

1. "Planning for a funeral in Japan," *Japan Today*, July 1, 2013, https://www.japantoday.com/category/opinions/view/planning-for-a-funeral-in-japan.

2. J. Soble, "Japan's newest technology innovation: Priest delivery," *New York Times,* September 20, 2016.

3. A. Sundararajan, *The Sharing Economy* (Cambridge, MA: MIT Press, 2016).

4. L. Fedor, "Tech investors taste success in food delivery," *Financial Times*, July 6, 2016.

5. Morgan Stanley Research, "Rent-a-car meets tech: Head-on collision" (New York: Morgan Stanley, September 4, 2014).

6. C. Ghosn, personal interview with Venkat Sumantran, Paris, May 26, 2015.

7. P. LeBeau, "Americans holding on to their cars longer than ever," CNBC, July 29, 2015.

8. "How the Germans drive and shop," Spiegel Online, April 30, 2008.

9. D. Runkle, personal interview, Detroit, July 12, 2014.

10. D. Johnson, "Japan's 'kuruma banare' dramatically decreasing new car sales," LeftLaneNews.com, May 23, 2008.

11. S. Shaheen, D. Sperling, and C. Wagner, "Car sharing in Europe and North America: Past, present and future," *Transportation Quarterly* 52, no. 3 (1998).

12. D. Miller, telephone interview with Venkat Sumantran, September 15, 2015.

13. Forbes, "Explaining the Avis take-over of Zip Car," January 2, 2013.

14. D. S. Evans and R. Schmalensee, *Matchmakers: The New Economics of Multisided Platforms* (Boston: Harvard Business School Press, 2016).

15. J. Stein, "Strangers crashed my car, ate my food and wore my jeans: Tales from the sharing economy," *Time*, February 9, 2015.

16. Turo, Leading car rental marketplace, RelayRides, rebrands as Turo. Press release, November 3, 2015.

17. R. Lieber, "Fatal collision makes car-sharing worries no longer theoretical," *New York Times,* April 13, 2012.

18. P. Mercer, "The Australian company unlocking parking in city centres," *BBC News,* February 6, 2017.

19. Evans and Schmalensee, *Matchmakers*; and G. G. Parker, M. W. Van Alstyne, and S. P. Choudary, *Platform Revolution: How Networked Markets Are Transforming the Economy— And How to Make Them Work for You* (New York: W. W. Norton, 2016).

20. E. Martin, S. A. Shaheen, and J. Lidicker, "Impact of carsharing on household vehicle holdings, *Transportation Research Record: Journal of the Transportation Research Board* 2143 (2010).

21. PhillyCarShare, https://en.wikipedia.org/wiki/PhillyCarShare.

22. PricewaterhouseCoopers, "The sharing economy: Sizing the revenue opportunity," PwC.co.uk, 2016.

23. J. Bert et al., "What's ahead for car-sharing?" (Boston: Boston Consulting Group, February 2016).

24. W. Hook, personal interview with Venkat Sumantran, New York, July 8, 2014.

25. C. Lane, "Car-sharing: A vehicle for sustainable mobility in emerging markets," *ITDP Journal,* December 14, 2015.

26. Taxis, https://en.wikipedia.org/wiki/Taxis.

27. New York City Taxi and Limousine Commission, http://www.nyc.gov/html/tlc/html/about/about.shtml.

28. J. Barro, "New York City taxi medallion prices keep falling, now down about 25 percent," *New York Times,* January 7, 2015.

29. N. Kumar, "Uber driver convicted in rape case," *The Hindu* (New Delhi), October 20, 2015.

30. S. Jorgensen and P. Melendez, "Kalamazoo shooting suspect has outburst, ordered to stand trial," CNN, May 21, 2016.

31. B. Fung, "Uber is about to pay its U.S. riders $28.5 million: Here's why," *Washington Post,* February 11, 2016.

32. C. Isidore, "Judge rejects $100 million settlement between Uber and drivers," *CNN Tech,* August 19, 2016.

33. CNBC, "Taxi owners, lenders sue New York City over Uber," November 17, 2015.

34. E. Newcomer, "Uber China rival Didi Kuaidi raising $1 billion at valuation of more than $20 billion," Bloomberg, February 24, 2016.

35. A. Abkowitz, "Uber sells China operations to Didi Chuxing," *Wall Street Journal,* August 1, 2016.

36. Z. Rodionova, "UberPOOL gets more than 1 million customers," *The Independent* (London), June 7, 2016.

37. R. Wauters, "Ride-sharing has arrived in Europe, and the race is on between BlaBlaCar and Carpooling.com," tech.eu, February 7, 2014.

38. Ford Smart Mobility, "Ford partnering with Global Cities on new transportation," press release, September 9, 2016.

39. J. Aguilar, "Centennial teams up with Lyft for rides to light rail station," *Denver Post,* August 15, 2016.

Chapter 11: CHIP Mobility

1. R. Karlgaard, "Paul Baran, the Cold War and the birth of the Internet," *Forbes*, March 28, 2011.

2. C. C. Cheong and N. Loh, "Transport policies and patterns: A comparison of five Asian cities," *Journeys*, September 2013.

3. M. Martinez, "Faraday Future unveils 1,000-HP electric concept racer," *Detroit News*, January 5, 2016.

4. M. P. Regan, "Robo advisers to run $2 trillion by 2020 if this model is right," Bloomberg, June 18, 2015.

5. K. Entenmann, personal interview with Venkat Sumantran, Berlin, September 22, 2016.

6. J. Hagel, telephone interview with Venkat Sumantran, November 20, 2015.

7. E. Brynjolfsson, interview with Venkat Sumantran and Charles Fine, Cambridge, MA, May 2, 2016.

8. Andrew Ryan, "Cost and convenience will be the mobility priorities," *Fleetnews.co.uk*, July 23, 2015.

9. G. Silberg, interview with Venkat Sumantran, Chicago, September 16, 2015.

10. T. Piketty, *Capital in the Twenty-First Century* (Cambridge, MA: Harvard University Press. 2013).

11. Statistics Denmark, https://www.dst.dk/en/Statistik/emner/biler/nyregistrerede-og-brugte-biler.

Chapter 12: Implementing CHIP Mobility: The Roles of Stakeholders

1. Climate Group, *Agile Cities* (London: Metropolis, 2013).

2. Global Property Guide, "World's most expensive cities," http://www.globalpropertyguide .com/most-expensive-cities, 2016.

3. S. Nair, "NCR urbanisation: Delhi remains the epicenter," *Indian Express*, September 12, 2015.

4. H. Riedel, "Chinese metro boom shows no sign of abating," *International Rail Journal,* November 19, 2014.

5. N. Balwit, "A growing Seattle goes all in on transit," *The Atlantic* via Citylab.com, January 5, 2017.

6. Ibid.

7. P. Erickson and P. Tempest, "Advancing climate ambition: How city-scale actions can contribute to global climate goals" (Stockholm: Stockholm Environment Institute, 2014).

8. Ajuntament de Barcelona, "Pla de Mobilitat de Barcelona, 2013–2018," June 11, 2016.

9. World Bank, "Cities on the move: A World Bank urban transport strategy review, 2014" (Washington, DC: World Bank, 2014).

10. EU EPA-Polis, "Polis-EPA parking report" (Brussels: EU EPA-Polis, 2011).

11. World Bank, "Cities on the move: A World Bank urban transport review" (New York: World Bank, 2002).

12. J. Leape, "The London congestion charge," *Journal of Economic Perspectives* 20, no. 4 (2006): 157–176.

13. Climate Group, "Faster, smarter, greener: The state of city innovation on climate change and other urban challenges," Agile Cities report, Climate Group and others, May 2013, https://www.theclimategroup.org/sites/default/files/archive/files/Agile-Cities-Report -Full-FINAL(1).pdf.

14. P. Gott, telephone interview with Venkat Sumantran, October 26, 2015.

15. A. Greenfield, "Helsinki's ambitious plan to make car ownership pointless in ten years," *The Guardian*, July 10, 2014.

16. PRT Consulting, "Why has Masdar Personal Rapid Transit (PRT) been scaled back?," blog post, PRTConsulting.com, October 16, 2010, http://www.prtconsulting.com/blog/ index.php/2010/10/16/why-has-masdar-personal-rapid-transit-prt-been-scaled-back.

17. Ford, press release, September 9, 2016.

18. K. Entenmann, personal interview with Venkat Sumantran, Berlin, September 22, 2016.

19. Ibid.

20. G. Nelson, "BMW adapts to a changing view of driving with ReachNow," *Automotive News*, April 18, 2016.

21. B. Ford, "A future beyond traffic gridlock," TED Talk, TED.com, May 2011.

22. Ford Motor Co., press release, Dearborn, MI. March 11, 2016.

23. Ibid.

24. M. V. Copeland, "Bill Ford: Venture capitalist," *Fortune*, June 28, 2010.

25. M. Schulz, personal interview with Venkat Sumantran and David Gonsalvez, Detroit, June 11, 2014.

26. A. Mackenzie, "All change at Ford: What does Jim Hackett's appointment as CEO mean?," *Motor Trend*, May 22, 2017.

27. C. Baraniuk, "CES 2017: Car-makers choose virtual assistants," *BBC News*, January 6, 2017.

28. N. Gibbs, "German auto firms try to nurture Silicon Valley boldness," *Automotive News*, November 22, 2015.

29. T. Higgins, "Apple hairball? Ex-GM CEO says building cars may not be worth it," Bloomberg.com, February 18, 2015.

30. 100RC Rockefeller Foundation, "Nissan partners with 100RC to prepare cities for autonomous vehicles, electric cars, future mobility." Press release, Las Vegas, January 5, 2017.

Conclusion

1. J. Hagel, *Navigating a Shifting Landscape: Capturing Value in the Evolving Mobility Ecosystem* (Westlake, TX: Deloitte University Press, 2016).

Index